Russia's

20th Century

Russia's 20th Century

A Journey in 100 Histories

Michael Khodarkovsky

BLOOMSBURY ACADEMIC
LONDON · NEW YORK · OXFORD · NEW DELHI · SYDNEY

BLOOMSBURY ACADEMIC
Bloomsbury Publishing Plc
50 Bedford Square, London, WC1B 3DP, UK
1385 Broadway, New York, NY 10018, USA

BLOOMSBURY, BLOOMSBURY ACADEMIC and the Diana logo are trademarks of
Bloomsbury Publishing Plc

First published in Great Britain 2019

Cover design by Adriana Brioso
Cover image: © Christina Hägerfors

A catalogue record for this book is available from the British Library.

A catalog record for this book is available from the Library of Congress.

ISBN: HB: 978-1-3500-9145-0
       PB: 978-1-3500-9142-9
       ePDF: 978-1-3500-9141-2
       eBook: 978-1-3500-9143-6

Typeset by RefineCatch Limited, Bungay, Suffolk
Printed and bound in India

To find out more about our authors and books visit www.bloomsbury.com
and sign up for our newsletters.

To all those who, against all odds, retained their moral compass and never gave up their vision of Russia as a democracy governed by the rule of law and respect for human rights.

Contents

Part III The Democratic Experiment

Acknowledgements

Some years ago, in a used bookstore in Chicago, I picked up a book by Günter Grass entitled *My Century*. In 100 stories from 1900 to 1999, Grass spins a masterly yarn around great events as well as little-known episodes from German history. It occurred to me that this might be an interesting new way to look at Russia's turbulent history in the twentieth century. Unlike Grass, who mixed fact and fiction, I wanted to write a history book that would reach a general reader but, like Grass, I chose to include issues that may already be familiar together with those that remained a little-noticed footnote to history.

My major debt, therefore, is to Günter Grass, who despite a controversy late in his life, remains one of the literary giants of the twentieth century.

I am grateful to Rhodri Mogford at Bloomsbury for his full-throated and enthusiastic support of my project. I am also thankful to my colleagues, Ben Eklof and Semion Lyandres, and three anonymous reviewers for their helpful comments and suggestions.

My son, Loïc, was the first victim of my prose, as he diligently and effectively made his way through the first draft of the book. Insa Blanke, Chris Kubiak, and Michelle Navarre Cleary did the rest. I am particularly grateful to Jeffrey Glover for his meticulous copy-editing and for making the book a better read.

My editor at the *New York Times*, Marc Charney, taught me that whatever is expressed in 1,200 words can be rendered just as effectively in 1,000, a skill that became useful both in writing a column for the paper and in a book manuscript.

Like every writer who tackles a big topic, I owe a debt of gratitude to so many of my colleagues, past and present, who over the decades have produced numerous studies on all aspects of Russian-Soviet history and culture. In our post-Enlightenment age of information overload and mega data it is easy to lose sight of one's own contributions to human knowledge. Yet I want to reassure them that their scholarly efforts, and hopefully mine, were not in vain.

I owe special thanks to my colleague and friend Viktor Ostapchuk, who throughout the years made sure that I was aware of the Ukrainian perspective.

Finally, I am grateful to my wife Insa and our children, Loïc and Tosya, for being a daily pleasure in my life.

Illustrations

Introduction

Quo Vadis?

Is Russia "a riddle wrapped in a mystery inside an enigma" as the British Prime Minister Winston Churchill famously described it? A state driven by "messianic expansionism," according to the Nobel Peace Prize winner Andrei Sakharov? A civilization stuck between apocalypse and revolution, in the words of the twentieth-century Russian philosopher Nikolai Berdyaev? Or is it simply a space defined by its vast size, imperial ideology, intertwined cultures, cohabiting civilizations, and deeply traumatized people?

A reader may find some answers to these questions in this unusual book that consists of 100 vignettes, one for each year of the twentieth century. The vignettes touch on different themes from the history of the Russian Empire and its successors, the USSR and post-Soviet Russia. One could think of this book as a mosaic wherein each year represents a small piece that, when taken with the others, coalesces into a large picture of Russia's tortured path through the last century.

Readers, regardless of how much or little they may know about Russian history, will find something new and different in this book. Each vignette offers an insight into Russian society and culture. Those interested in particular topics, whether it be Soviet ideology, culture, economy, anti-Semitism, nationalism, or political violence, will discover common threads that will take them through the entire century. In the end, each vignette will allow a curious reader to further explore a specific theme and interest.

The stories I chose to tell are influenced by decades of studying Russian history, but also by my own experience growing up in the Soviet Union in the 1960s and 1970s. I wanted to tell the lesser-known stories that cast a big shadow over what some may consider the great Soviet achievements: universal literacy, free medicine and education, industrial and nuclear superpower status, women's emancipation, victory over Nazi Germany, a formidable military force, space exploration, and sports. All this is set in the shadow of the exceptional human and social cost of the Soviet socialist project and the new society it created—one based on habitual lies and violence.

The heroic narrative of Soviet history quickly crumbles when one looks behind the slogans and lofty rhetoric: universal literacy and education were driven by ideological indoctrination, free medical care led to corruption and inefficiency, industrialization propelled by military ambitions resulted in a grossly distorted economy in a country which was unable to feed its own population, women's emancipation meant a daytime job without changing the traditional role of women, victory in the Second World War was achieved at a staggering human cost that could have been avoided, space exploration could not be separated from Soviet propaganda, and neither could sport, where a focus on medal counts at international competitions led to harsh training programs and reliance on performance-enhancing drugs. The Soviet experiment was one of the most radical and violent cases of social engineering. For what underpinned the Soviet vision of human nature was a belief in one indisputable truth which could be imposed on malleable humanity.

The way people see their collective history may be the best general indicator of a nation's health and ailments. Self-criticism and periodic re-examination of the past are signs of a mature society and a healthy democracy. By contrast, manipulating, airbrushing, and mythologizing the past are clear symptoms of malaise in societies whose leaders are using history to legitimize their rule. For most of its modern history, Russian has fallen into the second category. This book looks beyond the historical myths by re-examining some well-known stories and introducing new ones.

For example, the vignette *1903—The Pogrom* describes the notorious violent outbreak against the Jewish community in the city of Kishinev, an event that prompted an exodus of Jews from the Russian Empire and a huge international outcry. Another vignette entitled *1957—Sputnik* also describes a well-known historic event. Yet few are aware of how Moscow used the launch of the Earth's first artificial satellite as a propaganda victory over the US.

Other stories remain little known. *1921—Chemical Weapons and Concentration Camps* tells the story of the Bolshevik leaders' use of poison gas against rebellious peasants and the creation of Soviet concentration camps at a much earlier date than was previously believed.

Similarly, *1977—Moscow Bombings* addresses several bomb explosions on the Moscow subway in January 1977. At the time, the authorities blamed the deadly explosions on Armenian nationalists, but it appears more likely that the KGB planted the bombs with the intention of blaming Soviet dissidents for the terrorist act so it could dismantle the dissident movement.

Another vignette *1984—"Iron Maiden" Behind the Iron Curtain* tells the story of the first western rock concerts behind the Iron Curtain and their phenomenal impact on Soviet youth. The Soviet Union might have been more undermined by Western pop culture and rock music than by the arms race.

Different readers may be interested in different topics, but all will find common threads. One such thread is the brutal nature of the Soviet political system, which defined Russia and the Soviet Union throughout the century. From the moment he seized power, Lenin and his government were determined to establish a dictatorship of one party and one vision.

No document is more revealing of the Bolshevik Party's intentions than the decree entitled "Concerning the Press," issued by the new government on October 28 (November 9 of the contemporary calendar) the day after it came to power. Warning that "words could be as dangerous as bombs and bullets," the decree banned all publications deemed as counter-revolutionary. Within two months, 122 publications had been shut down; by August 1918, an additional 340 publications had been outlawed. Freedom of the press ceased to exist and would not resume until after the collapse of the USSR some seven decades later.

By contrast, one may recall Thomas Jefferson's 1787 dictum in which he stated that the basis of government was the opinion of the people and that "were it up to me to decide whether we should have a government without newspapers or newspapers without a government, I should not hesitate a moment to prefer the latter." One hundred and thirty years later, Lenin chose the opposite of Jeffersonian democracy: government without free press, dictatorship instead of democracy.

Having set out on a radical course, the Soviet regime relied on violence and the repression of those who stood in its way. From the first days of the Bolshevik government, in the chaos of war and revolution, the regime prioritized policies that would become the two principal pillars of the Soviet system: mass propaganda and political repression; the latter appeared as the Soviet Secret Police (the future KGB) which was founded less than two months after the revolution.

The extraordinary human cost of the Soviet experiment provides another thread in the book. The level of systematic violence and brutality inflicted upon the Soviet people remains without precedent. The horrific atrocities of Nazi Germany, the mass violence during Mao's Great Leap Forward and the

Cultural Revolution in China, genocides in Cambodia and Rwanda, the British-induced famine in India, Congo's civil wars, and the post-Second World War repressions in Eastern European countries were all relatively short-lived. No other people has been subjected to such relentless waves of terror, death, and despair for such a sustained period of time as the people of the USSR were throughout the twentieth century.

Furthermore, with the exception of Nazi Germany's invasion in 1941, the death and violence were unleashed not by some foreign power, but by the Soviet government, which for decades devoured millions of innocent lives among its own citizens. The most recent estimates put the number of victims who perished in sustained campaigns of deadly violence and deliberate genocide during the first three decades of Soviet rule at well over 30 million: Revolution and Civil War (8 million dead), famines (1932–1933 over 7 million and 1946–1947 over 1 million dead), deportation of prosperous peasants (15 million deported with unknown number of dead), deportation of 3.5 million ethnic minorities (1.5 million dead), 6 million dead in penal colonies and labor camps, and 1.5 million executed in purges. This excludes the massive war-related casualties that for both the Russian Empire in the First World War (over 3 million military and civilian dead) and the Soviet Union in the Second World War (over 27 million military and civilian dead) were much higher than those of other belligerents.

These numbers are hard to fathom. They are also imprecise and may even be larger because the authorities under Stalin and after him deliberately underreported the numbers of the dead. Whatever the exact numbers, a simple gruesome fact remains: tens of millions of innocent victims died as the result of Soviet policies, with the Communist Party presiding over the mass murder of its own people.

"A single death is a tragedy, a million deaths is a statistic," was a typically cynical and ruthless remark attributed to Stalin. This "statistic" did not include the millions who survived torture and the unspeakable cruelties of the Soviet labor camps and penal system. But what kind of a society, one asks, emerges from this calculus of evil? How does a society survive such a gaping demographic hole, a trauma of broken social ties and norms, and inhumane psychological and emotional stress? These deep wounds, both individual and collective, take generations to heal under the best of circumstances.

Stalin's death in 1953 brought a dramatic change: criticism of him was now permitted, millions of people who were imprisoned in penal labor camps were released, and torture was forbidden. Yet propaganda and repression continued to march in lock step. To be sure, victims of the post-Stalinist Soviet regime were no longer counted in millions, but tens of thousands continued to be harassed, exiled, and imprisoned.

The web of prisons, labor camps, mental institutions, intimidation, censorship, denial of career opportunities, exile abroad, and assassinations continued to suppress dissenting voices. Yet now, instead of arresting writers, the authorities were arresting their novels; rather than a bullet to the head, Soviet intellectuals were now more likely to die from a heart attack, as both their work and careers were viciously destroyed by party hacks. This was a measure of progress.

The USSR was an Orwellian society where political reprisals, a shortage of consumer goods, and ideological conformity made fear and distrust a common currency. The basic human qualities of honor and dignity were subsumed by the state which controlled every aspect of Soviet society. The average Soviet citizen was condemned to live in a schizophrenic world of denial, where the constant, never-ending struggle to reconcile official lies with daily reality became the new normal. Little wonder that so many found solace in a bottle of vodka.

The fact that the Soviet Union was an empire of nations is another thread that readers will follow throughout the book. Founded on the remnants of the Russian Empire, the Soviet government initially encouraged the emergence of distinct national and ethnic identities, but after the Second World War, subjected the same peoples to a campaign of Russification. In the 1960s, national movements among the USSR's different peoples began to chip away at the unstable national edifice. In time, the initial clamor for greater cultural autonomy and resentment against ethnic Russian supremacy grew into a demand for national sovereignty and eventually led to the country's peaceful dissolution.

By the mid-1980s, the model of a Soviet socialist society was bankrupt. With 75 percent of its economy belonging to the military-industrial complex, the country could not meet the needs of its people, who no longer believed official propaganda. Mikhail Gorbachev's attempts to rescue the USSR through democratic reforms failed, and in 1991, for the first time in its history, Russia became a democracy guaranteeing basic human rights and freedoms to its citizens. But the early jubilant mood quickly disappeared under the weight of everyday privations. To many Russians, democracy stood for the privatization of the state economy and led to the emergence of robber barons on the one hand and jobless millions on the other.

Russia's brief experiment with democracy in the 1990s also coincided with an economic depression that was comparable to the Great Depression in the US and with a loss of international prestige. It was not surprising that more people were finding a greater appeal in the ideas of unreconstructed Communists and hardcore nationalists. All along, the FSB—the renamed but fundamentally unchanged KGB—was plotting a comeback. In 2000, Russia's fragile democracy came to a grinding halt with the arrival of Vladimir Putin and the restoration of many Soviet policies and values.

Russia entered the twenty-first century as a society with unprecedented social traumas of war, revolution, mass political repression, famine, disastrous public health and alcoholism, a failing economy, and millions of lives broken by the political hypocrisies of the Soviet regime and a ruthless economic transition during the post-Soviet era. But above all, Russia was a society that, throughout the century, had become unmoored from the humanistic and religious values of Western civilization. It was at this juncture that Russian people began their search for a new national identity, economic stability, and strong leadership.

It is my hope that those who choose to set out on this journey through Russia's twentieth century will also find clues to a better understanding of Russia in the twenty-first.

Part I

The Empire Must Die

1

Autocracy Wrestles with Change

1900
Writers

The beginning of the new century found Russia's great writer, Lev Nikolaevich Tolstoy, at his house in Khamovniki, an old district of Moscow. Tolstoy believed that city life was a punishment and preferred to stay at his country estate in Yasnaia Poliana. Yet various social engagements and business matters compelled him to spend time in Moscow.

Tolstoy was not well. The aging and tired Russian writer was in a melancholy mood. Treated like a god by fellow writers and like a tsar by peasants, Tolstoy played the role of the wise, old, and unpredictable man. A welcome interruption from his daily routine came on January 13 with a visit from a young writer, Aleksei Maksimovich Peshkov, better known under his pen name Maxim Gorky ("gorky" literally means "bitter").

The two writers were separated by what seemed like a chasm of age and experience: at seventy-two Tolstoy was the most venerable Russian writer, while the thirty-two-year-old Gorky was a rising literary star. Yet the two had a clear bond: they both had a great sense of affinity with the common people. Born into wealth and nobility, Tolstoy had chosen to reject "the sins of materialism" in search of moral self-improvement and to idealize peasant virtues. A carpenter's son and an orphan since he was eleven, Gorky's early life was one of misery and hardship; the privation of downtrodden working men and women became the main subject of his work.

Their meeting in early January 1900 was important for both writers. Tolstoy felt rejuvenated by the enthusiasm of the young writer, while Gorky was inspired by the enormity and profoundness of Tolstoy's personality.

Russian writers: Leo Tolstoy, Maxim Gorky, and Anton Chekhov in the Crimea.

Later that year, Gorky traveled to the Crimea to visit another ailing Russian writer, Anton Pavlovich Chekhov.

Chekhov was sick, very sick. He had tuberculosis but denied it until he suffered a major hemorrhaging of the lungs in 1896. Chekhov was a practicing physician and knew that he did not have many years left. His health required a warmer climate, and Chekhov decided to spend more time at his newly built summer house in the Crimean resort of Yalta.

Until Chekhov's death in 1904, the house was a magnet for the best of Russia's intelligentsia: writers, composers, singers, actors, and painters all visited Chekhov at Yalta. Yalta and its environs were studded with the mansions and palaces of top government officials and members of the imperial family. While both Russia's governing and intellectual elite shared the same corner of the Crimean Peninsula, they continued to live in parallel worlds, which never seemed to have overlapped in the Crimea or elsewhere.

In the following years, Gorky and Tolstoy would return to Yalta to spend numerous days in conversation with Chekhov over the fate of Russia and humanity. At the dawn of the twentieth century, these three great Russian writers represented different strands of Russian philosophy and culture. Within several decades, the new Soviet ideology that came to dominate most of the twentieth century in Russia would leave little room for the universal love of Tolstoy or the psychological humanity of Chekhov. In the Soviet Union, they would be made into cultural icons prescribed for restricted viewing by a captive audience.

Only Gorky would live to see the most radical transformation of the country from the oppressive autocracy of the tsars into the brutal dictatorship of the Communists. In some sense, he absorbed both the monumental moral weight of Tolstoy's philosophy and the deep humanity of Chekhov. He would never feel entirely comfortable with the Soviet cultural dogmas. Yet, at the beginning of the twentieth century, his search for justice turned Gorky into the bard of a new and rising class, the proletariat.

1901
Workers

On May 1, 1901, more than 1,000 workers at the Obukhov metal works in St. Petersburg did not show up for work. The Obukhov factory—the main

Russian workers at the turn of the century.

manufacturer of guns and artillery for the Russian Navy—was a large state enterprise employing between 6,000–7,000 workers. To some Social Democrats, the relatively low participation of workers in the May Day walkout was a clear sign of the immaturity of the Russian working class. To others, like Lenin and his comrades, who insisted on greater centralization of the party, it was a promising beginning that was destined to grow with improved leadership and better organization among the workers.

Yet, to the factory administration, which consisted of military personnel, a walkout for political reasons was the perfect way to get rid of the troublemakers. In the days that followed, several dozen workers were fired, and rumor had it that more were to go. But instead of calming the waters, the administration's hard line had the opposite effect. The recently founded St. Petersburg Worker's Organization secretly organized a general strike. On May 7, the factory came to a full stop. Within several hours, roaring crowds spilled into the neighboring streets demanding the right to celebrate Workers' Day on May 1, an eight-hour working day, and better working conditions.

Various attempts to pacify the workers failed. When the deputy director of the factory, Colonel Ivanov, tried to reason with the workers, he had to run for safety. The local police commander, who arrived with several detachments of gendarmes, foolishly confronted the workers and was also forced to beat a hasty retreat. Only the arrival of a director of the factory, Major-General Vlasiev, calmed the crowds. He commanded the workers' genuine respect, and was prepared to listen to their complaints. They told him that they had decided to launch a strike in sheer desperation after all their requests had been ignored by the administration; he was their last hope. The fact that the workers put their trust in him left Vlasiev deeply moved and he promised to leave immediately for the Naval Department to raise their issues with the Minister.

Two hours went by with no news from Vlasiev or anyone else. In the meantime, a squadron of 150 horse-mounted Cossacks and more gendarmes arrived on the scene. When the workers ignored the order to disperse, the Cossacks moved against them with their whips and sabers ready. But the intimidation did not work. Instead they were met by a hail of stones and had to retreat. By 6 pm, the government had dispatched 200 armed troops to join the Cossacks and gendarmes. According to witnesses, the commander opened fire without warning. Shooting directly into the crowd finally had the desired effect: the workers fled in different directions carrying with them the dead and the wounded. The official casualties were three dead and more than twenty wounded.

Yet the confrontation was not over. The workers retreated only to build barricades and to begin taking apart the streets to arm themselves with stones. Almost 2,000 workers from the neighboring factories arrived to support the strikers. The skirmishes continued for several more hours but, in the end, the unarmed workers were no match for the whips, sabers, and rifles of the government forces. The crowds were dispersed, the strike was over, but the news of the bloody events shocked the public.

The violent encounter at the Obukhov metal works was only the beginning. Lenin and his followers criticized the St. Petersburg Workers Committee and its platform of "work, bread, life and freedom." To Lenin, the lessons of the Obukhov strike were obvious: economic and social demands were not enough; to become successful, the workers needed to organize into a political party.

But before Lenin and his fellow radicals within the Social Democratic party could harness the workers' movement to their own ends, strikes broke out in numerous industrial centers of the Russian Empire. The twentieth century opened in Russia with unprecedented social upheaval. Whether it was a revolution in the making, no one could predict.

1902
Peasants

While the workers took to the city streets, the countryside too became a battleground between the peasants and the authorities. The failed crop in the summer of 1901 and the harsh winter that followed triggered peasant riots across many regions of European Russia. There were persistent rumors of "the second freedom," a new land reform, which, unlike the abolition of serfdom in 1861, would finally provide peasants with decent land allotments.

Skillfully tapping into a despair and discontent among the peasants, Russia's nascent socialist parties resolved "to bring the class-struggle to the countryside." In the winter of 1902, an unprecedented number of leaflets appeared in the villages across Russia. These referred to the anniversary of the abolition of serfdom on February 19, 1861 as "the day of the great lie to the people" and called for an uprising.

The disturbances first began in the Poltava province in eastern Ukraine. In late March 1902, dozens of peasants from neighboring villages descended on the Karlovka estate belonging to the great grandson of the emperor

Russian peasants. Photo by SPUTNIK/Alamy Stock Photo.

Paul I, Prince G. G. Meklenburg-Streletskii. The estate was completely defenseless, and the looting and violence continued for eight days. The peasants arrived in their carts and loaded them up with looted potatoes and hay. The telephone line was cut, hay stacks were burnt, and the managerial staff attacked. Only desperate telegrams from the estate manager secured the arrival of a battalion of Russian troops who quickly restored order.

If Karlovka was quickly pacified because it belonged to a member of a royal family, other estates were subject to the continuing wave of violence with no immediate relief in sight. Across the villages of the Poltava and Kharkiv provinces, the peasants raided the granaries, storage barns, and animal pens on the estates of the large landowners. Peasants often arrived accompanied by women and children and carted away grain, potatoes, tools, and cattle.

Most of the violence was directed towards seizing property, not against the individual landowners and their managers. The peasants often believed that the tsar approved of their actions and that redistributing property and seeking justice was government sanctioned. Even when the troops arrived, many peasants initially believed they had been sent to protect them and to supervise the redistribution of property.

In the following month, peasant raids and looting spread to other parts of the Russian Empire: the provinces of Saratov and Tambov in central Russia and the regions of southern Ukraine and Bessarabia. Everywhere, the main underlying issue was the same: land plots that were too small to sustain a peasant family. In the wake of the abolition of serfdom in 1861 and subsequent land reforms, the peasant plots continued to shrink. In the early 1900s, for example, 49 percent of land in the Poltava province was owned by the landowners, who comprised 1.5 percent of the population, while the remaining 51 percent of land was distributed among the peasants, who comprised 91 percent of the population. In other provinces the statistics were similar.

During the investigations of the peasant revolt in 1902, the assistant prosecutor in the Kharkiv province described one scene that captured the substance of the unrest. When peasants arrived to loot his property, a landlord confronted the crowd and asked why they wanted to ruin him. The reply was: "You alone have 100 desiatinas (about 300 acres), while we have one desiatina per family. Go ahead and try to live off one desiatina, then you will see how we would feed you." The "40 acres and a mule" promised to the freed American slaves, was beyond the wildest dreams of the Russian peasant.

The spreading peasant revolt became a matter of grave concern in the capital. After all, peasants constituted 85 percent of the empire's population and a large peasant uprising was a frightening prospect. In mid-April, the newly appointed Minister of the Interior (top police official), Viacheslav von Plehve, arrived in Kharkiv to assess the situation in person. To restore order, the government ordered combat military units into the lawless provinces. In the following weeks, the peasant movement was harshly suppressed. Soldiers responded to violence with even greater violence: firing at the crowds of peasants and raping peasant women. Thousands of peasants were arrested and brutally beaten and flogged; 960 were put on trial. To compensate the landlords, the peasants were to pay large sums collected as a special tax.

By early summer, the riots were largely contained. To prevent any future disturbances among the peasants, the government introduced a series of draconian measures. Governors were instructed to watch for sedition, courses offered at the local self-government schools were cancelled in case they encouraged revolutionary ideas, rural police were boosted, and more gendarmes were assigned to the countryside. The overzealous governor of the Poltava province went even further and submitted a proposal to deport the Poltava peasants to Russia's Asian territories. Both Plehve and Nicholas II approved the project, which would have resettled 600,000 peasants (22 percent of all Poltava's peasants). The outbreak of the Russo-Japanese War and the 1905 revolution prevented the government from putting this plan into action.

While the peasant disturbances of 1902 were relatively minor in comparison with the social upheaval that would shake the Russian Empire in the following decade, they were critical in crystallizing certain issues for different political players and social groups. Above all, a growing realization dawned among the peasants that their hope for "the second reform" was just an illusion. They still believed that the tsar was kept in the dark by his officials and that he would have helped them, had he known their true plight. But even this naive faith in the tsar that for centuries sustained autocracy would not last long.

Russian authorities drew their own conclusions. They resolved to deal with any discontent not through negotiation and reform, but through brute force. Initially, this approach seemed to work, but it too proved to be an illusion.

To the Russian middle class of liberals and progressives, the peasant revolt was an ultimate manifestation of the despair and injustice prevailing in the countryside. They strongly believed that the impoverished peasant men and women, who could not feed their families and were close to ruin, could hardly be held responsible for looting the property of the wealthy landlords. Even the prosecutors in charge of investigating the violence expressed sympathy for the peasants in their official reports.

Finally, Russia's socialists, who agitated for a violent uprising, decided to make the peasants their central cause. In 1902, led by Viktor Chernov, they formed a Socialist Revolutionary Party (SR) that was dedicated to agrarian socialism and sought a just division of land that would turn peasants into tenants.

The Party of the Social Democrats, who less than a year later would further split into the Bolsheviks and Mensheviks, had a different idea. The peasant disturbances of 1902 had convinced the Social Democrats that the peasants' vision was limited to their own plot of land or their village. As such, they were poor revolutionary material. The burden of the socialist revolution would fall on the shoulders of the industrial working class, the proletariat, led by the party of professional revolutionaries, while land would be nationalized and managed by the state.

1903
The Pogrom

The deep economic crisis in the Russian Empire between 1900–1903 soon translated into a new wave of anti-Semitism. In 1903, the St. Petersburg newspaper *Znamya* (*The Banner*), founded by the ultra-nationalist and virulently anti-Semitic publisher P.A. Krushevan, began to serialize *The Protocols of the Elders of Zion*. This notorious pamphlet, likely composed by Krushevan himself, alleged that there was a worldwide Zionist conspiracy to control governments around the world. It would have given a different meaning to the "world wide web," had the term existed at the time.

What Krushevan could not say explicitly in St. Petersburg, he could in his hometown, Kishinev, where his daily, *The Bessarabian*, directly appealed to Christians to finish off the Jews. Kishinev was the capital of Bessarabia, a small sliver of land in the empire's southwest corner, which today overlaps with the territory of Moldova. Bessarabia was a part of the Jewish Pale of Settlement, and Jews comprised 12 percent of the region's 220,000 people. In Kishinev, the Jewish population reached almost 50 percent.

In the spring of 1903, using blood libel as a classic means to incite violence against the Jews, *The Bessarabian* insinuated that a recently murdered child had been a victim of the Jewish sacrificial rite of Passover. But when the murderers were arrested within a few days, the case for violence fell apart. Another opportunity to incite violence arrived in February 1904, when a teenager was found dead with multiple stab wounds in a small town near

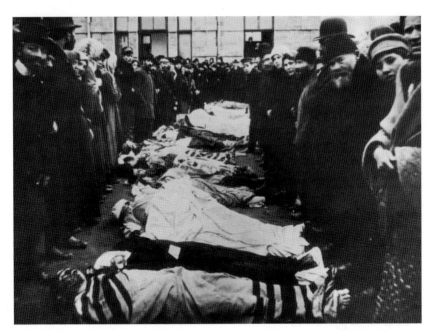

Victims of the Kishinev pogrom. Photo by Hulton Archive/Getty Images.

Kishinev. The newspaper again accused the Jews, while numerous leaflets found in Kishinev and neighboring towns called for the destruction of "the bloodsuckers who live off the Russian blood." Once again, the murderers were found, but appeals "to kill the Jews and save Russia" continued.

There were rumors that the government sanctioned violence against Jews on holidays, and that the tsar had issued a secret order to avenge Christian blood. In daily encounters, Christian neighbors often told Jews that they had little time left anyway: "Come Easter, we shall cut your throats."

Deep anti-Semitism was, of course, prevalent at the very top of the Russian government. Russian government. "The Jewish Question" became a thorn in the side of Alexander III and his son, Nicholas II, both notoriously anti-Semitic Russian emperors. Future Russian Prime Minister Sergei Witte recalled a conversation he had with Alexander III. Witte offered a ruthless argument for a coherent policy towards the Jews: if one could drown them all in the Black Sea, it would be fine. But since one could not, one had to deal with them.

By this time, the word *pogrom* had already entered the gruesome vocabulary of the Russian Empire. The assassination of Tsar Alexander II on March 13, 1881 prompted the familiar accusations, and a wave of pogroms rolled across the towns and villages of southern and eastern Ukraine throughout the early 1880s.

The frightened Jews of Kishinev did not yet know that they were about to become victims of another pogrom that would shock and horrify the world. Violence was in the air, and the Jews repeatedly sent petitioners to the governor, the police chief, and the archbishop to seek protection from the authorities. Their petitions were plainly ignored.

As expected, the pogrom began on Sunday, April 6, the first day of Easter. After a day of celebration accompanied by much eating and drinking, a crowd began to gather in the square in front of the church. Around 4 pm, the agitated crowd moved into several Jewish neighborhoods, smashing windows and beating up Jews. At this point, the pogrom could have been easily prevented, but the authorities showed no sign of restraining the crowd.

In the early hours of the following day, a large crowd of rioters took to the streets. A new rumor that the tsar had sanctioned a three-day pillaging and looting of Jews convinced the crowd that they could continue to destroy Jewish neighborhoods with impunity. Many arrived by train from neighboring small towns and suburbs and quickly joined the local vandals. Armed with axes, crowbars, pipes, metal rods, and clubs, they split up into bands of fifteen to twenty people. The police and passers-by watched silently as they began breaking into Jewish shops and houses, destroying merchandise and furniture, tossing out personal belongings, and torching the buildings.

By the early afternoon of April 7, the streets were littered with broken glass and porcelain, blood-soaked goose feathers from ripped pillows and mattresses, overturned child carriages, and torn books. Another rumor that Jews had ransacked the cathedral and killed the priest sent hordes of drunken men into a new frenzy. Cudgels, metal pipes, and knives were used against old men, women, and children. Screams, some vainly begging for mercy, others in horror at the rape, pillage, and murder, filled the streets of Kishinev. The corpses brought to the hospital were covered in blood and feathers, their skulls broken, faces crushed, ribs and limbs missing.

As the pogrom unfolded, the governor did not bother to leave his residence to assume control, the chief of police ignored the Jewish pleas, the military patrols insisted that they had no orders to intervene, and policemen idly watched and occasionally encouraged the rioters. Yet when several groups of Jews organized for self-defense, the police and military ordered them to disband. By the end of the day, 49 Jews were dead, over 500 were wounded, several women had been raped, 1,350 houses—about one-third of the entire city—had been ransacked, and total damages exceeded 1 million rubles.

The initial official reports and nationalist press blamed the Jews for the outbreak of violence, alleging that they had provoked the rampage. The courts tried to muddle the case through various restrictive procedures and rulings. Instead of a single case, for example, the court divided the proceedings into 22 separate cases to make it appear as if these were small, disconnected acts of hooliganism. Despite protests from lawyers, the hearings were not open to the public.

Yet in the wake of the judicial reforms of 1864, which for the first time created a legal profession in Russia and put its judicial system on par with those in Europe, fully suppressing or manipulating the issue was no longer possible. Some of Russia's best lawyers participated in the case and continued to press the authorities for a full investigation. They filed numerous successful appeals challenging the decisions made by the authorities.

The court procedures lasted for a year. Prosecuting the rioters and perpetrators proved to be difficult. In the end, many defendants were acquitted; only a small number were found guilty. The governor of Bessarabia, R. S. von Raaben, was transferred to St. Petersburg, where he continued to serve in various capacities and was later promoted and decorated. No other official suffered any serious consequence.

The Kishinev pogrom provoked worldwide condemnation. The foreign press covered the case in detail. The US president, Theodore Roosevelt, personally chastised Nicholas II about his brutal treatment of Jews, and notes of protest were sent from the State Department and the British Foreign Office. The brazen indifference of the Russian authorities to the plight of their Jewish subjects also galvanized democratic forces within Russia. Among those who raised their voices to denounce the Russian government, none had greater moral authority than Leo Tolstoy. Three weeks after the Kishinev pogrom, Tolstoy accused the Russian government of lies and violence. The government's complete indifference in the face of the brutalities perpetrated against Jews, Tolstoy charged, was no different from the Ottoman government's attitude towards Armenians.

Tolstoy was right. The authorities made little effort to prevent another wave of pogroms, which claimed the lives of more than 2,000 Jews between 1903 and 1905. Despite the outcry in the Western press or perhaps because of it, the emperor, Nicholas II, remained silent, confirming in the minds of many that he, like his father Alexander III, personally shared the virulent anti-Semitism of many of his officials.

While the pogrom revealed the pervasive and violent anti-Semitism of the Russian imperial authorities, it also provoked a new awakening among Jews both within and outside Russia. Some would immigrate to the US, South America, and Palestine, others formed self-defense groups, still others embarked on the path of war with the tsarist government by joining the growing ranks of the revolutionary parties: the Jewish Socialist Bund, the Socialist Revolutionary Party, and the Russian Social Democrats (shortly to be known as Bolsheviks and Mensheviks). Those in the Russian government who believed that controlled inter-ethnic and religious violence would prevent revolutionary chaos were achieving the opposite result.

1904
War with Japan

Russia's sound defeat in the Crimean War (1853–1856) gave the government only a small pause in its ceaseless expansion. St. Petersburg now directed its efforts further east, conquering most of Central Asia throughout the 1860s and securing more territory in the Far East in the 1880s. By 1900, through a series of treaties, leases, and concessions, Russia was able to wrestle away from a powerless China the effective control of much of Manchuria and acquire trade privileges in Korea. Unable to rely on a naval force locked in a

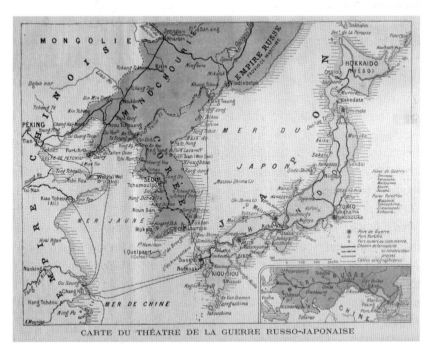

Map of the theatre of the Russo-Japanese War, 1904. Photo by The Print Collector/Alamy Stock Photo.

few inferior ports, Russian authorities decided to rely on the imperial army. In 1898, Russians had begun construction of the Eastern Chinese Railway, a new section of the Trans-Siberian Railroad linking Harbin in Manchuria with the newly leased Liaodong Peninsula in the northern China Sea. The railroad was completed four years later, giving the Russians access to two warm-water ports: the newly built port at Dalniy (Dalian) and the nearby naval base at Port Arthur (Lüshunkou).

Russia's rapid expansion was viewed with resentment in Tokyo and increasing alarm in China, Britain, and the US. In November 1901, a former Japanese Prime Minster, Prince Ito, arrived in St. Petersburg with the informal proposal to sign a peace treaty, which would recognize Japan's interests in Korea and allow Russia's control over Manchuria. Confident in the superiority of Russian arms, the emperor refused the offer.

In the following years, the Japanese government made continuous efforts to find a negotiated solution to the issue, only to face deliberate delays and obstruction. When Tokyo's last attempt and specific warnings failed in December 1903, Japan was ready for war.

On February 8, 1904, the Japanese fleet launched a surprise attack on the Russian ships at Port Arthur; a few hours later, Japan formally declared war. Blockading Port Arthur allowed the Japanese troops to land near Incheon in Korea and quickly occupy Seoul and the rest of the peninsula. Russian troops were further demoralized when after several unsuccessful attempts to break the blockade, the Russian flagship, with the fleet's commander Stepan Makarov onboard, struck a Japanese mine and sank. On May 1, the Japanese army stormed the Russian positions and crossed the Yalu River into Russian-controlled Manchuria. Suddenly, some in St. Petersburg began to realize that this might not be the "small victorious war" they had hoped for.

During that year, Russia suffered a series of relentless and crushing defeats on land and at sea. In August 1904, the Russians made another unsuccessful attempt to break through the Japanese blockade and bring their fleet to Vladivostok. During the battle, a Japanese shell scored a direct hit on the flagship's bridge, instantly killing the newly appointed Russian commander, Admiral Wilgelm Witgeft. With several ships damaged, the Russians retreated to Port Arthur. In December 1904, the Japanese army was finally able to capture one of the key bastions dominating the harbor, and using long-range artillery, they shelled and sank most of the Russian Pacific Fleet. On January 2, 1905, the commander of Port Arthur, General Anatoly Stessel, and his garrison surrendered to the Japanese. Port Arthur would never again come under Russian control.

At the same time, in Manchuria, the Russian army was retreating further north in hopes of regrouping at Mukden while waiting for reinforcements, which were slow to arrive because some sections of the Trans-Siberian Railroad were not complete. The Japanese did not wait. In what became known as the Battle of Mukden, 340,000 Russian and 280,000 Japanese troops confronted each other. This was the largest battle since Napoleon's defeat at the Battle of Leipzig in 1813. During the three weeks from late February to early March 1905, the Japanese troops overwhelmed the Russian flanks and inflicted heavy casualties. Facing encirclement and having lost 90,000 men, supplies, and artillery, the Russian commander ordered a retreat. For the next ten days, the remaining units of the Russian Manchurian Army kept marching north, avoiding captivity and complete destruction.

Despite the endless string of demoralizing news, the worst was yet to come. Early in the war, in October 1904, the emperor had reluctantly decided to dispatch the ships of the Baltic fleet to relieve the siege of Port Arthur. Leading the newly formed Second Pacific Squadron was Admiral Zinovii Rozhdestvenskii. Sailing 18,000 miles around Africa, the Russian fleet reached the southeast coast of Vietnam in French Indochina in late April 1905.

Disheartened by the news that Port Arthur had fallen to the Japanese several months previously, Rozhdestvenskii decided to move the fleet to Vladivostok. The longer and safer route would have taken his fleet east of Japan; the shortest route lay through the Tsushima Strait, between the southern tip of Korea and Japan. With crews exhausted from the long journey and the warships in need of maintenance, Rozhdestvenskii chose the shorter path. The Russians were hoping to slip through the Strait under the cover of night but were spotted by the Japanese.

On May 27, the Japanese fleet under Admiral Togo attacked the Russians with devastating results. During the two days of the Battle of Tsushima, which in its size and significance was comparable only to the Battle of Trafalgar, virtually the entire Russian fleet was either sunk or captured. Only three Russian warships reached Vladivostok. The Russians lost all their battleships and most of their cruisers and destroyers; 4,380 sailors were killed and 5,917 were captured. The Japanese lost three torpedo boats and 117 sailors killed. The Japanese navy proved to be superior to the Russian in every regard. Even to the most hardened war supporters in St. Petersburg, it became clear that the war was lost.

On September 5, 1905, with the US president Theodore Roosevelt serving as a mediator, the Russian delegation headed by Count Sergei Witte signed a peace treaty with Japan in Portsmouth, New Hampshire. Russia ceded to Japan the Korean peninsula, the Liaodong Peninsula with Port Arthur, the southern half of the Sakhalin Island, and agreed to evacuate Manchuria.

In his memoirs, which he prudently kept outside of Russia, Sergei Witte recalled that the war, which resulted in huge losses of territory and bitter humiliation, was entirely avoidable. The Russian intransigence came from the usual combination of denial and wishful thinking. The emperor had ignored numerous warnings of the escalating crisis in Manchuria and the need to settle it peacefully. Instead, he was influenced by a group of high-ranking Russian officials, known as the Bezobrazov clique, who had a personal investment in the timber concessions in Korea and advised him against any compromise with Japan.

Perhaps the most influential man in the government, the Interior Minister Vyacheslav von Plehve, had his own reasons to stay the war course. Shortly after the war broke out, the War Minister Aleksei Kuropatkin accused Plehve of being the only member of the government cabinet who shared the views of Bezobrazov and other political adventurists in clamoring for war. Plehve's response was as straightforward as it was cynical: "You do not know the situation in Russia. To stop the revolution, we need a small, victorious war." Assassinated by a terrorist bomb in July 1904, Plehve did not live to see how the "small victorious war" had turned into a large and humiliating defeat, bringing about the very social storm that he had tried to avert. In 1905 a revolution started in Russia.

1905
The Crisis

By the end of this year, the entire Russian Empire, from Poland to the Far East and from the Baltic to the Caucasus, was in the throes of revolution. The spark that ignited it was the massacre of hundreds of unarmed demonstrators, shot in cold blood by government troops near the tsar's residence at the Winter Palace in January 1905. The news of "Bloody Sunday," as the event became known, spread quickly through the capital and the country. The government could no longer contain the crisis that had been looming for years.

Strikes paralyzed the country. Workers demanded better working conditions, higher wages, and an eight-hour working day. Riots and disturbances swept through the countryside, where many peasants were compelled to live off

A city street during the 1905 revolution. Photo by Apic/Getty Images.

insufficient allotments and demanded redistribution of land. Numerous non-Russian peoples of the empire raised their voices in protest against the oppressive Russification policies and called for equality and autonomy. Radical ideas found increasing appeal among students, intellectuals, and workers and propelled the socialist parties to the political center stage. Russia's military defeats, rising bread prices, and a failing economy brought the empire to the brink of collapse. Both high-ranking Russian officials and foreign observers alike warned that the existing regime might not survive.

In the fall of 1905 the situation became desperate. The conservative faction of the Russian ruling elite was trying to persuade the tsar that military dictatorship was the only solution. The liberal faction pressed for major reforms that could modernize Russia and save it from collapse. As always, Nicholas II was indecisive. His personal preference was for military dictatorship but, given the state of the Russian military, demoralized by defeats and infected with revolutionary ideas, he had no confidence that the military could restore order.

Reluctantly, the tsar agreed with the proposal of the liberal camp championed by Count Sergei Witte. On October 17, 1905, Nicholas II signed the Manifesto on Improving State Law and Order. For the first time in the country's history, the imperial Manifesto granted basic civil liberties and freedoms of speech, assembly, association, press, and religion. It proclaimed universal male suffrage and the creation of the Russian parliament (the Duma) as a fully representative legislative body.

The October Manifesto sent shockwaves through Russian society. The liberal press and the centrist political parties were jubilant and proclaimed the beginning of a constitutional order with a truly representative government. For the conservative and reactionary groups, the Manifesto spelled the beginning of the end of autocracy and traditional order. The socialists, too, denounced the Manifesto on the grounds that it did not address the concerns of the working people and preserved the autocratic power of the tsar. Whatever the reaction, one could not deny that the Manifesto signaled a sharp break with the past and an uncertain future for the eroding power of autocracy.

Yet the Manifesto failed to achieve its principal and immediate goal—to mitigate the continuing violence and chaos and restore order on the streets. In fact, the suddenness with which the Manifesto was announced resulted in the outbreak of more disturbances and violence throughout the country. The socialist and liberal parties called for more strikes. The peasants interpreted the Manifesto as the right to seize more land and property from the landlords. Several military units mutinied, and many others were considered unreliable. The old ethnic and religious hostilities erupted anew into bloody clashes, such as those between the Armenians and Azeris in the Caucasus and the Poles and Russians in the Western borderlands of the vast empire. As always, the Jews represented the easiest target for reactionary rage, and numerous pogroms, often incited by local authorities, followed.

Prior to the October Manifesto, Sergei Witte had warned that Russia, which had no civil rights before, needed to be gradually prepared for such a dramatic transformation. It seemed that he was right, and Russia was now teetering on the edge of a revolutionary abyss. It was up to him to save the Russian Empire, as the feckless and dispirited tsar appointed Witte as new prime minister.

1906
The Tsar's Speech

The October Manifesto, which granted civil rights and a representative assembly, the Duma, was a victory for the liberal, educated, and professional classes. But for the working masses, the promise of freedom and liberties

Tsar Nicholas II speaking at the opening of the Duma. Photo by Fine Art Images/Heritage Images/Getty Images.

remained too abstract. The specific demands by the factory workers and peasants remained unaddressed, as did the concerns of the non-Russian peoples of the empire. Agitated by the radical left parties, the workers took to the streets and the peasants continued to rampage in the countryside.

In December 1905, the revolution reached its pinnacle, and the regime once again appeared to be on the brink of collapse. The epicenter of the revolution was Moscow, where the Bolsheviks' call for a violent overthrow of the regime succeeded in transforming the strikes into an armed insurrection. Realizing that liberal reforms were not going to stop the violence, the government responded with brute force, dispatching military units and the Cossack cavalry to crush the uprising and restore order. The uprising in Moscow, the largest and best organized, stood no chance against elite military units that used heavy artillery to pulverize the barricades. By the end of December, with several districts lying in ruins and over 1,000 dead, Moscow was quiet.

At that moment, those within the tsar's close circle who had argued against the October Manifesto won the argument: the use of force seemed to be more effective in achieving stability than the path of reform. Nicholas II, always inclined to listen to his conservative advisors, had signed the Manifesto only as an act of desperation. As the situation in the country changed, he began issuing a series of edicts, which one by one took back some of the promises of the Manifesto. Unable to exert his influence over the tsar and the direction of the government, Prime Minister Sergei Witte resigned on April 22.

The First State Duma that was about to be convened became the main threat to the established order and to the centuries-old autocracy of the Romanov dynasty. On April 23, just four days before the inaugural session of the First Duma, the tsar issued the Fundamental Laws. While often heralded as the first Russian constitution, the Fundamental Laws greatly diminished the authority of the Duma, declawed some of the reform promises, and preserved significant powers of the tsar, giving him, among other things, the power of a veto and the title of the "supreme autocrat."

Before convening their first meeting at the Tauride Palace, the members of the First Duma were invited to the throne room of the Winter Palace for the inauguration. Sitting on the throne in full regalia, the tsar made a short statement. It lasted for three minutes, was full of generalities, and squarely placed the emperor above the Duma and its deputies. It did not bode well for the future Duma.

The political composition of the First Duma surprised everyone: the tsar and his government because the right-wing parties they supported were routed; the centrist party of the Constitutional Democrats (Kadets) because they won an overwhelming majority; and the Bolsheviks and other radical left parties, who found themselves sidelined because they had boycotted the Duma, which they believed was a sham. Out of 478 deputies, the Kadets garnered 185, non-partisan deputies 112, various parties on the left 132, and the extreme right 0. The Duma was also remarkable for its wide representation of the non-Russian regions of the Russian Empire, including 32 deputies of the Polish National Democrats and 30 Muslim deputies.

No less surprising was the social composition of the Duma. The largest contingent proved to be the peasantry, with 231 deputies; the nobility had 180; the rest was divided between the lower middle class, Cossacks, and merchants. Even though he was disappointed with the outcome, Nicholas naively believed that the Duma would be friendly to the government because the peasants always loved their tsar. When told that the peasants were demanding land and might rebel, Nicholas calmly replied: "Then the army will pacify them."

The First Duma was the most liberal and representative of the four that would be convened and disbanded before the 1917 Revolution. But it stood no chance against the overwhelming hostility of the government and the tsar. During its short-lived existence between April 27 and July 8, the Duma was able to pass one bill of no significance. While debates took place on the floor, they could never materialize into legislation because of the obstruction from the upper chamber of the Duma, the State Council. Most members of the State Council as well as the government ministers were appointed by the tsar and had no incentive to collaborate with the center-left Duma. When the Kadets attempted to confront the government, the emperor simply disbanded the Duma on July 8, 1906. On the same day, Nicholas appointed a new prime minister. His name was Petr Stolypin.

1907
The Great Tiflis Robbery

The Bolsheviks and other leftist parties, who boycotted elections to the First Duma, resolved not to make the same mistake again. When the new elections to the Second Duma were called, parties on the left participated fully and successfully. As a result, the Second Duma emerged more radical than its predecessor, with 47 percent of the deputies representing the left block. Once again, the government was unprepared for such results and made sure that the Second Duma would be just as powerless as the first one. Three months into its existence, Prime Minister Stolypin demanded that the Duma hand over fifty-five deputies from the social democratic parties, who were allegedly plotting a coup against the government. Hours later, Stolypin ordered the arrest of the accused deputies and disbanded the Duma on June 3, 1907. The event became known as the "Stolypin Coup" and the prime minister would soon be referred to as Russia's Bismarck, after Germany's "Iron Chancellor," Otto von Bismarck.

The government charges were not without foundation. The radical left, and the Bolsheviks in particular, were plotting violent acts even as they were debating issues in the Duma. One such event stood out because of its brazen nature and long-term consequences. On June 26, 1907, a Bolshevik-organized heist netted 341,000 rubles (over $3.5 million in today's currency). It became known as the "Great Tiflis Robbery."

In April 1907, the high-ranking Bolsheviks, Vladimir Lenin, Leonid Krasin, Alexander Bogdanov, Maxim Litvinov, and Joseph Stalin, met in Berlin where, among other issues, they discussed ways to raise funds for purchasing arms. Their solution was a series of robberies, or "expropriations" as the Bolsheviks called them. One of the largest "expropriations" was entrusted to Stalin, who had experience in organizing robberies. Stalin and his Armenian childhood friend and notorious criminal, Simon Ter-Petrosian, known as Kamo, planned the operation. Their target was a bank in Tiflis, the capital of a region already known for its violence. In 1907 alone, there were 3,060 terrorist acts in the Caucasus, 1,732 of which were armed robberies.

An informant at the Tiflis branch of the State Bank notified Stalin that on June 26, the bank was scheduled to receive a large sum of money. When the stagecoach transporting the cash entered the Yerevan Square, where the bank was located, the robbers were already in position dressed as peasants and armed with bombs, grenades, and revolvers. At the same time, the gang's leader, Kamo, appeared in the square riding in an open carriage and dressed in the uniform of a cavalry captain. At a signal, the bombs and grenades were thrown at the security guards. In the midst of the loud explosions and the dead and mutilated bodies of the soldiers and horses, the robbers were able to seize the bags of cash, throw them into a carriage driven by Kamo, and escape from the scene before police reinforcements arrived. On his way from Yerevan Square, Kamo ran into a police patrol rushing towards the scene of the robbery. Without hesitation, Kamo yelled that the money was safe, and the police should rush to the Square. Thinking Kamo was a military officer, the police quickly obeyed.

The operation left around forty dead, many wounded, and much property destroyed. But it also brought 341,000 rubles into the party's coffers. As far as the Bolsheviks were concerned, "the expropriation" was an unqualified success. There was, however, one hitch. Most of the money came in 500-ruble notes which were traceable because their serial numbers had been recorded and were known to police.

Moving this large sum of money was no simple matter. At first, the cash was sewn into a mattress that was moved between several safe houses. Later the money found its way into the director's couch at the Tiflis Meteorological Observatory. The director later claimed that he never knew about it. Such a couch stuffed with cash could have been a nice complement to the twelve chairs stuffed with family jewels that were the subject of Ilf and Petrov's immortal 1928 novel, *The Twelve Chairs*.

Eventually, Kamo personally brought the cash to Lenin, who at the time was in Finland. Some of the money was in small denominations and unmarked. Lenin delegated Kamo to travel to Europe to purchase arms and ammunition with the unmarked bills. Kamo bought arms in Belgium and detonators in Bulgaria. After he arrived in Berlin, he was betrayed by a

Bolshevik informer working for the Russian Secret Police and was arrested with a suitcase full of detonators.

Since the money could not be exchanged in any of the Russian banks, Lenin, who had recently fled Finland and settled in Switzerland, instructed his comrades to go abroad and exchange the money at several European banks simultaneously. Betrayed by the same informer once again, those dispatched to exchange the bills were arrested in New York, Paris, Stockholm, and Munich. Only Krasin, who had hired a forger to change the serial numbers on his bills, succeeded. In the end, the money that the Bolsheviks obtained with so much blood and effort was unusable and had to be burned. The Tiflis robbery, which had initially appeared to be a great success, proved to be a fiasco.

Most significantly, the Tiflis robbery exposed a deep rift within the Russian Social Democratic Labor Party (RSDLP). For four years, the party had been divided into two factions: the Bolsheviks, who promoted violence and a socialist revolution, and the Mensheviks, who advocated more moderate means in line with the rest of the social democratic movement in Europe. When the party delegates had convened in London for the Party's Fifth Congress in May–June 1907, there was hope that both factions could reconcile their differences. Among the many issues that divided them was the issue of "expropriations." Lenin and some of the militant Bolsheviks argued that armed robberies were a legitimate way to raise money. The Mensheviks opposed violence and were able to get the overwhelming majority in Congress to pass a resolution condemning "the expropriations."

Despite the resolution, Lenin and his followers had formed a secret committee and continued to plot a series of armed robberies across Russia. The Tiflis robbery took place just weeks after the Fifth Congress ended. Shocked by Lenin's duplicity, the Mensheviks were furious. From then on, reconciliation was neither possible nor sought. With the cunning and ruthless nature of the Bolshevik leaders on full display, the Bolsheviks and Mensheviks parted ways and traveled along different roads towards the Russian revolutions of 1917.

1908
Father John of Kronstadt

Not long before his death in 1894, the Russian emperor Alexander III, in a conversation with Countess A. A. Tolstaya, inquired who were the most remarkable and popular people in Russia. The emperor added that he knew how honest she was and could trust her opinion. When Tolstaya mentioned her cousin, the writer Leo Tolstoy, Alexander III was not surprised, but when he asked her again who else might fit the bill, she mentioned Father John of Kronstadt. The emperor confessed that he had forgotten about him, but quickly agreed with the choice.

It was hardly accidental that these two men, one of Russia's greatest writers and one its most popular priests, would be mentioned in one breath. They both spoke for the poor and downtrodden, but their reaction to Russia's social ills placed them at opposite ends of society. Tolstoy condemned autocracy and the official church that supported it. Father John sought redemption within the church and under the guidance of the tsars. The fate of these two popular giants said much about the church and the role it played in early twentieth-century Russia. As an opponent of organized religion and the state, Tolstoy was excommunicated in 1901; despite several attempts to have him readmitted, the church refused to reconsider its judgment. By contrast, after Father John's death in December 1908, the government immediately authorized steps to canonize him, eventually leading to his sainthood.

Who was Saint John of Kronstadt? He was born Ioann Ilyich Sergeev in 1829 in a remote village in the Arkhangelsk province. Coming from the poor family of a local sacristan, Father John was able to finish the parish school in Arkhangelsk and earn a scholarship to St. Petersburg Theological Academy. By the end of 1855, he was a married and ordained priest at a parish in Kronstadt, Russia's large naval base in the Baltic Sea.

Father John's priestly life coincided with a period of broad social discontent: the Great Reforms initiated by Alexander II in the 1860s, the incessant terrorist acts by left-wing radical groups, the conservative reaction to violence, and the revolution of 1905. Like other imperial institutions, the church could not escape the wave of social change and reforms.

Ever since Peter the Great abolished the title of Patriarch in 1700, the Russian Orthodox Church had increasingly become part and parcel of the imperial government. Church affairs were administered by the Holy Synod, which was supervised by an appointed lay administrator, the Ober-Procurator, who over time began to report directly to the tsar. By the late eighteenth century, most of the church land had been confiscated; the emperor had become the official head of the Orthodox Church, which was declared "the first and foremost" in Russia's multi-religious empire.

Incorporating the church into the governmental bureaucratic structures meant that changes within the church closely mirrored changes within the government. For example, during the reign of the pious Tsar Alexander I, church matters and public education were combined into one Ministry because "Christian piety should always serve as the foundation of a true education." In the first quarter of the nineteenth century, there was a proliferation of missionary activity, with over 100 editions of the Bible translated into the 29 languages of the empire's non-Christian population. With the arrival of the reactionary policies of Nicholas I, missionary activity was largely scuttled, a recently founded Bible Society closed, ecclesiastical censorship tightened, and the debates within church periodicals limited to purely spiritual matters.

In 1861, the Minister of the Interior, P. I. Valuev, initiated church reforms that had a significant social impact. Through several legislative acts, the government successfully erased the boundaries that for centuries had defined the clerical estate. Seminary students were now allowed to enter the universities, the children of priests were accepted into gymnasia and military schools, and all Orthodox Christians were eligible to study at the seminaries. By 1875, almost half of university students came from the seminaries. Hoping to restructure religious education, the government even looked to Europe to see how education in the seminaries and religious academies could be improved.

After the assassination of Alexander II in 1881, the government once again backtracked from the course of liberalization and reform. The appointment of Konstantin Pobedonostsev as the Ober-Procurator of the Holy Synod signaled the return of a conservative reaction, Russia's "unshakable autocracy."

It was against this background that Father John searched for his own path within the church. His choice was an ascetic life and hard work on behalf of the destitute. He was involved in the temperance movement, in providing jobs and shelter for the poor, and distributing alms to the needy. Word of his healing powers spread quickly, and the small town of Kronstadt became a pilgrimage site visited by multitudes from all over the empire.

Father John became known as "a holy defender" of the little people, a humble champion of the poor, who in his emotional sermons called for mutual responsibility and openness to others. His appeal seemed to have crossed religious boundaries; he often received letters from Jews, Muslims, and Catholics, who asked for his prayers and help. His reputation reached its peak when, in 1894, he was summoned to the tsar's palace in the Crimea to administer to the dying Alexander III.

In the last decade of his life, Father John's politics moved further to the right, as he witnessed the 1905 revolution and the radicalization of Russian society accompanied by increasing violence. He eventually gave his wholehearted support to the far-right movement by blessing the banners of the radical anti-Semitic organization, the Union of the Russian People. It was said that Father John condemned Russia's influential statesman, Sergei Witte and writer Leo Tolstoy, as the two men responsible for destroying Russia. To the end, Father John remained a faithful defender of autocracy and continued to be revered as a charismatic leader of a conservative church and true Orthodox people. In this sense, Father John epitomized the standing of the church in imperial Russia. The church, which for centuries had found itself in the tight embrace of the government, had little choice but to rise and to fall with it.

1909
The Bosnian Crisis

Barely four years after Russia's debacle in the Far East, Russia suffered yet another humiliating international setback—this time in the Balkans.

It was hardly a secret that for centuries Russia's tsars and patriarchs had dreamt of returning the magnificent city on the Bosphorus to its proper name, Constantinople, and to its proper place at the heart of the Christian world. Apart from historical nostalgia, the strategic importance of Istanbul and the Straits of Bosphorus and Dardanelles was apparent.

Throughout the nineteenth century, the European powers had increasingly taken advantage of the "sick man of Europe," the declining Ottoman Empire. Under the pretexts of Christian solidarity and, later, Pan-Slavic brotherhood, Russia engaged in naked territorial aggrandizement in the Caucasus and in southeast Europe. Several international treaties that were meant to set limits on Russia's expansion failed to do so. Only the direct military involvement of the British and French, in what became known as the Crimean War of 1853–56, brought about Russia's defeat and halted its unbridled expansion.

A two-decade respite followed, during which Russia conquered most of Central Asia before returning its attention to the Ottoman borderlands. The Russo–Ottoman War of 1877–78 witnessed Ottoman defeats in both the Balkans and the Caucasus. Once again, the European powers intervened to stop Russia and prodded the Ottoman sultan to sue for peace. Yet even after Russia accepted the truce, her troops continued to move towards Istanbul. Only an appearance of British warships off the coast of the city changed the minds of the Russian commanders.

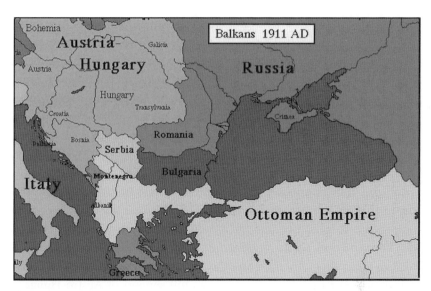

The Balkans in 1911.

The Russians were stopped, none too soon, having reached the small Ottoman village of San Stefano (today Yeshilköy) on the outskirts of Istanbul. Here, in 1878, no more than 12 miles away from the Sultan's palace, the Ottomans had signed the Treaty of San Stefano, surrendering much of their territory to the Russians in the Caucasus and recognizing their losses in the Balkans to Serbia, Romania, and the newly formed Bulgaria. Alarmed by Russia's success, the European powers convened the Congress of Berlin in the summer of 1878, where they succeeded in containing Russia's newly gained influence in the region.

Trying to break away from the constraints imposed by international treaties, Russia pushed to revisit the issue of the Straits. Since Russia's defeat in the Crimean War, the Black Sea had been demilitarized and no warships allowed through the Straits. With Russia's rebuilt Black Sea fleet bottled up there, the issue became more urgent.

In July 1908, the Russian Foreign Minister, Alexander Izvolskii, sent a letter to his counterpart in the Austro-Hungarian Empire, Count Alois von Aehrenthal, offering to amend the Treaty of Berlin by letting Vienna annex Bosnia-Herzegovina and the district of Novi Pazar (today a district in southwest Serbia) in exchange for "opening the Straits" to Russian warships. This triggered the Bosnian crisis.

Aehrenthal responded positively but with a slightly different proposal: Vienna would annex Bosnia-Herzegovina and in exchange would withdraw its troops from Novi Pazar. The issue of the Straits should be discussed separately. What happened when the two met to discuss the issues at the Buchlov Castle in the mountains of Moravia remains murky. Izvolskii later claimed that Aehrenthal fooled him, calling him a dirty Jew due to rumors that the Aehrenthals had Jewish roots. The rumors, incidentally, were wrong. Others believed that Izvolskii was dishonest about the course of negotiations and that when his plans ran afoul of the emperor's inner circle, he changed his tune by blaming Aehrenthal.

The government in Vienna followed up on its original proposal, and on October 6, 1908, it annexed Bosnia and withdrew from Novi Pazar. The Austro-Hungarian move in Bosnia quickly unraveled the fragile peace in the Balkans. Bulgaria declared independence, prompting complaints from the Ottoman Porte. Serbia mobilized its army, demanding a reversal of the Bosnian annexation. Britain refused to revisit the issue of the Straits much to Russia's consternation, and Germany's full support of Austro-Hungary muted the issue.

When the Russians balked at the Austro-Hungarian annexation of Bosnia, Vienna leaked several documents revealing that over the last 30 years Russia had agreed to give Austro-Hungary a free hand in Bosnia-Herzegovina and Novi Pazar. St. Petersburg was thoroughly embarrassed. For years, it had publicly assured Serbia that it supported its claim to the same region in the name of Orthodox and Slavic solidarity. Suddenly, Russian rhetoric turned out to be just a cynical political ploy. On March 23, 1909, Russia formally accepted the annexation of Bosnia-Herzegovina. Eight days later, Serbia too was compelled to accept the annexation and demobilize its troops.

In April 1909, a formal amendment to the Treaty of Berlin was signed in Europe's various capitals stipulating the annexation of Bosnia-Herzegovina by the Austro-Hungarian Empire. It was not the kind of amendment that St. Petersburg wanted. Bosnia was annexed by Austro-Hungary, while the Black Sea fleet continued to be denied access to the Mediterranean. Russia was bitter, but powerless to change the terms of the treaty. Serbia was livid about losing the territories it believed were to form a part of Greater Serbia. Any previous thought of reaching a compromise with Vienna proved to be an illusion. The lines of the Serbian-Russian alliance against that of Austro-Hungary-Germany were clearly drawn. In retrospect, the Bosnian crisis of 1908–1909 proved to be a prelude to the First World War, which, five years later, would engulf the European continent and neighboring regions in the bloodiest military conflict the world had ever seen.

2

Wars and Revolutions

1910
Tolstoy's Death

The news that Leo Tolstoy was nearing his death in the provincial town of Astapovo in Kaluga province reached St. Petersburg in November 1910 and immediately rang alarm bells at the highest levels of government. While to the rest of the world he was known as a great writer and a voice of universal moral authority, in Russia, Tolstoy was regarded as a sort of secular prophet, whose unsparing criticism of the autocracy and the Orthodox Church made him both popular and dangerous. Would his death cause mass disturbances and demonstrations? For the authorities, this was no idle question.

Russia's Prime Minister Petr Stolypin urged the Holy Synod to consider what they might do in case of Tolstoy's death. Members of the Synod discussed the issue in numerous sessions, but when the Procurator of the Synod had finally raised the possibility of giving Tolstoy a Christian burial, the bishops balked. They pointed out that Tolstoy showed no signs of repentance since the church's encyclical of 1901, which had effectively excommunicated him.

Throughout the years the church found itself in a difficult predicament when dealing with Tolstoy. While the 1901 encyclical condemned Tolstoy for his heretical views, the majority of his readers were not sure why the church had decided to punish the great writer. As his books were censored and all references deemed inappropriate were expunged, to readers his work seemed only to contain a humble religious message of sin and redemption. Tolstoy's death presented the church with the same uneasy challenge: denying a Christian burial to an immensely popular public figure was to invite questions from many Russian believers, yet to embrace the man who denounced the church and was considered a heretic seemed too much to ask.

Tolstoy in his study two years before his death.

It was Tolstoy himself who came to the church's rescue. In his will he specifically forbade any Christian references or the presence of a priest at his funeral. The church officials were still looking for any sign that Tolstoy might repent and change his mind in his final hours. A day after Tolstoy died, a priest named Parphenii arrived at Astapovo. He told a police officer that he had been sent by a personal order of the tsar and the Holy Synod to find out whether there were any indications that Tolstoy intended to retract his false beliefs and accede to an Orthodox funeral. He was told that there were none.

The news of Tolstoy's death on November 20, 1910 spread quickly at home and abroad. While the country was in mourning, the authorities were preparing for mass disturbances. A high official of the Interior Ministry was secretly sent to observe the situation at Astapovo, where an armed unit of gendarmes had been positioned a few days earlier. Police from the neighboring regions were placed on alert.

In Moscow, the authorities forbade any official signs of mourning, and the police were instructed to pay attention to what kind of ribbons were bought for the wreaths. Thousands of mourners were stuck at the train station since the police refused to allow extra trains to Astapovo. Mass rallies were forbidden in Moscow, St. Petersburg, Warsaw, and other cities. Nonetheless, about 5,000 students, intelligentsia, and peasants made their way to Yasnaia Poliana, Tolstoy's estate, where he was buried on November 24. Police were present at the funeral, and a group of mounted gendarmes was positioned in the nearby forest.

Tolstoy's will was respected. There were no priests, no wax candles, no icons, and no crosses. He was the first public figure in modern Russian history to be buried without an officiating priest.

Tolstoy's death and burial stood in sharp contrast to that of his arch enemy, Father John of Kronstadt, who was among the most vociferous voices in arguing for Tolstoy's expulsion from the church in 1901. Both Leo Tolstoy and Father John became immensely popular public figures as humble champions of the poor and oppressed. But the two chose very different paths. Father John sought redemption within the church and defended autocracy. As a result, the church canonized him, and the imperial authorities embraced Saint John of Kronstadt wholeheartedly. Leo Tolstoy denounced the church and the ruling political order and sought to replace corrupt clerical and secular institutions with brotherly love, peace, and tolerance. For this he was disowned by the church and rejected by authorities.

Tolstoy died a lonely giant, critical of both the old regime and the new ideologies of anarchism, socialism, and communism that were poised to replace it. In the end, Tolstoy's moral philosophy, with its appeal to universal human values, outlived both the police society of imperial Russia and the infinitely more repressive Soviet system that followed it. Called by Mahatma Gandhi "the greatest apostle of non-violence," Tolstoy's ideas were taken up by Gandhi and Martin Luther King in a bid to transform the world history of the twentieth century.

Paradoxically, while lionized for his literary achievements in his own country, Tolstoy's moral philosophy and political ideas never took root in Russia. Russia's history in the twentieth century would prove to be anything but non-violent.

1911
Terrorism

On the night of September 14, 1911, the Kiev City Theater was hosting a gala performance of Rimsky-Korsakov's opera *The Tale of Tsar Saltan*. The audience included Tsar Nicholas II accompanied by his two eldest daughters, as well as many high-ranking government officials. They had arrived in Kiev to attend the unveiling of a monument to Alexander II, who had abolished serfdom exactly fifty years before. Also attending the opera was Russia's prime minister, Petr Stolypin. During the second intermission, a young man named Dmitrii (Mordekhai Gershkovich) Bogrov approached Stolypin and shot him twice. Four days later Stolypin was dead, and with him died the last hope for saving the monarchy and modernizing the empire.

Petr Stolypin was and remains a controversial figure in Russia. To some, he was a brutal policeman appointed in July 1906 by Nicholas II to suppress revolutionary movements and restore stability to the empire. To others, he exemplified a reformer, who wanted to modernize Russia by ending traditional peasant communes and creating American-style independent farmers.

The assassination of Stolypin was yet another high point in a long history of terrorist activity in Russia. Its origins can be traced to April 1866, when Dmitrii Karakozov, a drifter and a member of a revolutionary group, made the first attempt to assassinate Alexander II. Amateur as it was, this assassination attempt inspired other radical revolutionaries to do the same. After seven unsuccessful attempts on his life, Alexander II was finally killed in March 1881 when his carriage was ambushed and blown up by several members of the radical "People's Will" organization.

With anarchism and political terrorism in the air, it was Sergei Nechaev's 1869 manifesto *Catechism of a Revolutionary* which outlined a vision of rational terror. Nechaev proposed creating a list of the most important

One of the assassination attempts on Prime-Minister Pyotr Stolypin. Photo by Keystone/Getty Images.

government officials and leaders, whose assassination would deprive the autocracy of its ablest people and eventually bring about its downfall. In the years before the Russian revolutions, the radical left consciously deployed terrorism as a weapon against the regime, just as a century later, Nechaev's work influenced the rise of the Black Panther Party in the US and the Red Brigades in Italy.

Harsh repression, increased surveillance, and the expansion of the police force in the wake of Alexander II's assassination helped to reduce acts of terrorism in the last two decades of the nineteenth century. Perhaps the best known was a plot to assassinate Alexander III in March 1887. It was disrupted by the arrest of conspirators ready to throw bombs at the tsar's carriage passing through the main thoroughfare of St. Petersburg. Among the leaders, who were refused pardon and hanged, was Alexander Ulianov, the elder brother of Vladimir Lenin.

A new wave of terrorist violence began in 1901, shortly before the emergence of the Socialist Revolutionary Party (the SR) and its military wing, which was bent on continuing the terror campaign. In 1901, the Minister of Education, Nikolai Bogolepov, was shot and killed by a student. A year later, Dmitrii Sipiagin, the Minister of Internal Affairs, was shot and killed by a young anarchist dressed as an officer. Sipiagin's successor, Viacheslav von Plehve, became the object of a failed assassination attempt in 1904. A year later, a group of Socialist Revolutionaries succeeded in killing him with a bomb thrown at his carriage. In 1905, the tsar's uncle, Grand Duke Sergei Aleksandrovich, was killed by a terrorist bomb. During the revolution of 1905–1906, the SRs greatly expanded their list of targets, adding regional governors, high-ranking military officers, mid-level civilian officials, and policemen. In 1906 alone, the SRs killed eighty-two government officials.

It was at this time that Nicholas II appointed Stolypin to deal with the violence and restore order. Almost immediately, he became a target of the revolutionaries. On August 25, 1906, several bombs exploded during a reception at his country residence. Stolypin escaped with slight injuries, but twenty-eight others were killed. His fifteen-year-old daughter was badly injured, while his three-year-old son sustained light wounds.

Stolypin responded in kind. In the following five years, hundreds of those suspected of revolutionary involvement were hanged, thousands exiled, the press heavily censored, the courts reigned in, and the electoral law altered to make the Duma more compliant. In the end, Nicholas II lost confidence in Stolypin, who antagonized not only the left but also right-wing groups that had initially supported him.

It was not surprising that opinions on who was behind Stolypin's murder differed. Some believed that he was murdered by Socialist Revolutionaries, who could not forgive him for setting in motion the reforms that were destroying traditional peasant communes, which they believed could easily transition into a socialist economy. Others thought that it was the work of right-wing groups, who had begun to see Stolypin as an unreliable defender of autocracy, one whose reforms threatened their radical conservative agenda and the old order they tried to preserve. Still others saw his murder as the result of his harsh Russification policies. The trouble was that Stolypin's murderer, Bogrov, could fit any of these profiles. He was a Jew, a double agent, a member of the SRs, and a onetime informer for the tsar's Secret Police.

In a 1906 interview with a British historian, Bernard Pares, Stolypin said: "I am fighting on two fronts. I am fighting against revolution, but for reform." Famously called a "conservative liberal," Stolypin's reforms did not seek to create a democratic order but to modernize and strengthen the monarchy. Just as the terrorist bombs that killed Alexander II thirty years earlier scuttled the path of further reform in Russia, Stolypin's assassination in 1911 left the country adrift in a sea of change.

1912
The Lena Massacre

In mid-April, newspaper headlines throughout the world were preoccupied with one story: a ship that was believed to be unsinkable and an event thought unimaginable. On April 15, the *Titanic*, the largest passenger liner in the world, struck an iceberg on its maiden voyage across the Atlantic and sank. Out of the 2,224 people aboard, fewer than one-third were rescued. A ship that was believed to be the pinnacle of ship-building went down and with it some of the grandees of the British and American elite.

But in Russia, the news of the *Titanic* was quickly replaced by a headline describing a large-scale massacre that had taken place in a distant corner of Russia. On April 17, the Russian military, summoned to deal with the miners' strikes at the Eastern Siberian goldfields, opened fire on some 2,500 protesters: 270 miners were killed and nearly as many were wounded.

The conditions at the goldmines, which were run by the Lena Gold Mining Partnership, a private joint-stock company, had been deteriorating for some time. The labor was extremely hard, the temperatures freezing, and the company had a complete monopoly on the miners' lives. They worked 15–16 hours a day, inhabited overcrowded, unfit-for-living barracks, suffered extremely high accident rates, had few doctors, were paid in coupons valid only in company stores, and were often fed rotten food. Indeed, it was the latter that sparked the strike in March 1912. By mid-April, the number of the striking miners had reached 6,000. They demanded the basics: an eight-hour work day, better pay, and improved working conditions.

The outrage over the massacre was widespread and it split Russia's business community. Some businessmen, led by banker and industrialist, Pavel Riabushinsky, demanded reforms and a greater role for businessmen in politics. Even the usually pliant Duma had to take on the issue and launched its own investigation into the Lena affair. The head of the Duma's fact-finding mission was Alexander Kerensky, a bright young lawyer, whose findings won him many acolytes among the Duma members. Kerensky rose as quickly as he would fall. In 1912, he was elected to the Duma as a moderate member of the Socialist Revolutionary Party, and in 1917 he became head of Russia's Provisional government, which lasted only eight months before being overthrown by Lenin's Bolsheviks.

Kerensky, and his nemesis Lenin, drew very different conclusions from the Lena incident. For Kerensky and most Duma members, it was a lesson in corrupt labor practices and the government's heavy handling of the protest. For Lenin, however, the incident reaffirmed his unshakable faith in the revolutionary potential of the industrial working class and a forthcoming proletarian revolution. As fate would have it, Lenin and Kerensky were born in the same provincial town on the Volga River, Simbirsk, renamed after Lenin's last name into Ulianovsk in 1924. Their fathers were both public school administrators, and their families knew each other well. Yet while Kerensky and Lenin each formed a starkly different view of the future, it was Lenin's more radical vision that prevailed in October 1917.

1913
The Romanovs

When the church bells rang during the Orthodox Christmas in January 1913, they also rang to mark the beginning of what was to be an extraordinary year—the 300-year anniversary of the ruling Romanov dynasty. A specially issued imperial manifesto declared a broad amnesty to prisoners, aid to the poor, imperial donations to charities, cancellation of debt for small business owners, and free food and entertainment during the celebrations. The imperial mint struck a series of commemorative coins, architects and sculptors worked to build new monuments and chapels, and the church held special services throughout the Russian Empire.

Early in the morning of February 21, 1913, twenty-one salvos of a cannon announced the beginning of the official celebrations that continued until the fall. Services in honor of the emperor were held in churches and cathedrals, but also in St. Petersburg's choral synagogue, the grand mosque, and the Buddhist temple (datsan), the latter two still under construction. It was a grand display of the empire's diversity and the alleged loyalty of all its subjects. In other cities, there were feasts for the commoners and balls for the gentry, military parades and cross processions; everywhere there were imperial flags and portraits of the emperor.

Particularly sumptuous celebrations took place in Kostroma, a provincial town northeast of Moscow, which occupied a special place in the history of the House of Romanov. It was from here that the founder of the dynasty, Michael Romanov, was called upon in 1613 to come to Moscow to accept the tsar's crown. Throughout the centuries, Kostroma enjoyed the special patronage of the royal family. On the occasion of the jubilee, the municipal authorities opened the Romanov museum and the Romanov hospital, while the State Duma passed a resolution to found the Romanov Pedagogical Institute in Kostroma, a co-ed, tuition-free institution to train teachers.

In May, the emperor and his family set out on a journey through the towns most closely associated with the Romanovs. By train and boat, they visited the old Russian towns around Moscow and along the Volga River. In each of the towns, they presided over events dedicated to their dynasty. In Vladimir, they were present at the opening ceremony of a hospital and groundbreaking of the Trinity Church; in Kostroma, they attended the groundbreaking for an ambitious monument to mark 300 years of the Romanov House; in Iaroslavl, they were present at the ceremony to open the Romanov Bridge, the first steel bridge across the Volga; in Rostov, Nizhnii Novgorod, and Moscow, the Romanovs attended church services, watched the parades and processions with icons, gave banquets, and received local gentry and merchants.

To an unaware observer, Russia might have appeared a happy and prosperous place, where commoners and nobles alike worshipped the tsar as their glorious ruler and a father to his people. Even Nicholas II might have

Three-hundredth anniversary of the House of Romanovs. Photo by Science History Images/Alamy Stock Photo.

succumbed to the power of the illusion created during the jubilee year, which reinforced his faith in the future of the empire.

Yet behind the festivities and celebrations was a society deeply divided and discontented. Peasants were restless, factory workers radicalized, political freedoms stifled, the Duma incapacitated, the military slow to modernize, the non-Russian peoples chafing at the Russification policies, the church subservient to the monarchy, and the emperor weak and ineffective. In 1913, Russia was already staring into the abyss, at the time visible only to a few.

Outside of the Russian Empire, there was one city where equally splendid celebrations and festivities took place. This was Belgrade, the capital of the resurgent Serbia. While the Metropolitan of Belgrade, Dimitrije, was attending festivities in St. Petersburg, special services in honor of the Romanovs were held in Belgrade's Cathedral. Among the guests were the eldest son of the Serbian King, Peter I, members of the Serbian cabinet, and Russian residents in Belgrade.

The bonds between St. Petersburg and Belgrade had been forged in the late nineteenth century and had grown into a close alliance in the first decade of the twentieth century. It was a perfect union with mutual interests couched in terms of the Pan-Slavic and Pan-Orthodox brotherhood. Russia used Serbia to project its Balkan interests, which were to take advantage of the Ottoman retreat and frustrate Habsburg ambitions. Belgrade, however, was fully dependent on Russia as an ally supporting the Serbian nationalist drive to reconstitute the Greater Serbia of long-gone days.

In fact, while the celebrations continued in Russia, the Second Balkan War broke out in June 1913. By early August the war was over, with victorious Serbia doubling its territories and emerging as the most powerful state in the Balkans. As Russia's satellite in the Balkans with an ever-increasing appetite for expansion, Serbia was eyed nervously by the Habsburgs and their German ally. The stage was set for another conflict that would become the First World War.

1914
Tannenberg

On June 28, 1914, two shots rang out in the streets of Sarajevo, a provincial town in a distant corner of southeastern Europe. On this day, which marked the 525th anniversary of the Battle of Kosovo and the beginning of the Serbs' long submission to Ottoman rule, a group of Serbian terrorists stood ready to assassinate the heir apparent to the Austro-Hungarian throne, Archduke Franz Ferdinand. The plot did not go as planned, but in the end, one of the six terrorists, Gavrilo Princip, succeeded in firing two shots, killing Ferdinand and his wife.

In the following weeks, the rhetoric and actions of the belligerent powers escalated rapidly. After receiving assurances of support from Germany, Austro-Hungary sent Serbia an ultimatum. Serbia, secure in Russia's full

Russian prisoners of war. Photo by Press Illustrating Service/FPG/Archive Photos/Getty Images.

support, refused to comply. On July 28, the government in Vienna declared war on Serbia. Russia announced a troop mobilization, which it had secretly begun three days earlier. Despite warnings from Germany, Russia continued with its military preparations.

Russia's early mobilization was seen by all parties as an act of war. It challenged the basis of the Schlieffen Plan, the German war plan, which was designed for Germany to avoid war on both fronts at the same time. Given Russia's large spaces and general inefficiency, the Schlieffen Plan presumed that Germany would have enough time to defeat France and then quickly move troops to the Eastern front against Russia. The beginning of Russia's secret mobilization on July 25 was a critical moment, which transformed a possible local conflict into a world war. Within a week, all major powers were at war: the Entente alliance of Britain, France, and Russia poised against the Central Powers, the alliance of Germany and Austro-Hungary. Only four weeks after the assassination in Sarajevo, the entire continent was engulfed in the First World War.

The nationalist propaganda machines assured their respective peoples that theirs was a just cause and that victory would be quick and sweet. On

August 17, Russian troops invaded the German province of East Prussia and the Austro-Hungarian province of Galicia. Two weeks later, the Russian army suffered the first humiliating defeat of the war at the Battle of Tannenberg.

On the eve of the war, the Russian army was the largest in Europe with 1.42 million soldiers. Germany feared the Russian "steamroller" but was also aware that the Russian army was poorly equipped and slow to move. Nonetheless, the advancing Russian troops outnumbered the Germans by almost two to one, and the Germans chose to retreat to avoid encirclement.

Two Russian armies, respectively under the commands of Generals Pavel von Rennenkampf and Alexander Samsonov, moved forward confidently. The Germans were aware that the two Russian commanders harbored deep-seated grudges towards each other dating back to the days of their service in the Russo-Japanese War, 1904–1905. Most astonishingly, the commanders communicated through unencrypted telegraph messages. It turned out that the Russians were short of cryptographic equipment and trained wireless telegraph operators. The intercepted communications allowed the Germans to anticipate the Russian troops' every move.

Russian armies proceeded to advance with little coordination and created a wide gap between themselves. The Germans were quick to exploit the situation and launched an attack on August 26. Unable to maintain supplies to the bulk of his army, General Samsonov ordered a retreat. Two days later, Samsonov's army found itself surrounded and pounded by the German artillery. Samsonov's appeal to Rennenkampf to come to his aid arrived too late. By August 30, four days after the battle began, Samsonov's army had been completely routed: 78,000 Russian troops were killed or wounded, 92,000 troops and 350 guns were captured, and only 10,000 had escaped. By contrast, the Germans suffered 12,000 casualties. General Samsonov committed suicide.

A week later, Rennenkampf's army was defeated at the Battle of the Masurian Lakes and was forced to withdraw to the pre-war border between Germany and Russia. Just one month after the declaration of war and great public enthusiasm, tens of thousands of Russian soldiers were either dead or wounded, the Russian invasion of Germany had failed, and the war no longer looked like a walk in the park. The first weeks of the war revealed the Russian military's chronic inability to supply troops. It also made clear that Russia's overwhelming numerical superiority was not enough against the smaller but better trained and equipped German army.

1915
Dreams of Tsargrad

The first two decades of the twentieth century were referred to as the Silver Age of Russian poetry: the time of an enormously creative outburst of the Russian avant-garde that pushed the boundaries of accepted genres and experimented with new styles and ideas. The outbreak of the war came as a surprise to most Russian modernists, and it channeled their energy towards comprehending the war and Russia's role in the world. Once Russia was at war, the reaction of this literary elite occupied the entire spectrum: from enthusiastic patriotism and joy to depression and despair.

In the summer of 1914, Anna Akhmatova warned of "the approaching frightening times" and "many fresh graves." A year later, when one could already see the first consequences of the war, Velimir Khlebnikov wrote that "the forests of Siberia will not suffice to make enough crutches." Others bemoaned the war's unjustified butchery (Andrei Belyi) and condemned the fervor of Russian messianic chauvinism (Zinaida Gippius and Dmitrii Merezhkovskii).

Yet there was another camp of Russian modernists who wholeheartedly supported Russia's war efforts. The most ardent supporters of the war were the neo-Slavophiles, a group of modernists who saw the war as Russia's holy cause. A writer, Viacheslav Ivanov, stated unapologetically in an interview in December 1914: "I believe this war to be holy in its inner essence and a war of liberation, and I regard it as something very positive." This was a continuation of the traditional Slavophile ideology that claimed Russia as God's chosen nation, blessed and destined for a historic mission.

If Ivanov saw Russia's apocalyptic Christianity as the foundation for establishing a universal Church, his literary colleague and fervent supporter of the war, Fedor Sologub, believed that together with China, India, and Japan, Russia formed a part of the "mystical East." By juxtaposing East and West, Europe and Asia, Sologub, like Ivanov, found a special role for Russia, far and apart from Europe.

Valerii Briusov represented yet another strand of the neo-Slavophile ideology. For Briusov, the war was a battle between the Germans and the Slavs. Similar to the French and British, Briusov too saw the Germans as barbarians, the descendants of Attila the Hun. But the "barbarian army" had a high technological standard, thus the war, for Briusov, pitted a mechanical, automated society in the shape of Germany against the living human spirit of the Slavs. By contrasting the spiritual Russian soul with inhuman Western technology, Briusov was merely reviving the old Slavophile claim of Russia's exceptionalism.

It was natural for the neo-Slavophiles to condemn Western imperial ambitions while backing Russia's own imperialist designs. This was particularly true in the south where, for centuries, Russia had dreamt of returning the Ottoman capital, Istanbul, to its previous name of Constantinople or, as the Russians referred to it, Tsargrad, the City of the Tsar. In addition to the messianic vision of restoring Orthodox Christianity to the former Byzantine lands, Istanbul and the Straits of Bosphorus and Dardanelles had an immense geopolitical significance. Whoever controlled the Straits controlled direct access from the Black Sea to the Mediterranean.

Throughout the nineteenth century, it was the British Navy that stood between Russia's designs and Ottoman resistance. The conflict indirectly led to the Crimean War of 1853–56, in which Russia suffered a humiliating loss at the hands of the British and French militaries. Two decades later, in yet another Russo-Ottoman War of 1877–78, the Russians soundly defeated the Ottomans and, after agreeing to a truce, continued to march towards Istanbul. Once again, it was only the dispatch of British battleships that made the Russian troops stop, this time within seven miles of the city, where they signed the Treaty of San Stefano. Among other things, the treaty ceded to Russia Armenian and Georgian territories in the Caucasus, but it made no concession on the Straits.

Now that the British, French, and Russians found themselves on the same side in the First World War, the Russians seemed to be very close to turning their old dreams into reality. On March 18, 1915, Britain, France, and Russia signed a secret document, known as the "Constantinople Agreement," in which the allies promised that, upon their victory, they would hand Istanbul and the Straits to Russia. The old dreams and new realities meant that Russia was within reach of a great historic prize.

1916
Rasputin

As Nicholas II and his family celebrated their last Christmas at the Winter Palace in St. Petersburg, there was no customary exchange of presents between the imperial family and the rest of the Romanovs. The relationships between the Romanovs had begun to fray as Nicholas II and his German-born wife, Alexandra, learned that some of their cousins had conspired against them.

Indeed, as the war went from bad to worse, there were plots against Nicholas II and his circle. Some conspirators sought to depose Nicholas II or force him to abdicate. Others believed they could save both the imperial family and Russia by getting rid of an embarrassing outsider at the court with too much influence over Nicholas and Alexandra. Several plots were hatched, and one finally succeeded: the assassination of Grigorii Rasputin.

Nicholas II and Alexandra's only son, Aleksei, suffered from hemophilia, an incurable genetic blood disease, which had killed many of Alexandra's relatives. With no effective medical treatment available, a desperate Alexandra turned to a holy man: Grigorii Rasputin.

It seemed indeed that Rasputin was able to stop Aleksei's bleeding, and he thus made himself indispensable to the imperial family. Yet to many in the capital, Rasputin was no more than a charlatan who exercised an inordinate influence over the imperial family. Without any justification, Rasputin was blamed for the current situation: for convincing the emperor to assume the

Grigorii Rasputin.

position of commander-in-chief against the advice of his own government, for selecting inefficient cabinet ministers, and for being altogether responsible for turning the tsar's attention towards mysticism and away from the successful prosecution of the war. Moreover, the imperial family's association with the man, whose reputation for sexual debauchery and drunkenness became the stuff of legends, had become increasingly embarrassing to the ruling elites.

When new rumors emerged that the tsar, influenced by Alexandra and Rasputin, was ready to sign a unilateral peace treaty with Germany, the plotters could wait no longer. The three conspirators: 29-year-old Prince Felix Yusupov, the Grand Duke Dmitrii Pavlovich, the tsar's nephew, and the Grand Duke Nikolai Mikhailovich, the tsar's cousin, resolved to dispose of Rasputin once and for all. All three were known to be homosexuals, and apparently Yusupov, who was married but who struggled with his sexuality, had previously sought Rasputin's advice. Instead, Rasputin, who seemed to have been bisexual, tried to seduce him.

The plotters, joined by the right-wing Duma leader, V. M. Purishkevich, decided to invite Rasputin to Yusupov's palace on the banks of the Moika River under the pretext of meeting Yusupov's beautiful wife, the Grand Duchess Irina Aleksandrovna. There they planned to poison him and dump his body into the river. As planned, on December 16, Rasputin arrived in Yusupov's car and was led to the basement salon. There, awaiting the Duchess, he drank several glasses of poisoned wine and ate pastries filled with cyanide. Yet, an hour later, the poison seemed to have had no effect on him. In desperation, Yusupov grabbed a pistol from his writing desk and shot Rasputin, who issued a wild scream and collapsed on the floor. Believing that he was dead, the conspirators left the room to make preparations for the disposal of his body. In the meantime, Rasputin regained consciousness and made his way out into the courtyard. When Purishkevich saw Rasputin staggering through the snow towards the gate, he shot him two more times and finally killed "the holy man." The conspirators then dumped the corpse, weighed down with iron chains, into the river, where it washed up on the shores of the Neva River two days later.

In Russia's aristocratic circles, the news of Rasputin's murder was greeted with joy and relief. Many considered it a patriotic act. Sixteen members of the Romanov dynasty signed a petition to the tsar asking him to forgive the Grand Duke Dmitrii's participation in the plot. Nicholas rejected the appeal, pointing out that no one had the right to engage in murder. The Grand Duke Dmitrii was exiled to Persia, and four other grand dukes were banished from the capital. If the plotters hoped to free the emperor from unhealthy influences and to invigorate Russia's war effort by murdering Rasputin, they were mistaken. Nicholas drew closer to his own family, isolating himself further from Russian aristocracy and the concerns of the war. The year ended with failed attempts to rescue the empire by a coup at the top. A change would come in 1917, but it was far more dramatic than members of the aristocracy hoped for. Two revolutions would sweep away first the monarchy and then a nascent democracy.

1917
"Down with Autocracy, Down with the War"

As the father to his people and the embodiment of the empire, Nicholas II continued to believe in his divine infallibility. Detached from the rapidly unfolding events around him, the tsar failed to realize that he had lost support among both the political parties in the Duma and the war-weary Russian people.

Storming of the Winter Palace. Photo by OFF/AFP/Getty Images.

February 1917 began with a workers' strike and demonstrations demanding bread. Harsh cold temperatures put a dent into already meager supplies of coal and flour in Petrograd, the Russified form of St. Petersburg that had been adopted since the beginning of the war. Within a few days, the shelves were empty, and the city authorities announced the beginning of rationing. On February 22 (March 7 new style), the workers at the Putilov factory, the largest industrial enterprise in the capital, declared a strike. Three days later, the entire city was shut down, with women, white-collar workers, and students joining the strikers. The demands for bread were now replaced with the slogans "Down with Autocracy" and "Down with the War." When the city's military commander ordered troops to disperse the demonstrators, the soldiers refused. The Duma established the Provisional Committee and the socialist parties formed their own Council (*Sovet*, usually spelled in English as *Soviet*) of the Workers.

On March 1, the emperor, on his way from the Military Headquarters (Stavka) to join his family at their summer residence near Petrograd, was diverted to the army's headquarters in the north, where the Army Chiefs and some Duma deputies urged him to abdicate without delay. He did so the next day in favor of his brother, Grand Duke Mikhail Aleksandrovich, who then declined the crown. The Empire no longer had an emperor. The Duma had now formed a Provisional Government, which placed Nicholas and his family under house arrest. Dramatically, three centuries of the Romanov autocracy came to an end.

While a revolutionary Petrograd was celebrating the downfall of the Romanovs, the second slogan of the socialists and insurgent soldiers demanding an end to the war was yet to be realized. The Provisional Government was preoccupied with dismantling the old regime and heralding a new, democratic Russia. Indeed, within several months, it passed a dizzying array of laws endowing Russian citizens with basic rights and freedoms. Yet its power was heavily circumscribed by a competing source of authority—the Soviets, Councils of the Workers' and Soldiers' Deputies—who were in charge of the nuts and bolts of the war economy.

The competing powers of the Provisional Government and the Soviets generated a political crisis that, seven months later, culminated in yet another revolution, or a coup, in which the Bolsheviks seized power. In early April, the leader of the Bolsheviks, Vladimir Lenin, arrived in Petrograd and quickly assessed the situation: the February Revolution had brought down autocracy and established a democratic republic; it was time to move towards the next stage, the socialist revolution prophesied by Karl Marx. Lenin had little respect for what he called "the bourgeois freedoms" enacted by the Provisional Government and determined correctly that the real power rested with the Soviets. But the Soviets were dominated by the socialist parties of the Mensheviks and Socialist Revolutionaries. Therefore, Lenin concluded, the task of the Bolsheviks was to infiltrate and prevail in the Soviets, get rid of the Provisional Government, and make the Soviets of the Workers, Soldiers, and Agricultural Laborers (the new groups that Lenin added) the only source of legitimate authority in Russia. His plan succeeded spectacularly.

Before Lenin's arrival in Petrograd, the Bolsheviks had little influence and were a small party of 24,000 members. By October, the Bolsheviks had become the most powerful party in Petrograd and Moscow and dominated many Soviets, as their membership grew nine-fold. In part, the party's iron discipline and relentless propaganda accounted for its success. But mainly, it was Russia's economic collapse and continuous failure on the battlefield that helped propel the Bolsheviks and their anti-war agenda to the forefront. In June, after yet another Russian offensive against Germany had ended disastrously, strikes and mutinies among the soldiers and sailors became widespread.

After much controversy and debate within the party, the Bolsheviks were ready to seize power on the night of October 25. With a blank shot from the battleship Aurora, troops loyal to the Bolsheviks stormed the Winter Palace, the seat of the Provisional Government. The members of the government were arrested and the Petrograd Soviets assumed the legitimacy of a new Bolshevik regime. This was the beginning of the socialist revolution in Russia, that theorized by Marx and put into practice by Lenin. Arguably, it was also the most decisive event of the twentieth century, and the one that radically changed the history of Russia and the world around it.

1918
The Red Terror

On October 13, 1918, on the eve of the first anniversary of the October Revolution, the Patriarch of Moscow and All of Russia, Tikhon, bravely wrote to the authorities: "The entire year you are holding in your hands state power and preparing to celebrate the first anniversary of the October Revolution, but the rivers of blood of our brothers' murdered on your orders are crying to heaven and compel us to tell you the bitter word of truth." He

Nicholas II and his family. Photo by Universal History Archive/Getty Images.

was right. A virtually bloodless October Revolution quickly evolved into a violent and bloody civil war that during the next three years would claim millions of lives. By various estimates, the number of those who perished from war, repression, wanton violence, disease, and famine varies between eight and fifteen million people.

Resistance to the Bolsheviks' seizure of power came from many quarters: a dismayed nobility, a shocked urban bourgeoisie, the Cossacks and military officers, clergy and prosperous peasants, and even from some among the Bolsheviks' own power base of workers and soldiers led by other socialist factions. Lenin never had any illusions about a power struggle. He postulated early on that to secure their victory, the Bolsheviks needed to establish "a dictatorship of the proletariat." On December 20, 1917, less than two months after the revolution, the Bolsheviks founded the Extraordinary Committee to root out the enemy. Led by a devoted Polish Bolshevik Felix Dzerzhinsky, the Extraordinary Committee, or Cheka, as it was commonly known, became a notorious precursor of Russia's ominous state Secret Police, the NKVD (People's Department of Internal Affairs), later the KGB.

It was on July 16, 1918 that the Bolsheviks showed their true colors to the stunned and dismayed world. On this day, under orders from the Kremlin, the entire royal family of the Romanovs, including the tsar, his wife, their five children, together with their doctor, cook, maid and a servant, were shot and bayoneted in cold blood in the distant Siberian city of Yekaterinburg. The First World War had also brought to an end the rule of the Ottoman, Hapsburg, and German imperial households, but none of them suffered a fate so cruel and wanton as the Romanovs.

There was a civil war, and the Bolsheviks, no doubt, were under siege, facing armed uprisings by sailors, soldiers, and civilians in Russian towns, peasant resistance against the forceful requisition of grain, foreign troops and the White armies, and anarchy and banditry in the countryside. There were assassination attempts against the Bolshevik leaders. The first failed attempt to assassinate Lenin took place in January 1918. On August 17, a prominent member of the Bolshevik Central Committee and the chief of the Petrograd Cheka, Moisei Uritsky, was assassinated by a military cadet avenging the execution of his friends. Two weeks later, a second attempt on Lenin's life left him partly paralyzed by a bullet lodged deep in his neck. The suspected assassin, Fania Kaplan, a member of the Socialist Revolutionary Party, was arrested and promptly executed without any investigation or trial.

It was in this febrile atmosphere that the Bolshevik leadership resorted to a campaign of Red Terror, publicly announced in the Bolshevik paper, the Red Gazette, on September 2, 1918. The Red Terror was an auspicious beginning for the mass political repressions that would later come to define the political system created by the Bolsheviks. This specific campaign of terror lasted throughout the Civil War and did not abate until 1922. The logic of the Red Terror was simple—to eradicate the counter-revolutionaries. Yet, because the counter-revolutionaries and conspiracies seemed to be everywhere, the mass terror was intended to intimidate and subdue the entire population of Russia. Lenin personally argued that any enemies were to be publicly hanged, and the news of executions spread as far as possible. The enemy was everywhere: the nobility of the old regime, well-to-do peasants and Cossacks, the middle classes, which chose to side with the White Army, and the workers and soldiers who mutinied. Those suspected of disloyalty were either to be executed or placed in concentration camps.

Dzerzhinsky's statue in front of the KGB headquarters.

Atrocities were common: seized hostages, arrests without charge, and widespread torture. When not enough suspects were arrested, the Bolshevik leadership demanded more, setting up quotas for the "enemies of the revolution." Within two months, 10,000 to 15,000 people had been summarily executed. The Red Terror proved to be very red indeed.

The Bolsheviks might have tried to drown their deeds in the rhetoric of lofty communist ideals and militant propaganda, but the facts remained: the revolution unleashed rivers of blood, and nothing could stop the Bolshevik leaders from pursuing their violent course.

1919
Mass Violence Against Cossacks

The Civil War had become a laboratory of violence for the Bolsheviks, who learned to see carnage and brute force as ordinary policy tools. Counter-revolutionaries, prisoners of war, professionals accused of sabotage, peasants who refused to surrender their grain and livestock, all shared the same fate: arrest and execution. It was also at this time that the Party used mass violence against a specific social group, the Cossacks.

Historically, Cossacks emerged on Russia's southern frontiers as communities of freebooters, mostly peasants who had fled the authorities in search of freedom and a new life. They settled in a no-man's land between different empires and formed democratic communities of warriors, who lived off war and booty. By the late eighteenth century, the expanding Russian Empire was able to impose its rule over the Cossacks and turn them into Russia's irregular military. Eventually, the Cossacks became Russia's separate military class with substantial privileges of owning land and retaining a degree of administrative autonomy. In return, they became highly loyal to the autocracy. They were often deployed to suppress protests, and in time acquired their typical image as the tsar's violent servitors, riding their horses into crowds while lashing demonstrators with their signature whips.

As such, the Bolsheviks held a particular animus towards the Cossacks. On January 24, 1918, the Party's Central Committee issued a secret order that recognized that there was no other way to establish Soviet rule in the Cossack regions but by a merciless and total annihilation of Cossack leadership. The instructions were specific, indicating point-by-point the prescribed measures that would later serve as a blueprint for the larger-scale violence deployed during collectivization campaigns in the countryside during the 1930s.

The Cossacks. The Protected Art Archive/Alamy Stock Photo.

The order of the Central Committee instructed local Bolsheviks to conduct a campaign of mass terror against affluent Cossacks and all those who resisted Soviet policies. The Bolshevik leaders, supported by armed units, were to confiscate grain and other agricultural products and to disarm all Cossacks. Any Cossack found to have arms after the deadline was to be shot. While death and terror awaited prosperous Cossacks, the Party ordered a massive resettlement of poor peasants on Cossack lands. Finally, the directive encouraged local Bolsheviks to follow these instructions without compromise or half measures.

Yet if the Bolsheviks hoped to suppress resistance with their ruthless policies, they achieved quite the opposite. All Cossacks, both rich and poor, rose up against the forceful confiscation of their property and resettlement of newcomers on their land. One Cossack region after another rebelled and joined forces with the White Army to fight against the Bolshevik regime. The Bolshevik response was more violence. The head of the Red Army, Leon Trotsky, dispatched a punitive expeditionary force with instructions to destroy Cossack villages and kill any Cossacks who offered resistance.

Within a year, the Cossack revolt had been suppressed. The traditional autonomy of the Cossack communities along the Don, Terek, and Kuban rivers was dissolved. Many Cossacks fled together with the retreating White Army. Many were later captured by the Bolsheviks, but a few managed to escape from Russia. It is estimated that among the Don Cossacks alone, with a pre-Civil War population of 1.5 million people, as many as 500,000 were killed or deported. No one knew then that what seemed like a terrible tragedy was only a prelude to a far greater human calamity. Barely a decade later, collectivization, the Party's violent campaign of introducing socialism to the countryside, would utterly ruin the peasantry, killing millions by force and famine and deporting more millions to Siberia.

Part II

Utopia in Power

3

Socialism Delayed

1920
Congress of the Peoples of the East

As the Civil War raged and hope for a revolution in the West began to fade, the task of promoting the revolutionary cause in the East became ever more important. After all, Russia was as much a part of Europe as it was of Asia. Naturally, in the minds of the Bolshevik leadership, it fell on Moscow to provide guidance to the peoples of the East stretching from Turkey to China.

The situation in the East, however, presented peculiar challenges. How was one to promote a socialist revolution in societies where the proletariat was absent, urban centers few, and the economy agrarian? It seemed that the situation defied the central premise of classical Marxism that stipulated that the working class would spearhead a socialist revolution in the developed European societies. Of course, Lenin had previously showed remarkable flexibility by arguing that, in fact, Russia, not the West, was destined to become the cradle of a socialist revolution because Russia constituted the weakest link in the chain of imperialism. Whether this was Lenin's creative adaptation of Marxist ideas to Russian circumstances or a cynical ploy to harness a Marxist theoretical base to his own ambition is anyone's guess.

The Bolsheviks' strategy towards the non-Western societies once again departed from mainstream socialist doctrines, which saw the East as backward and lacking an industrial working class, and therefore not ready for socialism. European Marxists believed that socialism first had to prevail in Western societies, which then would help less developed countries to become socialist. Lenin had no time to wait either for the revolutions in the West or an appearance of the proletariat in the East. The East, Lenin declared, was ready for a socialist revolution led by peasant masses.

It was with this in mind that the Bolsheviks convened the First Congress of the Peoples of the East that met in Baku, the capital of the newly declared Soviet Socialist Republic of Azerbaijan, in the first week of September. There were all together 1,891 delegates from different parts of the Russian Empire and the world. The largest contingents belonged to the Azeris (336 delegates) and Turks (273). The North Caucasus was mostly represented by the Lezgins (218) and Chechens (85). There were also 204 delegates from Iran, and smaller groups of Armenians, Georgians, Uzbeks, Tatars, Hindus, Arabs, Chinese, and others. Fifty-three delegates, less than 3 percent of the total, were women.

The delegates arrived dressed in their national costumes, so the Congress looked like a well-staged pageant. A contemporary critic, M.N. Roy, a prominent Indian revolutionary who believed that the East was not ready for socialism, dismissed the Congress as "the Zinoviev circus," after Grigorii Zinoviev, the Chairman of the Communist International (the Comintern) and the Baku Congress.

The Congress was conceived as a continuation of the Second Congress of the Comintern, which had just finished its work in Moscow in July 1920. The agenda of the Baku Congress, however, was to emphasize a national and anti-colonial struggle, to consider the agrarian question, and to promote the growth of the Soviets in the East.

Behind the lofty slogans of "a resolute struggle for freedom and independence of all peoples regardless of their race and skin color, and the elimination of human exploitation," the Bolsheviks faced a real challenge from the nationalist movements that swept through Asia. The Bolsheviks had to strike a delicate balance between joining those parties that represented nationalist and peasant movements, while also criticizing them for not being sufficiently socialist and radical.

In his bombastic opening speech on the first day of the Congress, Zinoviev offered a perfect example of this uneasy relationship. While welcoming and lauding the numerous delegates from Turkey for their successful anti-imperialist struggle, Zinoviev also criticized Mustafa Kemal, the future founder of modern Turkey, who later became known as Atatürk, for declaring the persona of the sultan and caliph as sacred and therefore inviolable. Zinoviev must have expected the Ottoman royal house to share the fate of the Romanov dynasty.

Eight days of passionate speeches called for an anti-imperialist and anti-colonial struggle and condemned the notion that the peasants were unable to govern the country. Curiously, the very last session was dedicated to the issues of women, who appealed for equality with men, abolition of polygamy, and the right to education and work. It seems that the women's agenda was met with little enthusiasm. The Bolsheviks did not immediately realize that the women in the East could serve as a critical tool in helping them to achieve their goals.

On September 8, the Congress finally concluded its work with an appeal to the peasant masses of the East to seize power and land, create the Soviet peasant republics of the East, and link them into one federation with the Soviet republics in the West. By 1923, as it became clear that a Bolshevik revolution had failed to spark similar events in Europe, the Party increasingly turned its attention to the East hoping for socialism to take root among the vast populations that would link Russia with India and China. In his speech at the Baku Congress, Zinoviev confidently proclaimed, "when the East begins to move, not only Russia but all of Europe will seem only a small corner of this vast scene." In stark contrast to classical Marxism, socialism was now expected to arrive in Europe from the less-developed societies of Asia.

1921
Famine, Chemical Weapons, and Concentration Camps

By the end of 1920, the Bolsheviks had achieved several crucial victories against the White and foreign armies. The short-lived and indecisive intervention by the Allied troops was over, the Polish army was pushed back, and the remnants of the White Army under Baron General P. N. Wrangel fled to the Crimea and were eventually evacuated to Istanbul. Yet many chose to remain in Russia and submit themselves to the mercy of the new regime in Moscow. But the Bolsheviks were not given to mercy. Within the last two months of 1920, an estimated 50,000 people, mostly civilians who followed the White Army, were massacred in the Crimea, making it the largest civilian massacre of the Civil War.

But just as the White Army was finally defeated, the government in Moscow found itself under a new kind of threat. This time it came from the very people who were supposed to support the Bolshevik cause: sailors, workers, and peasants.

Throughout the Civil War, in order to feed the cities and the Red Army, the Bolsheviks relied on forceful requisition of grain and other foodstuffs

Children at a camp in Samara, Central Russia. Photo by Topical Press Agency/ Getty Images.

from the countryside. By late 1920–early 1921, the Bolsheviks' expropriations, combined with chaos and violence, poor harvests, and famine, transformed the disgruntled peasant masses into an organized resistance army. The epicenter of this peasant unrest was the central Russian province of Tambov.

Organized by the Socialist Revolutionary Alexander Antonov, the Tambov peasant army included as many as 50,000 peasants and Red Army deserters. In the next few months, the uprising spread down the Volga River towards the cities of Samara, Saratov, Tsaritsyn, and Astrakhan and east into Siberia.

The Kremlin leaders became alarmed. Only a few months previously, they had ruthlessly suppressed a rebellion at the naval base of Kronstadt. There, provoked by diminishing food rations, a Bolshevik ban on workers' strikes, and liberal use of Cheka units, the sailors of Kronstadt convened a committee that presented Moscow with a long list of demands: freedom of speech and assembly, the right to organize trade unions and peasant associations, the release of political prisoners, the abolition of armed Bolshevik militias and guards at factories, and equal rations for all workers. The Bolsheviks immediately rejected the demands and charged the organizers of the Kronstadt committees with a conspiracy hatched by French counterintelligence. A week after the Committee submitted its demands, 60,000 Red Army troops, under General Mikhail Tukhachevskii, stormed Kronstadt. On March 19, 12 days after they began the assault, the Bolsheviks were in full control of Kronstadt. Thousands of Red Army troops died during the siege of this formidable naval base, and Tukhachevskii's retribution was swift: around 2,000 Kronstadt sailors were promptly executed and several thousand more dispatched to what would become an infamous prison camp at the Solovetsky Islands (Solovki) in the White Sea. The Kronstadt uprising was over.

Given his success at Kronstadt, Tukhachevskii was sent to Tambov at the head of 100,000 Red Army troops and Cheka units. He received specific instructions to pursue "the liquidation campaign of the Tambov province bandits." It was here that Tukhachevskii famously declared "a total war" against civilians, ordering his troops on June 11, 1921 "to shoot on the spot, without hesitation, any citizen refusing to give his name," "hostages in villages, where arms are hidden," and "the eldest sons of bandit families." The following day Tukhachevskii ordered the use of poison gas to flush the rebels out of the forests. During the summer and fall, he continued to use this gas against civilians. In July, the Bolsheviks opened seven concentration camps, which housed 50,000 prisoners, mostly elderly, women, and children. The monthly death rate from famine and disease was estimated at 15–20 percent of the prisoners.

Like the Kronstadt uprising, that in Tambov was eventually suppressed at a terrible human cost. Between 1920 and 1922, an estimated 240,000 people died in the Tambov province from war, mass executions, and imprisonment.

The Civil War and new Bolshevik policies had also created a famine that affected millions of peasants in the Volga River region. At least 1 million perished from hunger and disease, and many more would have died if not for a massive food aid program from primarily US international relief organizations. Even then, in the middle of the famine, the Soviet government diverted some of the relief supplies, and sold grain on the international markets to channel money into the industrial sector. No one knows how many lives were lost because of the Bolsheviks' priority of investing in industrial production, but the pattern was already clear: human lives, particularly those of peasants, deserved little consideration on the way to socialism.

1922
USSR

This was a pivotal year for Russia. The Civil War was largely over, and the Bolsheviks emerged victorious. But the country they came to rule was lying in ruins. Hunger, epidemics, unemployment, and lawlessness were only some of the challenges faced every day. To revive the economy and to avoid increasing anarchy, the government abandoned forced requisition of food, nationalization of all industries, strict central management, and other policies that were known as "War Communism." While succeeding in keeping the Red Army fed and armed during the Civil War, War Communism devastated the industries and the countryside and created huge popular discontent. With the war over, the Bolsheviks were forced to take a step back from their socialist vision of the future and allow private enterprise to rejuvenate the economy.

The Communist Party, as the Bolsheviks were now formally known, also had to adjust its expectations elsewhere. With the initial hope of socialist revolutions in Europe all but over, the Party moved rapidly towards installing Communist regimes in the former parts of the Russian Empire, which, in 1918, broke into several sovereign nation-states. By late 1921, Communist governments were in control of the newly formed Soviet republics of Ukraine, Belarus, and Transcaucasia. The Kremlin decided to form a union with these former parts of the Russian Empire and assigned the task to the Commissar (Head) of the People's Committee on Nationality Affairs, Joseph Stalin.

Stalin's initial idea was to incorporate these national republics into Russia. But Lenin strongly disagreed and criticized Stalin for his lack of sensitivity to the issue of national identity. Noting that many non-Russian peoples might see this as tantamount to Russification, Lenin plainly accused Stalin and his other supporter, the head of the Secret Police, Felix Dzherzhinski, of Russian chauvinism.

Lenin spelled out his vision of a new Soviet state in a series of letters written in the last months of 1922. He argued for strict rules to preserve and maintain the use of a national language in the republics, as well as for their full autonomy from Russia, with the exception of a common military and foreign policy. It was better to err on the side of being too accommodating to the non-Russians, Lenin argued, than to behave like imperialists and antagonize hundreds of millions of people in Asia, who might otherwise one day follow Moscow's lead. Lenin's opinion carried the day, and Stalin was compelled to make a change from "the republics incorporated into the Russian Federation" to "the republics joining the formal union together with the Russian Federation into a Union of the Soviet Republics of Europe and Asia."

Throughout December 1922, the Communist parties of the three national republics declared their intention to join Russia and to form a new Soviet entity. Finally, on December 30, Party delegates issued a declaration of the founding of the Union of the Soviet Socialist Republics (USSR). The Union was supposed to ensure "brotherly cooperation between peoples," eradicate colonial oppression, unite the republics against the world of capitalism into one socialist family, and provide for national security, economic development, and free national development. Sixty-nine years later, neither the founding principles nor the country itself survived, when the USSR broke apart into fifteen sovereign national republics that it initially had tried to unite.

1923
National Communism

Only a few months after the Soviet Union came into existence, Stalin's nationality policies already had their first victim. Mirsaid Sultan Galiev was one of the most prominent Muslim Tatar theorists and worked with Stalin at the Commissariat (Ministry) for Nationality Affairs. Together with several other Muslim Bolsheviks, he became a proponent of Muslim National Communism, an idea that sought to combine Islam, nationalism, and Marxism.

Straddling the fine line between religion, nationalism, and socialism proved to be a challenging and dangerous task in Soviet Russia. On the one hand, Sultan Galiev's Tatar compatriots accused him of forsaking his national and religious identity in favor of the Bolsheviks' internationalism and atheism, despite Sultan Galiev's argument that the Bolsheviks represented their interests better than any other political party. On the other hand, he tried to convince the Bolsheviks, who labeled him a Tatar nationalist, that Russia's Muslims required a special approach.

A rift between the national communists and Stalin was not new. Before being completely incapacitated by his illness, Lenin moderated Stalin's tendency towards Russian chauvinism and called for greater sensitivity to national questions. By the time the 12th Communist Party Congress convened in April 1923, Lenin was no longer capable of speaking or writing, and Stalin led the Congress to condemn the national communists in Georgia and Turkestan.

Sultan Galiev rejected Stalin's charge that nationalism of the non-Russian peoples was simply a reaction to the policies of the Great Russian chauvinism under the tsars. The roots of Tatar nationalism were old and complex, Galiev argued, and Tatar identity was both national and Islamic. At any rate, he maintained, given the deep grievances of non-Russians against a history of Russian domination, the emergence of socialism did not automatically end Russian colonialism.

Stalin was furious. Sultan Galiev's views directly contradicted his own views and nationality policies. Nine days after the Party's Congress, Sultan Galiev was arrested, making him the first member of the Bolshevik Party to be arrested on Stalin's orders. He was officially charged with entering into a secret correspondence with one of the leaders of the anti-Soviet rebels in Central Asia. Several months later, at the Communist Party meeting, Sultan Galiev was roundly condemned and expelled from the Party. He was later released and re-arrested several more times until he was finally shot in December 1940 on charges of anti-Soviet activity and spreading Pan-Turkic and Pan-Islamic ideas. His very name was turned into a label attached to any movement that was judged to have nationalist and Pan-Turkic aspirations.

Throughout the years, Stalin crushed any attempt by local nationals to naturalize Communism on their own soil and adopt different approaches to their own people. Instead, Stalin embarked on the policies of nativization (*korenizatsiia*), which were intended to promote local cultures and languages, while also promoting a non-Russian Communist elite loyal to a socialist agenda. But the tensions between Moscow and the non-Russian elites persisted because, to many non-Russians, Communism appeared to be dressed in a distinctly Russian garb, and Moscow's policies looked like a continuation of traditional Russian imperialism.

1924
The NEP

Two years after Lenin and his party decided to dismantle the economic policies of War Communism, the Russian economy rebounded beyond any expectations. The price of the economic recovery, from the Kremlin's point of view, was a tactical retreat from socialist policies. Lenin argued that it was an orderly retreat to his original idea of state capitalism and that the economic collapse threatened the Revolution much more than a temporary return to capitalism. By the time the 13th Congress of the Communist Party met in Moscow in May 1924, several initial decrees and concessions had now formed the basis of the New Economic Policy, better known as the NEP.

To understand the full impact of the NEP, one needs to realize the extent of the economic and social calamity that the years of Civil War and War Communism had brought to Russia. War Communism emerged out of the desperate need to feed the army and the workers during the Civil War. War Communism relied on the military administration of the economy, a harsh rationing system, elimination of markets, wholesale requisitioning of peasants' produce by armed squads, nationalization of industry, coercive mobilization of labor, and the widespread use of terror.

By the end of the Civil War in 1921, the Russian economy was barely a shadow of the Russian economy on the eve of the First World War: industrial production was one-seventh of the pre-1913 level, and agricultural production one-third. The population of the cities had shrunk to 40 percent of their pre-war levels. In St. Petersburg alone, where the population had stood at 2,347,000 in 1913, only 799,000 remained eight years later. The general productivity fell to 26 percent, production of steel 4.6 percent, cotton 5 percent, and the acreage of cultivated lands shrunk to 67 percent. The widespread famine, shortages, and epidemics resulted in a series of riots and uprisings and left the Party little choice but to change course.

In a country where 80 percent of the population lived in the countryside, the NEP had to begin with the elimination of coercive requisitioning of agricultural produce. Within a year, crops were growing again, food was available, and markets were thriving. In 1924, 70 percent of bread in Moscow was purchased from private traders.

ИЗ РОССИИ
НЭПОВСКОЙ
БУДЕТ РОССИЯ
СОЦИАЛИСТИЧЕСКАЯ
(ЛЕНИН)

NEP poster that quotes Lenin: "The Russia of NEP will become a socialist Russia." Photo by Fine Art Images/Heritage Images/Getty Images.

While much of the countryside was left to private entrepreneurs, the government refused to relinquish its control of the recently nationalized industries. Despite a desperate need to attract foreign capital to modernize industry, the government reluctantly issued some concessions to European companies to explore Russia's natural resources and import heavy machinery and everyday goods. But foreign capital also invited foreign influence and left many members of the Party uncomfortable and ambivalent about the NEP. In 1924, Russia's foreign trade was still only at half the level it was at in 1913.

By the mid-1920s, the NEP stabilized the economy and stimulated rapid growth of small businesses and cooperatives. But the swift recovery and rise in agricultural activity was not matched by similar improvements in heavy industry, which remained under tight government control. This inevitably led to huge disparities between the two sectors of the economy. The choice was between the privatization of industrial production or the nationalization of agriculture.

The Party was split on the issue. After Lenin's death in January 1924, Nikolai Bukharin became the most enthusiastic supporter of the NEP. But the Left wing of the Party, which was led by Leon Trotsky and supported by Stalin, was afraid of being overwhelmed by small businesses and a prosperous peasantry and eventually losing control of the economy. Their solution was to restore the central-command economy, privilege heavy industry, jettison foreign investments, and extract capital needed for industrialization from the peasantry. Bukharin, like Lenin, believed that the NEP was a long-term policy that would last for several decades before a socialist economy could take root. But Stalin had no patience. By 1928, the Russian economy had recovered enough to reach its 1913 levels, and Stalin decided that the NEP was no longer needed.

1925
Forging Cadres for World Revolution

"Comrades, permit me, first of all, to greet you on the occasion of the fourth anniversary of the existence of the Communist University of the Toilers of the East. Needless to say, I wish your University every success on a difficult road of training communist cadres for the East." These were the opening words of Stalin's speech on May 18, 1925, addressed to the students groomed to lead the revolutions in the colonial societies of Asia.

Like good missionaries, regardless of economic challenges or international concerns, Russian Communists spared no effort to spread their message, as they invested heavily in comprehensive propaganda at home and abroad. As hopes for a socialist revolution in Europe dimmed, the Party refocused its attention on the East. The Communist University of the Toilers of the East

(KUTV) was founded in February 1921, and a year after it was officially named after Stalin. Within several years, the KUTV opened campuses in Baku, Tashkent, and Irkutsk and began to publish the journal *The Revolutionary East*.

The three-year program included both theoretical and practical matters. The students studied Marxist theory, party organization and propaganda, law and administration, revolutionary tactics, socialist policies, and trade union organization. They also received military training in summer camps. The students were divided into two groups: those from the Soviet East (the Caucasus and Central Asia) and those from the rest of Asia (China, India, Turkey, Vietnam, etc.). One of the distinguished graduates of the class of 1925 was Deng Xiaoping, the future paramount leader of China. Other notable alumni included future members of the Chinese governing elite, the future president of Vietnam, Ho Chi Minh, and the Turkish poet Nazim Hikmet, to mention a few. China was of particular importance, and in 1928 Moscow decided to create a separate branch known as the Sun Yat-sen Communist University of the Toilers of China, where both Trotsky and Stalin were lecturers.

Similar schools emerged in the 1920s under the umbrella of the Comintern, an organization founded in Moscow in 1919 to promote Communism throughout the world. One such school was the Communist University of the National Minorities of the West, which, between 1922 and 1936, groomed several thousand Communist Party and trade union leaders of different nationalities. Another school, the International Lenin School, which existed from 1925 to 1938, graduated future Communist leaders of postwar Eastern Europe. Among them were the first leader of Communist Poland, Wladyslaw Gomulka, the president of Yugoslavia, Josip Broz Tito, the first leader of East Germany, Walter Ulbricht, a notorious head of the East German Secret Police (the Stasi), Erich Mielke, the last leader of East Germany, Erich Honecker, the Prime Minister of Bulgaria, Anton Yugov, and many others.

In his speech to KUTV students in 1925, Stalin warned the students about the dangers of extremes, or what he called "deviations." He advised the students not to overstate the international aspect of Communism by neglecting the local and national elements, and not to exaggerate the local at the expense of the international. Too much emphasis on the anti-colonial and national struggle was deemed a deviation to the Right, while too much preoccupation with the world Communist revolution was a deviation to the Left. Since Stalin made himself the ultimate arbiter of what constituted a deviation, anyone could be accused of misinterpreting the Party dogmas.

Indeed, throughout the purges of the 1930s, Stalin's sword fell to the right and left, and many who founded and taught at the Communist International Universities joined other numerous victims. Stalin's paranoia about the

Trotskyites and suspicion of their subversive activity in the Comintern eventually led him to shut down the International Universities. In 1939 the KUTV closed its doors, following the closure of other international Communist schools a few years earlier.

Despite the relatively short duration of the Communist Universities, they succeeded in raising the future Communist elites who later served to expand the world of Communism both in Eastern Europe and Asia. It was only in 1960 that Soviet leaders revived the idea of training the new anti-colonial and Communist generation and founded the Peoples' Friendship University in Moscow, the goal of which was to bring together young men and women from developing world. But with Communist China and the seemingly unstoppable march of Communism throughout Asia, the Kremlin's focus was now on Africa and its growing anti-colonial liberation movement. A year after it was founded, the University was named after independent Congo's recently murdered first Prime Minister, Patrice Lumumba.

1926
Creating Nations and Nationalities

The founding of the Soviet Union in 1922 was only the beginning of nation-building. Rejecting the Russian empire as "a prison of peoples," which denied non-Russians their own culture and identity, was easy. And so was casting the Party as the defender of non-Russian peoples. It was much harder to offer a plausible alternative to the discarded imperial policies of Russification. The Party had to find an answer to the formidable challenge of holding together an enormously diverse human tapestry consisting of hundreds of different peoples.

The Kremlin envisioned the new country as a federation of nations where larger, established peoples formed republics within the Soviet Union. However, it was less clear how to classify and organize literally hundreds of smaller peoples within these republics. Stalin's nationality policies defined ethnicity as a group of people bound to a specific territory. The problem was how to parcel the territories claimed by several ethnic groups.

To answer all these and other questions, the Party launched the first comprehensive census in 1926. The collected data included information about ethnic identity, sex, native language, occupation, literacy level, marital status, and physical and mental handicaps. In short, the census was a reflection of a vast social and national engineering project that was about to take place.

Preparing a census in a new Soviet reality was an extraordinary undertaking. The last census of the Russian Empire took place in 1897. Then, the residents were classified by their native language and religion. These two criteria were now in doubt. Religion was out of place in the new atheist state, and linguistic association was suspect, given the Russification policies under the tsars. The task to devise new parameters for national categories fell upon Russia's ethnographers.

Many months passed in lively debates about what constituted ethnicity, how to classify a myriad of indigenous identities, and what kind of questions would help the census-takers to establish one's ethnic identity. In the end, a state-sponsored evolutionary view of what constitutes a nation prevailed. The ethnographers agreed to divide all the peoples into "narodnost" (minor ethnicity) and "natsionalnost" (nationality, major ethnic group). These categories were fluid, however, and according to a Marxist paradigm of backwardness and progress, primitive peoples would eventually consolidate into minor ethnicities, minor ethnicities into a major ethnicity, and a major ethnicity into a nation.

The experts also created an official "List of the Nationalities of the USSR," which initially included some 600 names and was later reduced to about 200. Those who identified themselves as other than the ones mentioned on the List were deemed to be too small and were to be merged with the official nationalities.

All in all, the 1926 census provided the basis for the ethno-territorial structure of the USSR. All minor and major ethnic groups were given territories either as autonomous republics or as autonomous regions within the larger Soviet Republics. This process of dividing and consolidating the boundaries of the new ethnic territories continued throughout the 1930s.

The census also discovered the huge human toll that the years of war and revolution had exerted on the country. The population of the USSR in 1926 was 147 million, almost 20 million less than in 1914. Even if one were to exclude the population of the newly independent Poland and Finland, the demographic drop remained staggering.

1927
Orphans into Communists

Years of war and revolution had forced millions of children onto the streets of devastated Russian towns. By 1922, there were at least 7 million homeless

Anton Makarenko with students at his orphanage. Photo by ITAR-TASS News Agency/Alamy Stock Photo.

children in Russia. Most simply tried to survive by resorting to begging and occasional work. Others formed criminal gangs involved in petty theft and prostitution. The problem was urgent and challenging. The homeless children had to be removed from the city streets and made into new Soviet citizens.

To deal with the little runaways and orphans, the government decided to create educational labor colonies, where the homeless children would be supervised, educated, and brought up with Soviet values. One of the first of such colonies was founded in 1921 and was named in honor of the Soviet writer, Maxim Gorky. To head the new colony, the local authorities appointed an experienced teacher and educator, Anton Makarenko.

The first members of the colony were teenagers with difficult, often criminal pasts. The colony began its life in the abandoned estate of Wilhelm Trepke, a wealthy merchant of German origin. The estate was located near Poltava amidst the fertile lands of central Ukraine. The Trepkes fled after the revolution, and the local peasants pillaged the property. For several years the colony was in terrible shape with no furniture, fuel, and shortages of food. Makarenko complained that not far from them was the Dzerzhinsky commune, a similar children's colony under the auspices of the Soviet Secret Police, which was located in a former palace, had furniture, workshops, nineteen electrical engines, clothes, showers, baths, good bedrooms, and food. But the Ministry of Education, which was in charge of the Gorky colony, could offer little help. Makarenko's children had to rebuild the estate and provide for themselves, and by 1925, their numbers had grown from 30 to 130 children.

Anton Makarenko developed his own pedagogical approach to dealing with troubled children. He believed that schooling alone was not enough, and that one had to build an approach based on the children's personal vagabond experiences. What they needed, he argued, were explicit requirements and discipline, but also trust and respect. Labor and self-government were critical elements of Makarenko's pedagogy.

His approach proved to be very successful, yet critics abounded. In 1927, Makarenko wrote to Gorky bitterly complaining that the colony was under assault from all sides. The accusers charged that his colony was lacking class consciousness, even though 35 percent of the children had become members of the Young Communist League (Komsomol), and that his approach relied too much on the "old values" of honor, duty, pride, and self-esteem. The letter upset Gorky terribly, but he was powerless to intervene in the face of zealous Party officials.

The final attack on Makarenko and his pedagogy came from Nadezhda Krupskaia, Lenin's widow and one of the founders of the Soviet education system. At the Komsomol Congress in May 1928, she harshly criticized Makarenko and pointed out "that the role of the school was not only to teach, but to become the center of the Communist upbringing." After Krupskaia's attack, Makarenko was removed from his position as the head of the Gorky colony. After that, it was slowly transformed into a penal institution, with a high fence and barbed wire. The Soviet government's attempts to deal with homeless children had only limited success. In 1935, the Party was forced to revisit the issue with a new decree calling for the elimination of homelessness among children.

1928
Cultural Revolution's First Victims

In December 1928, members of the philosophical–religious society Resurrection were arrested in Leningrad and charged with belonging to a counter-revolutionary organization. This and other arrests of liberal intelligentsia marked the beginning of the end of the NEP, with its selective economic and intellectual tolerance. Together with an economic shift towards central planning, industrialization, and collectivization of agriculture, the Party began purging the intelligentsia and enforcing ideological discipline.

Founded in December 1917, on the initiative of the philosopher A. A. Meier, the Resurrection Society soon included some of Russia's best-known literary critics, historians, philosophers, artists, and writers. Initially, they met in a building belonging to the Free Philosophical Society, but by 1923 they were forced to relocate and meet in the apartments of various members.

Concerned with the impact of the revolution on religion, the society's main goal was "to prevent the destruction of Christian culture." The majority of the members nominally belonged to the Orthodox Christian church, but there were also some Protestants, Catholics, and Jews. All were interested in some sort of religious resurrection by combining Christianity and socialism.

Initially critical of the Russian Orthodox Church, which they believed was poorly suited for new Christian ideas, most members changed their attitude by the late 1920s, seeking closer ties with the Orthodox clergy and compelling the non-Orthodox members to convert. They continued to meet secretly on Sundays and promoted the teaching of Christian precepts among school children.

In 1928, as the Party launched its first Five-Year Plan to build a socialist society in the Soviet Union, there was no longer any room for those who did not share this vision. Following Stalin's speech at the 15th Communist Party Congress, which made the war against religion central to the Party's goals, the League of Militant Godless, which was an atheist vanguard of the Party, launched a new wave of anti-religious propaganda in the newspapers, schools, and factories. But for Stalin, propaganda alone was not enough.

Disregarding the advice of caution by Bukharin and other senior party members, who would soon be condemned as the Right Opposition, Stalin urged a wave of repression against the church and the faithful. Soon, the Secret Police were busy with mass arrests, exiles, and executions.

Members of the Resurrection Society were among the first to be arrested. Other non-official groups and societies were also closed, and their members charged with counter-revolutionary propaganda. Most were sentenced to three, five, or ten years' imprisonment and dispatched to concentration camps in central Russia. The rest were banished from living in the city and exiled. Some of the names of the victims are easily recognized: the literary critic Mikhail Bakhtin, the painter K.S. Petrov-Vodkin, the orientalist N.V. Pigulevskaia, the pianist M.V. Iudina, and the historian I.M. Grevs were just a few of those condemned.

The founder of the Resurrection Society, Aleksandr Meier, was sentenced to death, but his wife's connections to senior Soviet leaders helped to commute the death sentence to a ten-year prison term. He was sent to a remote prison at Solovki and a year later transferred to the construction site of the Belomor-Baltic canal. Released in 1935, he was then sent to work on the Volga-Moscow canal. Unlike some members of the Resurrection and other intellectual societies, who were able to return to Leningrad, adjust to the Soviet demands, and eventually pursue a successful career, Meier was banned from returning to any major city. He soon died, crushed, like the society he founded, by the unpredictable and cruel hand of Stalinism.

1929
War on Academia, the Intelligentsia, and the Church

By the summer of 1929, the full scale of the purges directed at the intelligentsia became clear. The first salvo came from a Marxist historian, M. N. Pokrovsky, the director of the Institute of the Red Professors and a recently elected member of the Soviet Academy of Sciences. Pokrovsky insisted that history, together with other academic disciplines, was an extension of class warfare. "It is time to launch an offensive on all fronts of science. The period of peaceful coexistence with the bourgeois science is over," he famously announced. The purges that followed decimated the Academy of Sciences and resulted in the arrest and exile of several hundred of Russia's best scholars, many of whom died in exile or were shot during the Great Purges of the late 1930s.

The series of purges that lasted until the winter of 1931 were triggered by the Academic Affair, a case fabricated by the Soviet Secret Police (then known as the Joint State Political Directorate, the OGPU). At the center of the Affair was a well-known historian, S.F. Platonov, a member of the Academy, the head of the Academy's Library, and the head of the prestigious Institute of Literature, the Pushkin House.

The purges began in January 1929, when several members of the Communist Party failed to be elected to the Academy. Under heavy pressure from state media and calls for reorganization, the Academy was forced to approve the membership of the rejected Communists. Nonetheless, a special investigative committee dispatched from Moscow to Leningrad, the seat of the Academy until 1934, found evidence of counter-revolutionary activity and fired 638 employees, over 30 percent of the entire staff. Among them was a man who had run the Academy throughout the 1920s, the Permanent Secretary of the Academy and renowned Orientalist, Sergei Oldenburg.

In early 1930, the State Police made the first arrests, which included Platonov and those close to him. He was condemned as a royalist and charged with plotting to restore the imperial family to the throne. By the end of the year, over 200 top academics from various disciplines in the humanities were under arrest. With no public trial, most were quickly sentenced to various prison terms and sent into exile; several were executed. They included some of the most famous names in Russian history and literature: Platonov (exiled to Samara, where he died in 1933), E.V. Tarle (exiled to Alma-Aty in 1931, but rehabilitated in 1937), S.V. Bakhrushin (exiled to Semipalatinsk, but allowed to return in 1933), M. K. Liubavskii (died in exile in 1936), and V.N. Beneshevich (exiled, pardoned, rearrested, and finally shot in 1938, together with his two sons and brother), to mention just a few.

No one could predict whether one would end up in the meat grinder of the Secret Police or on the glory billboard of a new socialist society.

The assault on the intelligentsia also took place in other parts of the country. In Ukraine, the Secret Police used the same approach. A case was fabricated, arrests were made, and severe sentences were passed to intimidate and eradicate the opposition. In this case, the students, professors, writers and other members of the Ukrainian intelligentsia were charged with belonging to "The Union for the Freedom of Ukraine." The trial took place in the Kharkiv opera theater, with forty-five defendants charged as leaders of the counter-revolutionary organization. Besides the defendants, several hundred others were found guilty, imprisoned or exiled. By some estimates, nearly 30,000 people were subject to repression in connection with this case. At the same time, a similar attempt to erase the national intelligentsia also took place in Belarus.

Nor was a wave of purges in 1929–1930 limited to academia. In another case, known as the Industrial Party Affair, over 2,000 engineers and managers at factories were arrested and charged with intent to cause damage to Soviet industry. Again, most were sentenced to lengthy prison terms, and some were shot.

The most violent assault, however, the authorities reserved for the church. The Second Congress of the Union of Atheists that took place in June 1929 had adopted a change from a religiously neutral education to a militantly anti-religious one. A series of decrees deprived the clergy of their pensions and took away their land. The church schools were closed, clergy arrested, and churches shut. In 1928, 534 churches were closed, and in 1929 that number reached 1,119. There were numerous pogroms of the churches, with destruction of icons and property. The Party's goal was no less than to destroy the church as a social institution.

This new phase in the government's anti-church and religious policies reflected a general struggle within the Communist party. A group of moderates—Anatoly Lunacharsky, Nikolai Bukharin, Aleksei Rykov, and Mikhail Kalinin—advocated for a long-term ideological struggle and a gradual winning of the hearts and minds of the people. Stalin and his clique, however, urged an immediate attack.

With Stalin's victories over his main rivals, Leon Trotsky and the Left Opposition in 1927 and Nikolai Bukharin and the Right Opposition in 1929, the Party settled on a militant approach aimed at the destruction of its enemies.

4

Stalin's Socialist Revolution

1930
Vladimir Mayakovsky

The purging of "bourgeois science" was accompanied by an aggressive attack against "bourgeois art." While it would take several more years before the Party declared socialist realism to be the sole official art form in the country, purges of any non-proletarian art had already begun in 1930.

Among the many artists who became victims of the vicious attacks, Vladimir Mayakovsky stood out. He was, after all, a poet of the Revolution. Early in his literary career, Mayakovsky joined a group of Russian Futurists, whose Manifesto called for throwing Pushkin, Dostoevsky, Tolstoy and others off "the ship of modernity." For Mayakovsky, the October Revolution was a fatal and welcome blow to old norms and values, and unlike other Futurists, he greeted it wholeheartedly.

In his poems, Mayakovsky unabashedly supported the Bolshevik cause and enthusiastically joined the Russian Telegraph Agency (ROSTA), where he designed propaganda posters. His energy seemed boundless. He wrote pro-revolutionary verses for newspapers, glorified the Bolshevik cause in booklets for children, and recited his poems in numerous talks and public rallies around the country.

Throughout the 1920s, Mayakovsky enjoyed great success. His unforgiving, scorched-earth style of poetry against the enemies of the revolution appealed to many Soviet high officials. But in 1928, the Party embarked on a course of building a socialist society, launching what some called, "a revolution from above."

In 1928, Mayakovsky, like many in the Soviet cultural elite, began to feel the official chill. The Party was no longer willing to tolerate futurism or any

Vladimir Mayakovsky with his lover, Lilya Brik, and without her in a later doctored photo.

other experimental styles. With the decision to embark on the construction of a socialist society, the only official style allowed in the USSR would be that which reflected the proletarian culture and served the cause of the Party. Thus was born the style of socialist realism.

The first indication of the rapidly changing winds came when Mayakovsky's friends, Lilya and Osip Brik, were not issued passports to travel abroad in January 1929. For many years, Mayakovsky had been romantically involved with Lilya, and all three, Lilya, her husband Osip, and her lover, Mayakovsky, remained best friends in a typical ménage à trois of the time. Mayakovsky, who in the past had used his fame to seek the intervention of high-ranking Soviet officials, did so again to help his friends. He sought and received a meeting with a powerful member of the Central Committee, Lazar Kaganovich. A few days later, Osip and Lilya had their passports and were allowed to travel.

While the intervention of Kaganovich helped his friends, a year later, no Soviet official was willing to get involved to save Mayakovsky. His two recent plays, *Bedbug* and *Bathhouse,* were a biting satire of opportunism and bureaucracy, and they did not go over well. The Russian Association of the Proletarian Writers harshly criticized the plays for lacking Soviet values.

To celebrate the twentieth anniversary of his literary career, four volumes of his collected works were released, and an exhibition was organized in the Writer's Club. Craving official recognition, Mayakovsky expected many high Soviet officials, and above all Stalin himself, to attend the exhibition. None came. Mayakovsky was increasingly referred to as *poputchik* (i.e., a fellow traveler who joined the Party's cause out of convenience, not sincere belief) and his poetry was deemed too obscure.

On April 14, 1930, Mayakovsky shot himself in the heart. His body and a handwritten note were discovered by his then-lover, the actress Veronika Polonskaia. The note read: "To all of you. I die, but don't blame anyone for it, and please do not gossip. The deceased terribly disliked this sort of thing. Mother, sisters, comrades, forgive me—this is not a good method (I do not recommend it to others), but there is no other way out for me. Lilya—love me. Comrade Government, my family consists of Lilya Brik, mama, my sisters, and Veronika Vitoldovna Polonskaia. If you can provide a decent life for them, thank you. Give the poem I started to the Briks. They will understand."

1931
The Palace of Soviets

Stalin's revolution was at full throttle and required nothing short of a complete and thorough transformation of society. Symbols of the past had to be replaced with new socialist icons. On June 2, 1931, the Party committee decided to build the Palace of the Soviets in Moscow. In time, numerous Palaces of Culture, Sports, Marriage, and Pioneers mushroomed throughout the country. Palaces for the people came to replace the palaces for the tsars. Yet there was only one Palace of the Soviets, which was meant to house the Soviet legislature, the Supreme Soviet of the USSR. So, the Party decided to build the Palace of the Soviets at the city's central location, where Moscow's main cathedral of Christ the Savior had stood for nearly half a century.

Of course, first the Cathedral had to be razed. The demolition began in August and was finished by December. Most of the treasures of the Cathedral were buried with the rubble. It was a perfect symbol of the new times—the house for the representatives of the happy Soviet people was to replace the house of God.

The contest for a design to replace it attracted a lot of international attention and was discussed in the Western press. Among the foreign architects who entered the competition were Le Corbusier, Armando Brasini, Walter Gropius, Albert Kahn, and twenty others. Soviet designers and architects entered over 200 concepts and designs. After several rounds of competition, the Soviet architect Boris Iofan was declared the winner. Le Corbusier was frustrated by his loss and complained to Stalin that the decision was an insult to the revolutionary spirit. He was yet to grasp that Stalin's revolution left no room for modern art.

Like so many others who pinned their modern ideas on the Russian Revolution, Le Corbusier, too, became bitterly disappointed. But unlike Mayakovsky, the Swiss-born Le Corbusier could choose to stay out of the Soviet Union. He eventually settled in France and became a French citizen in 1930.

Iofan's neo-classical design closely reflected the new architectural style preferred by the Party—socialist realism. Iofan had recently completed several buildings for the Party elite—a sanatorium in Barvikha, a suburb of Moscow and a popular summer destination for the Soviet elite, and a huge, block-size building that became known as the House of Government. There is little doubt that his connections to top Party officials helped to secure the prize.

But even Iofan's design remained mostly on paper. Stalin took a personal interest in the construction of the Palace of the Soviets and suggested various changes. Stalin wanted the Palace to be taller than the Empire State building in New York, at the time the tallest building in the world, and wanted it to have a statue of Lenin at the top. By the time Nazi Germany invaded the USSR in June 1941, only the foundation and some steel structures were in existence. The steel frames were then removed and used to defend Moscow. After the war, the site remained unused until 1958, when it was turned into the world's largest open-air swimming pool. Other Soviet-era projects for this space did not materialize until the collapse of the USSR brought about a radically new idea: the restoration of the demolished Cathedral of Christ the Savior. It was a fitting end to Soviet history: the Soviets never got their own palace, but the rebuilt Cathedral re-opened its doors in 2000.

1932
Children against Parents

In the summer of 1931, a thirteen-year-old boy named Pavlik Morozov denounced his father to the Soviet authorities. According to Pavlik, his father, who was the head of a village council in the Ural Mountains, was selling forged documents to peasants, who had been exiled to the region from their homelands in Central Russia and Ukraine. These newcomers were known as the *kulaks*: well-off peasants deported for resisting the government policy of collectivization. Pavlik's father was found guilty of providing the *kulaks* with the forged IDs that allowed them to travel home and was sentenced to ten years in a labor camp.

As a good pioneer and a member of the Young Communist League, Pavlik also participated in a campaign seeking to recover grain and other foodstuffs that local peasants might have withheld from the authorities. Pavlik discovered grain stashed away by his relatives and exposed his grandfather for hiding it. In revenge, Pavlik's relatives plotted to kill him, and on September 3, 1932, he and his younger brother were found murdered in the forest. The boy's grandparents, uncle, and cousin were arrested and shot. Pavlik became a martyr for the Soviet cause and an inspiration to all Soviet children.

Such was the story taught in all Soviet schools. It was meant to inspire the children to put the interests of the state above the family. Numerous statues to Pavlik were built around the country, streets were named after him, and books and songs were written about him. In the end, it turned out that the story was yet another myth concocted by the Soviet authorities. Unraveled in the 1990s following the collapse of the USSR, the story had many different versions, and story lines had shifted several times over the decades. The entire episode seems to have been a result of an ordinary family squabble, a criminal case, which was made into a "heroic pioneer" myth.

The Soviet propaganda machine required many myths, and that of Pavlik Morozov was created at a time when Stalin's collectivization campaign had run into stiff resistance from peasants. Millions of them had been forced to give their property to the newly formed collective farms. Those who resisted had their property taken away, were deported to Siberia, or executed. Stalin's violent campaign needed a new kind of propaganda. The pro-Communist abstract posters of the 1920s were now replaced by the Soviet hagiography of the 1930s, and Pavlik Morozov became the first such "Soviet saint." In a curious reversal of the old biblical story of Abraham's sacrifice of his son Isaac to God, the Soviets created a martyr from a child who sacrificed his father to the Soviet state. The message was meant to drive a wedge between the generations and to make it clear that nothing, not even family, could compete with loyalty to the Communist Party and Soviet state.

1933
Convict Labor

The 16th Congress of the Communist Party that convened in Moscow in June–July 1930 passed a momentous resolution: "to fulfill the Five-Year Plan in four years" and "to liquidate the kulaks as a class." Differently put, it meant to accelerate the pace of industrialization by all means possible and to wage war against the wealthy peasants. This aggressive directive was reinforced by a newly expanded penal code that allowed those found to be doing shoddy work to be sentenced to up to three years' forced labor, and those engaged in deliberate sabotage up to ten years. By broadly criminalizing the work environment, the government sent hundreds of thousands into penal colonies and created a huge reservoir of forced labor.

The man who founded the system of penal colonies and labor camps, the Gulag, was an old Soviet Secret Police hand, Matvei Berman. From 1932 to 1937 he was the head of all Gulag camps, and at one point, he boasted that he had 740,000 prisoners working on fifteen different projects. For one of these projects, a shipping canal between the White and Baltic Seas, he received the Order of Lenin, the highest possible Soviet award.

Known in Russia as the Belomorkanal, the 141 mile-long canal was the first major Soviet project completed almost entirely with convict labor. No less than 100,000 convicts were employed there during the twenty months of construction. Most prisoners lived in barracks, others in tents or other temporary dwellings. Many became sick and disabled as they worked in brutal conditions, digging the canal manually with the most primitive tools.

For Stalin, the Belomorkanal was the most visible and important project of the First Five-Year Plan. The large prison camps near the construction sites were conceived as re-education camps, and the Soviet government was eager to advertise the use of convict labor and its redeeming qualities to the "enemies of socialism."

Among the prisoners were intellectuals who had failed to support the Party, workers charged with sabotage, professionals whose loyalty was in doubt, and former Party members who had recently been purged from the Party ranks. The convict labor force was officially known as the "imprisoned members of the canal-construction army," evoking the image of the Red Army fighting for the Communist cause. This long, descriptive term for the convicts was eventually abbreviated in Russian as ZEK and has remained in unofficial use until now.

Given the high public profile of the Belomorkanal and the numerous propaganda posters that surrounded it, Stalin paid particular attention to the project. The Party's slogan "Five-Year Plan in Four Years" also applied to the Belomorkanal. Typically, human cost mattered little, and quality was secondary to the speed and value of the propaganda. In the summer of 1933, Party officials announced that the Belomorkanal had been completed in twenty months—four months ahead of schedule.

The Party named the Belomorkanal after Stalin and trumpeted it as a great victory for Soviet labor and socialism. After all, the Panama Canal was only 50 miles long but it had taken 28 years to build, and the 99-mile Suez Canal took ten years. Of course, out of 141 miles that connected rivers and lakes into one canal only 30 were man-made, and the mortality rate among the laborers exceeded 20 percent. Most importantly, the canal, built to shorten the voyage between the port of Archangel on the White Sea and Leningrad in the Baltic and to allow ships into the Volga River, failed in its main objective. Because of the haste and poor engineering, it proved to be too shallow to allow the passage of sea-going vessels.

But the thick fog of Soviet propaganda hid the fact that in both engineering and human terms, the canal was a disaster. The Party brought a group of popular Soviet writers to witness the completion of the canal and to describe

Convict labor at the Belomor Canal. The poster addresses the convicts: "Canal Army Soldier! Your prison time will melt from your hot work." Photo by Fine Art Images/Heritage Images/Getty Images.

the achievements of Soviet labor. They did so by creating a fiction that became one of the Soviet founding myths—the legendary success of the Belomorkanal.

1934
The Kirov Affair

On Sunday, December 2, 1934, the front pages of the Soviet newspapers carried an urgent government announcement:

On December 1, 1934, at 16 hours 30 minutes, in the city of Leningrad, in the building of the Leningrad Soviet (Smolnyi), the Secretary of the Central and Leningrad Committees of the Communist Party and a Permanent Member of the Central Executive Committee of the USSR, Sergei Mironovich Kirov, died at the hand of a killer sent by the enemies of the working class. The murderer has been arrested. His identity is being investigated.

Two days later, the government identified "the enemies of the working class" as members of the White Army, who were plotting terrorist acts against the Soviet people. Hundreds of suspects were rounded up and summarily executed, together with those who had previously been arrested under different charges and were already in jail. Two weeks later, the government found "enemies of the people" elsewhere and denounced Kirov's assassin, L.N. Nikolaev, as a follower of the Trotsky-Zinoviev-Kamenev counter-revolutionary Opposition.

In February 1956, during his famous "Secret Speech" denouncing Stalin, the Soviet leader Nikita Khrushchev pointed out numerous inconsistencies in the Kirov case: the assassin, Nikolaev, had twice been detained by the Secret Police near the Smolnyi, where he was found to have a gun, yet he was released without charge. On the day of the assassination, Nikolaev was in the corridor of Smolnyi, armed, and waiting for Kirov. When Kirov came out of the meeting, the head of his bodyguards, Borisov, who was supposed to have been with him at all times, was inexplicably far behind him. Borisov's car, which was driven to the interrogation, ended up in an accident in which only Borisov died; none of his guards had any injuries.

The details of the investigation and memories of contemporaries also raised more questions than answers. Shortly before the murder, the NKVD decided to reduce Kirov's bodyguard to four men. On the day of the assassination, Kirov had only one unarmed bodyguard, and he was not around. Reportedly, on the same day, Stalin called Nikolai Ezhov, his loyal henchman and soon-to-be head of the NKVD, to his cabinet. Apparently, Ezhov spent much of the day with Stalin, which was highly unusual. He left in the evening and immediately departed for Leningrad. Kirov was shot at 16:30. Shortly thereafter, Stalin travelled to Leningrad and brought an investigating team of his own. Stalin personally interrogated Nikolaev, after which his previous confession that he had been hired by some "fascist power" was changed to a new one in which he admitted that the leaders of the Opposition had placed the gun in his hand.

Amidst confusing and inconsistent official and unofficial accounts one is unlikely to find any direct link to Stalin. He certainly did what he did best—eliminate any paper trail and dispose of witnesses. The assassin, Nikolaev, was promptly executed on December 29, 1934. His wife, mother, brother, sister, and cousin were either killed or sent to labor camps. The mysterious man who provided Nikolaev with the gun and money was shot. Others were charged with negligence, given prison sentences, and eventually eliminated in the purge of 1937.

No one stood to benefit from Kirov's assassination more than Stalin. Kirov was considered to be Stalin's heir and was becoming dangerously popular among the Party elite, who supported his attempts to change the course of the Party. Only a month before his murder, members of the Central Committee approved his conciliatory gestures towards the Opposition.

It is not far-fetched to think that Stalin might have been taking a cue from another great master of death, Hitler. Five months prior to Kirov's murder, Hitler emerged as the single ruler of the Third Reich, after staging a putsch against his powerful rival in the Nazi Party, Ernst Röhm, in early July 1934. In December, Stalin too got rid of his main rival and placed the blame on the Opposition. At the end of December, the leaders of the Opposition, Kamenev and Zinoviev, were arrested and expelled from the Party for the second time. In January 1935, they were put on trial and found guilty of "moral complicity" in Kirov's assassination. They and their followers were given various prison terms until the summer of 1936, when, after a new public trial and forced confessions, they were shot. The Kirov murder was a mere prelude to Stalin's monstrous crimes during the Great Purge.

1935
Manufacturing Heroes

On November 17, 1935, Stalin spoke in front of 300 workers convened in the Kremlin. These were no ordinary workers, but an elite group celebrated for their hard work and efficiency. They were known as "Stakhanovites," named after Aleksei Stakhanov, a coal miner, who on August 31 of this year reportedly set a record by exceeding his quota 14 times and mining 102 tons of coal in less than six hours. Valorized by the Soviet press as a hero, he was soon followed by hundreds of similar exceptional workers, who would bear his name.

With Stalin's personal blessing, the convention laid the foundation for the Stakhanovite movement. The Stakhanovites were to become the vanguard of the Soviet economy, true representatives of the new socialist labor, who performed their feats for the cause of socialism, not for profit or material incentive. The Soviet propaganda machine trumpeted their success in breaking one record after another, all for the greater glory of the Soviet state and socialism.

In the Kremlin's design, the Stakhanovites were to become role models in more than one respect. Naturally, they were supposed to inspire other workers to emulate them in increased productivity. But the Stakhanovites also formed a new pantheon of Soviet heroes. Overnight, simple workers, peasants, teachers, and tractor-drivers became celebrities. Their smiling faces radiated happiness from numerous posters and newspaper pages, where they shared their enthusiasm with millions of their countrymen. Many of them would join the high ranks of the Soviet hierarchy, becoming deputies of the Supreme Soviet, fraternizing with top government officials, and growing into a true Soviet elite.

In the following decades, as enthusiasm alone was no longer sufficient to keep up the pace of productivity, the Stakhanovite movement sputtered. Soviet authorities tried to revive the movement under different names, creating the shock-worker brigades and dispensing such honorary titles as Shock Worker of Communist Labor.

In the 1930s, however, the government succeeded in manufacturing new, optimistic, and confident socialist heroes. And manufacturing it was! New evidence that emerged in the 1980s showed that the Stakhanovite movement was a government ploy; several people helped Stakhanov when he set his record, but the output was tallied only to him. Similar cases of heroic labor were propaganda fakes.

The November convention of the Stakhanovites was pronounced a success. Praising the achievements of the Soviet economy, Stalin announced in what would become a famous catchphrase: "Life has become better, comrades, life has become merrier." Indeed, it would become better for the workers and peasants, who worshipped their great leader and obeyed his commands. For others—many Party officials, military officers, and educated professionals—life was about to become a nightmare, as Stalin was preparing to launch the Great Purge.

1936 Constitution

On December 5, 1936, the 7th Extraordinary Congress of Soviets approved a new Constitution. A previous Constitution, which was adopted in 1924, sealed the birth of the USSR as a federative state. It mostly laid out federative structures, including that of a Joint State Political Directorate (OGPU): the Soviet Secret Police. Now that Stalin, at the 17th Party Congress in February 1934, had formally declared that socialism had prevailed in the USSR, a new Constitution was needed to match a new socialist society.

There was another reason why the Soviet government moved to adopt a new Constitution. After years of being an international pariah, Moscow was finally emerging from diplomatic isolation. In 1933, Washington and Moscow established diplomatic relations for the first time since 1917. A year later, the USSR joined the League of Nations in a bid to create an alliance against Nazi Germany. In exchange for growing international recognition, Moscow toned down the rhetoric of world revolution at the Comintern meetings and had to show that Soviet socialist society was progressive, fair, and democratic. In this sense, the new Constitution was yet another propaganda document.

Prepared for almost two years by numerous committees and subcommittees, the Constitution was put together with input from two different camps: Stalin, who saw Soviet society as being guided directly by the Party and bureaucratic state, and Nikolai Bukharin, who believed in a degree of economic autonomy from the Party and state and expanding the democratic rights of citizens.

The two visions could not be easily reconciled. For example, Bukharin introduced an article that would provide for the state-guaranteed right to work and freedom to choose professions and job locations. But such a clause would have made the 1932 law, which introduced an internal passport system with a fixed place of residence, unconstitutional. In the final drafts of the document, Stalin kept the right to work, but rejected the right to move around the country freely. In another example, Bukharin proposed an article guaranteeing safety from persecution when pursuing intellectual ideas in arts and sciences. That article was removed completely.

Nonetheless, the final document looked strikingly democratic and progressive. Soviet citizens were guaranteed the right to work with paid vacations, free education and health care, and equality of gender, race, and ethnicity. "In order to strengthen the socialist system," the Constitution guaranteed freedom of association, speech, press, meetings, public demonstrations, and religion (Articles 124, 125).

The Constitution also created a new legislative body, the Supreme Soviet, which consisted of two chambers and was modeled on western Parliaments. The Supreme Soviet's deputies were elected in a secret ballot through universal and direct suffrage.

In reality, however, none of these rights mattered. Direct voting was meaningless in a country with only one Party, the Supreme Soviet was a rubber-stamp body, and various freedoms, while guaranteed on paper, were outlawed. Some articles of the Constitution sounded like a cruel joke in the Stalinist USSR: Article 128, for example, guaranteed citizens' rights to privacy of their correspondence, residence, and personal life; Article 127 stated that "nobody could be arrested without an order from the court or prosecutor."

By the time the Constitution was approved in December 1936, hundreds of Stalin's victims had already been arrested on trumped-up charges and executed without trial. A few months later, hundreds of thousands more would perish in a campaign of mass arrests and executions. Stalin's Constitution, as it became known, was a bloodthirsty mockery of justice and a propaganda piece aimed at deceiving the world. The Party newspaper, *Pravda*, declared the constitution to be a triumph of Comrade Stalin and described him as "a genius of the new world, the wisest man of the era, and the great leader of Communism."

1937–1938
The Great Purge

To those few who could see through Soviet propaganda, it was apparent that Stalin's socialist society was based on mass violence, repression, and periodic purges of the Party ranks. Yet nothing could prepare even the critics for the terror campaign of political repression that became known as the Great Purge.

The scale of human destruction was shocking: by conservative measures, 1.3 million people were arrested during this time and over 681,000 were shot. But even more destructive was a constant and pervasive fear, a topsy-turvy world, where yesterday's executioner could become today's executed, where a patriotic speech today could be deemed counter-revolutionary tomorrow, and where cheerful government propaganda coexisted with bloody reality.

While the society was squeezed into a strait-jacket of socialist ideology and over 1 million victims were arrested, tortured, and killed, the most popular song in the country glorified the boundless Soviet motherland, where "life was getting merrier every day and people laughed and loved better than anywhere in the world." Written to celebrate Stalin's Constitution, the song's refrain concluded famously: "I do not know any other country where a human being can breathe so freely."

To survive in this netherworld of mass social schizophrenia, one had to learn how to reconcile the irreconcilable and suspend any critical judgment. This kind of cognitive dissonance became one of the central features of Soviet society, where the unbridgeable gap between reality and rhetoric was a constant part of life.

The year 1937 marked two decades since the Bolsheviks had come to power, and big celebrations were in order. The government commissioned numerous works of art, whose socialist realist style was to celebrate the achievements of the Revolution. Among them was music commissioned from a world-famous composer, Sergei Prokofiev, who had just returned to Russia after spending many years abroad. The result was a "Cantata for the 20th Anniversary of the October Revolution." It was conceived as a monumental work in ten movements, with two choirs and four orchestras, and was based on a text from the works of Marx, Engels, Lenin, and Stalin. Yet in the end, Prokofiev's music was deemed too modern to go with the words of classics of Marxism-Leninism, and the cantata was rejected. It was performed for the first time in 1966, long after the composer's death.

November 7th was the day of the anniversary, and it was marked by parades in Moscow's Red Square. Giant banners of Lenin and Stalin covered the towers and walls of the Kremlin. Stalin's cult of personality was on full display with numerous banners glorifying socialism and the wisdom of Comrade Stalin. Flanked by his loyalists, the great leader himself stood atop Lenin's mausoleum, gazing at the parade with the full confidence of someone who knew that no one could oppose his vision or will.

Two marshals, Semyon Budennyi and Kliment Voroshilov, led the military parade. They were among the five original marshals who had received this highest Soviet military rank in 1935, yet they were the only two to survive the purges. The first among the marshals to fall was Mikhail Tukhachevskii. He was arrested in May 1937, brought to Moscow, tortured, and was forced to confess to being a German agent and plotting against Stalin. In June, he, together with eight generals, was put in front of a special military tribunal. No defense attorneys or appeals were allowed. All defendants were found guilty of treason and promptly executed.

Among the members of the tribunal were Marshals Vasilii Bliukher and Alexander Egorov. They, too, would be arrested and tortured. Bliukher was charged with being a Japanese spy and was executed in November 1938, and Egorov died in prison in February 1939. Five other tribunal members at the Tukhachevskii trial were also shot.

The purges of 1937–1938 resulted in an unprecedented spike in suicides. Many chose to take their lives rather than face sudden arrest, torture, and the humiliation of a forced confession. The most significant suicide was that of Sergo Ordzhonikidze, an old Bolshevik of great stature among his colleagues. He was among the last to see through Stalin's murderous plans and to refuse to go along with them. After an argument with Stalin, he shot himself in February 1937. His death unleashed a wave of suicides. In 1937, there were 698 suicides in Moscow alone. There were 782 suicides in the Army in 1937, and this increased to 832 suicides in 1938. These numbers did not include other military services, and the official numbers are likely to be underreported.

On February 19, 1937, the front page of the Party's newspaper, *Pravda,* announced that Ordzhonikidze had died of a heart attack. The announcement was signed by twenty members of the Central Committee. Eleven of them would be killed in the purges. Three of the four doctors who signed Ordzhonikidze's death certificate were murdered the following year. On its twentieth anniversary, the Bolshevik revolution was devouring itself.

The victims included Soviet elite of all ranks: Party members, military officers, and government officials. No one could tell who would be next, or what charges they might face: belonging to a Trotskyite organization, engaging in anti-Soviet activity and propaganda, suspicion of espionage and foreign connections, being a church propagandist, a family member of the traitors, a counter-revolutionary, or a socially dangerous element. Any of these charges carried a death sentence or, at best, many years in the Gulag system of camps and special settlements.

While hundreds of thousands of victims were disposed of by a quick sentence of the tribunal, Stalin decided to hold show trials for the most prominent Communist leaders. The legal mastermind of the notorious show trials was the Prosecutor General, Andrei Vyshinsky. The trials were designed as a major propaganda piece and had nothing to do with law or justice. There were no defense lawyers and no evidence. The sentence rested on the confessions extorted from the defendants by threat and torture.

The first of the Moscow show trials took place in August 1936, where two prominent Bolsheviks, Lev Kamenev and Grigorii Zinoviev, together with fourteen other Old Bolsheviks, were found guilty of all sorts of unimaginable crimes: forming a terrorist organization, killing Kirov, plotting against Stalin, espionage, sabotage, and treason. All were promptly executed.

On March 15, 1938, Stalin finally disposed of his most popular rival, Nikolai Bukharin. Known as the Trial of the Twenty-One, Bukharin, together with twenty other prominent Bolsheviks, was charged with conspiring against the Soviet state. Among the specific charges were plots to assassinate Lenin and Stalin, to poison the iconic Soviet writer Maxim Gorky, and above all, treacherously to surrender Soviet territories to Germany, Japan, and Britain.

Neither Bukharin's confession, his last-minute appeal to Stalin to spare his life, nor the pleas from his fellow European Communists, changed Stalin's mind. Bukharin and the other twenty defendants were shot two days after the trial, and most members of their families were dispatched to the camps. The trial procedures and all related documents, like those of dozens of other trials, bore a surreal stamp: "Keep Forever." Did the monumental crime require an eternal safekeeping? Stalin too kept "forever" Bukharin's last note to him. Found in Stalin's desk after his death in 1953, the note contained only one shuddering line: "Koba [Stalin's nickname], why do you need me to die?"

1939
Hitler's Ally

On August 22, the Western governments woke up to shocking news: Nazi Germany and the Soviet Union had reached an agreement, and Germany's Foreign Minister, Joachim von Ribbentrop, was on his way to Moscow to sign a non-aggression pact.

The sense of betrayal and outrage at Stalin's duplicity was palpable. "London Staggered: Nazi-Soviet Pact Blow is Received in Anger and Stupefaction," ran the headline in the *New York Times*. The war in Europe now seemed inevitable. Indeed, several days later, on September 1, Hitler invaded Poland, and for the next seven years the world was plunged into the nightmare of the Second World War.

A joint military parade of the Nazi and Red Army troops in Brest during the invasion of Poland. In the center, Major General Heinz Guderian. Next to him is Brigadier Semyon Krivoshein. Photo by akg-images/Alamy Stock Photo.

For several months in the spring of 1939, Moscow was involved in negotiations with Britain and France. The Soviets insisted on both political and military treaties, which had to include a pact of mutual assistance in case of war with Germany. The British and French were weary of military obligations, and Moscow's unacceptable conditions over their alliance with Poland continued to divide both sides. At the same time, the Soviets entered secret negotiations with Hitler. In May, Stalin replaced his Foreign Minister, Maksim Litvinov, who was Jewish, with an ethnic Russian, Viacheslav Molotov, and instructed Molotov to purge the ministry of Jews. In retrospect, this was a clear sign of Stalin's intention of reaching a deal with Hitler.

When a new round of negotiations with the British and French began in Moscow in mid-August, the secret negotiations with Germany were already nearly complete. On August 21, Moscow suddenly broke off the talks with the British and French. Two days later, a smiling Stalin was looking over as Molotov and Germany's Foreign Minister, Joachim von Ribbentrop, signed a non-aggression pact in the Kremlin. A moment later, champagne corks were popped, and Stalin offered a toast to Hitler's health.

The pact was formally called the "German-Soviet Treaty of Friendship, Cooperation, and Demarcation." What Stalin and Hitler did not make public, and Moscow continued to deny until 1989, was that both sides also signed a secret protocol that divided Eastern Europe into spheres of influence. Finland, Estonia, Latvia, and part of Romania were to come into the Soviet sphere, and Poland was to be partitioned between Germany and the Soviet Union.

Poland stood no chance against the alliance of Hitler and Stalin. On September 1, German troops crossed the western border of Poland, and on September 17, the Soviets invaded from the east. Shortly before the Soviet invasion, Stalin suggested to Hitler that the second article of the secret protocol be amended so that no part of Poland remained outside German and Soviet-occupied territories. He specifically offered to change the demarcation line so Berlin would control the lands east of Warsaw and Moscow would acquire Lithuania. On September 27, Poland surrendered. A day later, Stalin and Hitler signed "A German-Soviet Treaty of Friendship and Borders Between the USSR and Germany." Attached was an amended copy of the secret protocol with a specific demarcation of the newly conquered territories. Poland ceased to exist.

While Hitler turned his attention to France and Britain in the west, Stalin proceeded to annex the eastern regions of Poland, the Baltic countries of Estonia, Latvia, and Lithuania, several regions of Romania that would later form Moldova, and parts of Finland, and executed and deported tens of thousands from the newly acquired territories.

In the end, Hitler duped Stalin. Two years later, Nazi Germany, ignoring the non-aggression pact, invaded the USSR. The invasion, the Nazi brutality on the Eastern front, and huge Soviet casualties allowed Moscow to present itself as an innocent victim of Nazism. It was not. As an ally of Hitler, Stalin bore full responsibility for unleashing the Second World War and for the millions of deaths across the continent.

5

War

1940
Leon Trotsky

By August 1940, things could not have looked better for Stalin. Hitler occupied most of Western Europe, had forced the surrender of France, and was bombing and preparing to invade Britain. In his sphere of influence, Stalin confidently continued to dismantle any resistance to Moscow and occupied new territories in Eastern Europe.

In March, after an initial humiliating defeat by the Finns in a brief Soviet–Finnish War, Stalin finally forced Finland to sue for peace and cede 10 percent of its territory. In April, in the notorious Katyn massacre, Soviet Secret Police units executed in cold blood an estimated 22,000 Polish prisoners of war, most of them the flower of Poland's elite military officers and intelligentsia. In June, Moscow occupied Estonia, Latvia, and Lithuania, exiled or murdered the countries' national leadership, and held rigged elections. In August, Stalin fully annexed the Baltic territories as well as parts of Romania.

By now Stalin enjoyed an unrivaled cult of personality and disposed of any Party or military leader who might present the slightest challenge or threat. Yet his main rival was still alive. Leon Trotsky, the legendary figure of the Bolshevik revolution, continued to condemn Stalin and his regime from his distant exile in Mexico. On August 20, the most welcome news reached the Kremlin—after more than a year of attempts to assassinate Trotsky, the plot had finally succeeded.

The most formidable revolutionary thinker and Lenin's heir-apparent, Trotsky was Stalin's first and most important rival from the early days of the revolution. Shortly after Lenin's death, Stalin's intrigues succeeded in having Trotsky removed from a powerful position at the head of the military. Two years later, Trotsky was expelled from the Politburo (the Party's executive committee) and exiled to the Kazakh capital of Almaty. In 1929, he was expelled from the Soviet Union and, for the next four years, found refuge in Turkey, on Büyükada Island, off the coast of Istanbul. Not feeling safe from the long arm of Stalin, Trotsky moved first to France, then to Norway, and finally settled in a suburb of Mexico City in 1936.

From Mexico, Trotsky continued his withering criticism of Stalin, who, he charged, had created a bureaucratic Soviet state which had nothing to do with true socialism. Having long resisted calls to found the Fourth Communist International for fear of splintering the Communist movement, Trotsky finally agreed to the idea because of what he believed was the Communist parties' inadequate response to fascism. In 1938, Trotsky founded the Fourth International in a direct challenge to the Third International, an alliance of the Communist parties under Moscow's strict control.

Not long after that, in March 1939, Stalin instructed the NKVD to murder Trotsky. Two attempts in January and May 1940 were foiled by his bodyguards. Then, on August 30, the Spanish Communist and Soviet spy Ramon Mercader, who previously had gained acceptance in Trotsky's household, came to visit him. When Trotsky leaned over to read an article, Mercader pulled out an ice pick that he had hidden in his raincoat and struck Trotsky on the head. Trotsky was taken to the hospital, and a day later was pronounced dead. Trotsky's wife, Natalia Sedova, later recalled that Trotsky told her before he died that Stalin had finally succeeded.

At home, Stalin continued his bloody orgy. A series of laws in 1940 stipulated harsh punishment for any minor transgression—being late to work by over 20 minutes, theft, petty crimes—all were punishable by death. The newspaper *Pravda* reported various cases involving minor crimes and the culprits' swift execution.

Stalin's ambitions were also on display outside the USSR. In November, Molotov flew to Berlin to meet with Hitler. During the meeting, he expressed Moscow's interest in annexing Finland, Bulgaria, Romania, and the Bosphorus and Dardanelles Straits in Turkey. Hitler talked in general terms about the spheres of influence but began to realize the extent of Stalin's appetite for a land grab. A month later, Hitler issued a secret directive to begin preparation for "Operation Barbarossa," a swift and overwhelming invasion of the Soviet Union.

1941
Moscow on the Brink

Panic and anger spread through Moscow on October 16, 1941. Stalin's gamble on an alliance with Hitler had suddenly collapsed when, on June 22, 1941, Hitler attacked without making any demands or declaring war. Warnings about the forthcoming German invasion had come from various quarters: from London, Washington, as well as from well-placed Soviet intelligence sources in Germany and Japan. Stalin chose to disregard them all. Why he put so much trust in Hitler is not entirely clear, but the question has prompted much speculation. Stalin profoundly misunderstood Hitler and miscalculated terribly. Even several weeks after the invasion, Stalin remained deluded about Hitler's intentions. He communicated in secret to Hitler that he was prepared to surrender some Soviet territories to Germany and would do more in exchange for peace. Berlin remained silent.

Stalin's mistakes and inaction brought about an unprecedented calamity. Within the first four months of the war, the Germans occupied Ukraine, Belarus, and the Baltics and laid siege to Leningrad. Three million Soviet soldiers became prisoners of war. Four million were dead, wounded, or missing in action. Most of the Soviet Air Force was destroyed, and the army was left with few tanks and cannons. German troops were only a few miles away from Moscow and poised to enter the city.

On the cold morning of October 16, Muscovites woke up to an eerily quiet city. All public transport was at a standstill, and the usually omnipresent police and government officials were nowhere to be seen. Government officials and ordinary people burned documents and their Party cards, lest they fall into German hands. Most government officials had already left for Kuibyshev (Samara), a city on the Volga River some 630 miles east of Moscow. Some machinery from Moscow's factories had already been disassembled and put into crates. The plan to blow up all the critical facilities in Moscow was ready. Much of the Kremlin was prepared for an evacuation, and Stalin's personal train was ready and waiting. No one knew whether he had decided to leave the city.

To the ordinary residents of Moscow, it seemed that the government was ready to abandon them. Rumors of Stalin's departure spread quickly, and for the first time in decades people began to voice their frustration, angrily denouncing Soviet leadership and government bureaucrats. This might have been the crucial moment of the war. If Stalin had decided to leave, the resistance might have collapsed. But he chose to stay. Within the next two weeks, the German military machine near Moscow ground to a halt, worn out by the stiff Soviet resistance, heavy casualties, muddy roads, frozen equipment, and a shortage of winter clothing, food, and fuel.

Throughout November, while the Germans struggled to supply their troops across the frozen plains of European Russia, the Soviets brought in fresh divisions from Siberia, regrouped, and launched a decisive counteroffensive on December 6. One month later, the German army had been pushed back 100 miles. It had suffered heavy casualties: 175,000 were either killed, wounded, or missing in action. But the Soviet offensive also came to a halt; the Soviet troops were suffering from exhaustion and had sustained heavy losses. Between October 1941 and January 1942, the Soviet losses were estimated at nearly 1 million casualties. The Battle of Moscow was won at an enormous human cost.

Not all who were killed fell on the battlefield. Stalin's killing machine knew no rest and continued its bloody work even as the battles raged. As Soviet troops retreated, they emptied city jails, systematically shooting prisoners, particularly political ones. In only one such case, Stalin ordered the execution of 163 prominent political prisoners on September 11, 1941 before the Soviets surrendered the city of Orel.

Even on that dark day of October 16, when the fate of Moscow was hanging in the balance, 300 Soviet officers, including several senior commanders, were summarily shot; twenty more generals were murdered on October 28. In November, the NKVD was given the right to issue extra-judicial death sentences. Several months later, on February 23, Red Army Day, forty-eight people, including seventeen generals, were executed.

1942
Not One Step Back

In the summer of 1942, Hitler launched Operation "Blue", intended to seize southern Russia and sever the routes that brought oil from the Caucasus and the US lend-lease supplies delivered via Iran. The central part of the operation was a rapid march towards Stalingrad to cut off retreating Soviet troops. Taking advantage of their superiority in armored divisions, the flat terrain, and the summer months, German troops advanced rapidly despite the stubborn resistance of the Soviet army. On July 19, Stalin ordered the

Stalingrad Defense Committee to prepare the city for war without delay. Several days later, the Germans took Rostov, a major city, and one month later, crossed the Don River on their final approach to Stalingrad. Only forty-four miles of arid steppe separated the German troops from Russia's main water artery, the Volga River.

In the face of the Soviet retreat and the possible loss of Stalingrad, on July 28, Stalin issued Order 227, which became known as "Not One Step Back." There would be no further retreat. Any commanders who ordered a retreat were to be promptly court marshaled; those who surrendered were to be considered traitors to the Motherland. Special units of about 200 men each were to be organized and placed behind the Soviet troops on the front line with orders to shoot the "panic-mongers and cowards who retreat." Penal battalions consisting of those "guilty of cowardice or any other crime" were to be sent on suicidal missions. In essence, this was classic Stalin—deploying fear and threat to achieve his goal with a complete disregard for human life.

Party authorities also mobilized Stalingrad's civilian population. Men and women between sixteen and fifty-five were organized into work brigades and marched out of the city to dig anti-tank ditches. Children, too, were used as a labor force. The newly set up tribunals tried as deserters any civilians who did not follow orders, condemned them as "traitors to the Motherland and Soviet people," and sentenced them to a minimum of ten years in labor camps. Those who did not denounce family members charged with desertion were also given a ten-year prison sentence.

When the threat of labor camps was not enough, propaganda filled the gap. One of the issues of the *Stalingrad Front* newspaper depicted a frightened girl with her limbs bound. The caption explained what would happen to her: Germans would rape her and throw her under a tank. The only way to prevent the fascists from raping Russian girls, the caption continued, was to kill the enemy.

Discipline had to be maintained at all costs. Stalin's quotation of Lenin from the early days of the Civil War was well known: "Those who do not assist the Red Army in every way, and do not support its order and discipline, are traitors and must be killed without pity." Around 13,500 Soviet soldiers were executed for treason during the battle of Stalingrad. Even so, desertions were common. In September alone, 446 people deserted to the Germans. Some were driven by hunger, others by a German promise to let prisoners return to their homes in the occupied territories.

The most unreliable troops were new detachments formed out of the Stalingrad factory workers. They were untrained and poorly armed. The NKVD blocking units were often put behind them and shot those who retreated. The frontline soldiers were considered disposable and received little support, while new equipment and more food went to fresh troops behind the frontline.

No one was spared in the battle, where signs of elementary humanity all but vanished. Hunger drove many to desperate acts. Among those struggling to survive were hundreds of orphans, who were willing to undertake dangerous tasks for a few crumbs. The German troops promised them food in return for filling their water bottles from the Volga, a mission that put them within range of Soviet snipers, who were ordered to shoot the children without hesitation. The precedent for this had already been set earlier in Leningrad, where Stalin had ordered civilians, whom the Germans used as human shields, to be shot.

The bloodiest battle in history, the Stalingrad campaign, resulted in nearly 2 million people killed, wounded, or captured. By early February 1943, the remaining German troops had surrendered. The Soviet victory was complete and marked a critical point in the course of the Second World War. Yet the enormous human cost of the victory showed, once again, that Moscow regarded human lives as easily disposable, and that none would be spared in the pursuit of victory or Stalin's agenda.

1943
The Enemy Within

Despite the debacle at Stalingrad, the German forces successfully contained any further advance of Soviet troops. It was only in early September that, fearing another encirclement, the Germans began to evacuate the region, allowing Soviet troops to regain control of the North Caucasus. Within the next few months, the lands and peoples liberated from Nazi control came to face an unprecedented wave of repression from their liberators. Hundreds of thousands of Soviet people, young and old, were rounded up within several days and deported to remote parts of Siberia and Central Asia.

Throughout the 1920s and 1930s, Stalin practiced his violent craft of death and repression on millions of innocent victims. The war gave him a new license to engage in mass deportations, this time of entire peoples. Shortly after the German invasion of the USSR, a government decree of August 28, 1941 ordered a resettlement of all ethnic Germans residing in Russia's Volga region. They were moved to special settlements in Siberia run by the newly founded Special Settlement Department of the NKVD. By early 1942, 1.3 million Volga Germans had been resettled in the Western Siberian regions, and 90,000 Finns were moved from the Leningrad region in 1941.

Previous deportations were aimed either at purging hostile social elements, such as the kulaks, clergy or intelligentsia, or preventing a war time collaboration of Germans and Finns with the enemy. The situation in the North Caucasus gave Stalin a new reason for deportations. The German troops were gone; the region was liberated. The deportation of entire peoples was simply a collective punishment for their alleged support of the enemy.

The first wave of deportations began in November 1943 with a small Turkic-speaking people, the Karachays. Over 72,000 ended up in special settlements in Kazakhstan and other Central Asian republics. Next, it was the turn of the Kalmyks, formerly a nomadic people in the northern steppe of the region. Dubbed Operation "Ulus," this deportation involved thousands of NKVD troops. From December 27–30, 1943, the entire Kalmyk population, about 104,000 in all, including women, children, and the elderly, were put on trains and shipped to Siberia in cattle cars.

Two months later, the NKVD decided to assume a greater challenge and deport the most numerous people in the region, the Chechens. The preparations began in October 1943 when tens of thousands of Soviet troops were brought in under the pretext of military maneuvers. Operation "Lentil" began on February 23, 1944, with the rounding up of the local population. As Chechnya was not occupied by the Germans, the Chechens' ostensible crime was not collaboration, but resistance to the Soviet regime. People were rounded up, put in Studebaker trucks, ironically delivered by the US as part of the lend-lease program, and brought to train stations, where freight trains were waiting for them. On February 29, the head of the NKVD, Lavrentii Beria, who had personally overseen the operation, reported to Stalin that 478,479 people, including 91,250 of the ethnic Ingush, had been put on 180 trains, most of which had already departed. Two weeks later, 39,000 ethnic Balkars followed the Chechens and Ingush into the special settlements in Siberia and Kazakhstan.

In the following months, several other Soviet minorities were uprooted from their homelands. The largest and best known were the Crimean Tatars. In May 1944, nearly 240,000 Tatars were shipped to Central Asia in the same way and for the same reasons as their brethren in the North Caucasus. The NKVD tactics during the deportations varied little. The deportation usually began in the early morning hours with a knock on the door. The residents were given between fifteen and thirty minutes to gather their belongings before being brought to the trains. Those who resisted were killed. Transported in cattle cars or sealed boxcars for days, the deportees had little food and water, and no access to toilets and medical care. The stories of horror abounded with children, the old, and the infirm dying in droves. Roughly 20 percent of the deported population died during transportation or within the first year of their resettlement. The NKVD report coldly noted that the deportees who died en route to their destination were mostly elderly and children, and "because of their age, their bodies lacked the necessary resistance to the changed climatic and daily factors."

Historically, deportation and ethnic cleansing has been motivated by the authorities' interest in seizing the land and property of an uprooted population. But Stalin's ruthless orders to resettle over 1 million people of different religious and ethnic backgrounds were driven by pure vindictiveness. While there was little enthusiasm for the Soviet regime among the deported peoples and many among them deserted the Soviet army, only about 10 percent had actively collaborated with the Nazis. Some had been won over by a relatively benign German rule in the region.

But hundreds of thousands of Russians, Ukrainians, and others also had good reason to hate Stalinist rule and many willingly joined the German side to fight against Soviet troops. The most notorious was the 100,000 strong Russian Liberation Army, which consisted mostly of Slavic deserters and prisoners of war and was led by a renowned ex-Soviet general, Andrei Vlasov.

Unable to deport large national populations, Stalin's wrath focused on the most vulnerable minorities. Their physical removal and the administrative abolition of their homelands was intended to break their national will and remold them into a loyal Soviet people. Indeed, their life in the special settlements was strictly controlled and their children were educated only in the Russian language.

Almost immediately after Stalin's death in March 1953, the Soviet government issued decrees easing the conditions of those in special settlements. Three years later, with Khrushchev's denunciation of Stalin's crimes, they were allowed to return to their homelands. Hundreds of thousands of deportees came back only to find that their homes had been seized by Russian and Ukrainian settlers. Hostility, tension, and an uneasy peace between the indigenous deportees and new Slavic settlers remained for decades.

Yet one people, the Crimean Tatars, was not included in the official amnesty of the "punished peoples." Their historic homeland, the Crimean Peninsula, with its beautiful landscape and valuable beaches, became a prime resort destination for Soviet citizens and the Kremlin elite. Between the new sanatoria and resorts for vacationing Soviet people, summer camps for children, and the official resort houses of the Party elite, there was no room for the Crimean Tatars. They would have to wait until the fall of the USSR before they could begin their journey home.

1944
The Siege of Leningrad

While in the south the Soviet Secret Police were loading a civilian population onto trains on their way to death and privation, Soviet troops in the north had finally relieved the long-suffering residents of Leningrad. After an unimaginable 872 days, the siege of Leningrad had finally ended on January 27, 1944.

Less than three months after the Nazi invasion of the USSR, Leningrad was completely encircled. To the south, it was cut off by German troops, which in some places were as close as 6.2 miles from the city. To the north, it was surrounded by Finnish troops, which advanced to the pre-Soviet-Finnish War border of 1940. Hitler gave explicit orders to enter and destroy the city only after the residents had been starved to death. The only remaining link to mainland Russia was a 100-mile long stretch of water along Lake Ladoga. All supplies for the residents and troops had to be delivered by watercraft in the summer and trucks traveling on ice in the winter. Moreover, the almost 1 million people who had been evacuated from the city during the siege also had to cross the lake. Lake Ladoga became known as the "Road of Life."

However, the route could not meet the defensive and civilian needs of the city. The German Luftwaffe bombed the supply convoys, and the city was under a constant artillery barrage. In the fall of 1942, the Germans brought the world's largest gun to Leningrad. Transported by rail, it could fire a seven-ton shell over twenty-nine miles. The bombardments and shelling were a fact of everyday life in the city, where a sign, famously preserved today, warned: "Citizens! This side of the street is most dangerous during artillery bombardments."

When a bitter cold descended upon Leningrad in the winter of 1942, the city's infrastructure ceased to exist: there was no water supply, no electricity, no heat, no transportation, and barely any food. During the winter of

Collecting the dead in Leningrad. Photo by 502 collection/Alamy Stock Photo.

1942–1943, an average of 100,000 people died every month from starvation, illness, and hypothermia. While the official number of deaths during the siege of Leningrad is listed as 632,253, most believe that the real number is at least twice as high.

During the extremely cold months of the winter of 1942, the food supply dwindled to its lowest level. The typical daily ration was 125 grams of bread, which consisted of less than 50 percent flour mixed with sawdust, wallpaper paste or other inedible ingredients. Even then, a ration card meant the difference between life and death; many were robbed and murdered for their cards.

Anything that could be eaten was consumed: animal fodder, toothpaste, boiled glue. Any source of protein was also quickly devoured: cats and dogs, rats and birds, were all eaten. There were numerous stories of mothers smothering one of their children to feed the others, or someone killing a relative to feed the family. More than 2,000 people were arrested and charged with cannibalism. Most cannibalism cases involved eating the corpses of those who were already dead.

Amidst these extraordinary privations, some continued to live well. Decades after the war was over, the published diaries of the survivors recalled that Party officials, their relatives, and friends continued to enjoy hot meals, lived in heated apartments, and lacked little in their daily lives. The responsibility for the high death toll from the blockade lay with the government and Party officials who had failed to make adequate preparations for the siege. Shortly before the encirclement was complete, Andrei Zhdanov, the regional head of the Leningrad Communist Party, was sending rosy reports to Moscow, while the evacuation of women and children and the stocking up of food was moving slowly and inefficiently.

Hunger, death, and destruction were everywhere, but people carried on. Dmitrii Shostakovich wrote his famous Symphony no. 7, which became known as the Leningrad Symphony. It was performed in the besieged city on August 8, 1942 and became a symbol of defiance and resistance in the most unimaginable circumstances. Several attempts to break the blockade failed. However, in January 1943 Soviet troops managed to seize a narrow land strip of six to seven miles along Lake Ladoga. The city was now able to receive more supplies. The worst seemed to be over, but it took another year before the blockade was lifted completely in January 1944.

Those returning to the city found Leningrad unrecognizable after a twenty-eight-month-long siege. All one could see were the ruins of buildings destroyed by shelling and fire, deserted streets, no animal life, and no parks or trees in the barren and cold land. Several old imperial palaces-turned-museums in the suburbs had been blown up and treasures and art works taken by the retreating German army. But it was the human landscape that was irreversibly altered. At the beginning of the siege, Leningrad's residents numbered 3.3 million. During the blockade, about 1 million were evacuated. When the blockade was lifted, there were 600,000 survivors in the city. The human toll of the siege of Leningrad was simply staggering.

Was it worth it? Was the French government wiser by surrendering Paris to the Nazis, thus sparing the city and its population? There is no simple answer. But even asking this question is not possible in today's Russia. When several Russian journalists raised the issue during a radio program in 2014, they immediately came under a heated attack from the government for being unpatriotic. Their program was taken off the air, and no similar issues have been raised since. Regardless of present-day judgments, the residents of Leningrad had no choice at the time. Hitler did not want their surrender, and Stalin would not allow it. In the end, it was the spirit of those who survived the siege against all odds that defined the city for years to come.

1945
The Rape of Germany

On May 8, the most devastating war ever to take place in human history finally came to an end in Europe. Defeated and destroyed, Germany was occupied by US, British, and French troops in the west, and Soviet in the east. Basking in the glory of victory, Stalin reached the peak of his popularity at home and abroad. Not one to miss an opportunity to trumpet his greatness, on June 22, exactly four years after the Nazi invasion, Stalin ordered a Victory Parade in Red Square. Two days later, the Soviet war hero and the country's most distinguished commander, Marshal Georgy Zhukov, opened the parade with a tribute to the great military leader, Comrade Stalin. Thousands of Soviet troops marched past Lenin's mausoleum, where, standing atop, Stalin and other Party leaders were proudly watching the parade. The event culminated in the memorable scene of Soviet soldiers throwing torn German regimental banners in front of the mausoleum. A documentary propaganda film of the spectacle was shown around the world, inspiring awe and admiration of the USSR and its military might.

What this documentary did not show was the price of the victory. Cheerful scenes of Moscow's Red Square teeming with men in military uniforms with glittering medals and decorations pinned to their chests hid a devastated landscape. The European part of the Soviet Union lay in ruins, cities were destroyed, fields were unplowed, and food was in desperately short supply. One-third of the national economy was destroyed, one-fifth of the country's population had been killed or wounded, and the drought and famine that followed would carry away another 2 million lives in 1946.

The Soviet victory in the Second World War—or the Great Patriotic War as it became known in the USSR—formed the core of Soviet identity for decades to come. Not surprisingly, given the propaganda value of the war and the Nazis' exceptional brutality towards the Soviet population, the Soviets' own war crimes were ignored and for decades remained a taboo subject. But the great Soviet liberating army was the same one that had committed vast atrocities against German civilians, raping millions of women, looting industries, and plundering cities and the countryside.

On June 6, 1945, Stalin appointed Zhukov to command the newly created Soviet Military Administration in Germany (SVAG). Special trophy battalions were charged with the removal of any valuable equipment, which was shipped to the USSR. In the following months, the trophy battalions systematically dismantled the German industrial infrastructure, shipping home trainloads of factory machinery, lab and communication equipment, livestock, agricultural products, art, rare books, treasure, and much more. Soviet officials reported that as of August 2, military authorities had shipped 1.28 million tons of "materials" and 3.6 million tons of "equipment." Rough estimates suggest that the Soviets stripped between 60 to 70 percent of the industrial and agricultural capacity in their zone of occupation. Still unsatisfied, Soviet authorities also collected reparations paid using various products.

None of this included the everyday plunder of German property by Soviet troops. Cars and bikes, furniture and musical instruments, sewing machines and cooking pots; anything that was of value to the destitute Soviet soldiers was unceremoniously taken away. Some of the seized items made their way back home to the USSR; however, most of them were destined for the thriving black market.

Soviet soldier seizing a bike from a German civilian in Berlin. Photo by Keystone/Getty Images.

Yet the most serious war crime committed by the Soviet troops was not looting and plundering, but the systematic raping of German women. Thousands of rapes took place in the newly liberated countries of Hungary, Poland, and Yugoslavia. But it was in Germany that the Soviet troops and their commanders abandoned any restraint. "It was an army of rapists," observed one Soviet woman who worked as a war correspondent. She noted that Russian soldiers were raping German females from age eight to eighty.

Apart from their traditional sexism, Red Army soldiers developed a moral justification for rape as revenge for German atrocities. Gang rape was the most common: some women were mutilated, and those who resisted were shot. The image of drunken Soviet soldiers prowling the streets of German cities in search of their female victims left an indelible mark on the survivors of the Soviet occupation.

The behavior of Soviet soldiers was well known to their superiors, who, while they did not encourage it, certainly made few efforts to stop it. When the issue came up in conversation with Stalin, he demurred with a benevolent smile, suggesting that the soldiers who had fought for so long should be allowed to have "a little fun."

This kind of fun resulted in the devastation of the Soviet zone of occupation. Hundreds of thousands fled, knowing that the arrival of Soviet troops meant the rape of women, killing of civilians, and looting and destruction of property. For the fleeing Germans, the Red Army was the embodiment of the imagined Asiatic Hordes. By 1946, Soviet authorities began to recognize that they needed to win over the remaining civilian population. Walter Ulbricht and other German Communist leaders who were brought from Moscow complained that the fear of Soviet troops and the dismantling of the German economy prevented them from "Sovietizing" the Soviet-occupied part of Germany. Their complaints reached the ear of Andrei Zhdanov, at the time the Chairman of the Supreme Council in charge of ideology, foreign policy, and propaganda.

Two factions within the Soviet government had a different vision for the future of the Soviet-occupied zone. One faction, led by Marshal Zhukov, believed in neutralizing Germany to prevent any future wars and thus encouraged Germany's economic despoliation. The other faction, led by Chairman Zhdanov, believed that German Communists should recreate a Stalinist society on German soil, and they needed resources to do it. Zhdanov's vision prevailed, and the pillaging of Germany stopped. The Soviet zone of occupation was soon transformed into Communist East Germany.

1946
Culture War as a Cold War

When, on March 5, 1946, Winston Churchill delivered his Iron Curtain speech with a stark warning about Soviet intentions, Stalin was not only busily consolidating his control of the occupied territories in Eastern Europe, he was also considering new ways to deal with domestic issues in the post-war world. The main challenge was reconciling the glorious victory of the Soviet army with growing awareness of the enormous human and material toll. Millions of demobilized Soviet soldiers were returning home, only to find famine and destruction. The pride and joy of victory were mixed with the uncomfortable realization that the victors were immeasurably more destitute than the vanquished.

Stalin resorted to a time-honored way of distracting Soviet people from the hardships of the daily life: unleashing anti-Western propaganda. In early 1946, he began to talk about the dangers of "kowtowing to the West" and the need to avoid "obsequiousness towards foreigners." Soon, Soviet leaders demanded that Soviet society be purged of contaminating Western influences. A brutal and venomous campaign denouncing the best of the Soviet cultural elite as stooges of the West was led by Chairman Andrei Zhdanov and became known as "Zhdanovshchina."

The first salvo of the campaign was issued by Zhdanov in his inflammatory speech condemning the work of several Soviet writers as being bourgeois and individualistic. He singled out the satirist Mikhail Zoshchenko for his hostility towards the Soviet system and called Russia's greatest poet Anna Akhmatova "a whore and a nun, in whom licentiousness is combined with prayer." Following Zhdanov's remarks, the Party's Central Committee adopted a resolution that condemned two magazines, *Zvezda* and *Leningrad*, for publishing the work of Zoshchenko and Akhmatova. The Party decided that Zoshchenko's work was vulgar, empty, apolitical, and devoid of ideas, while Akhmatova's poetry reflected bourgeois–aristocratic aesthetic values and was pessimistic and decadent. The resolution concluded that both writers were not marching in lockstep with the people, were harming the education of the young, and that their presence in Soviet literature was intolerable.

Stalin framed such issues in broader terms in his meetings with Soviet intelligentsia. The art forms of modernism, formalism, abstract painting, and sculpture were tools of the imperialist West intended to undermine Soviet values and wage an ideological war against the USSR. Stalin also connected socialist aesthetic values with Russianness and, by definition, those who espoused different forms of art became anti-Russian cosmopolitans.

In reality, Zhdanovshchina blacklisted those Soviet intellectuals whose work was known and praised in the West. Accusations of formalism were directed at many Soviet writers, critics, film directors, and composers. Russia's most famous composers, Shostakovich and Prokofiev, were among the latter. Several films of one of the founders of modern cinema, Sergei Eisenstein, were banned. While part II of his *Ivan the Terrible* was banned, the footage of part III was confiscated and most of it burned. Deeply distressed, Eisenstein produced nothing more and died from a heart attack in 1948.

Some were able to adapt to the new Party line. After Grigorii Kozintsev's film, *The Ordinary People*, was criticized and banned for dwelling on the hardships of the war years instead of instilling optimism, he quickly produced a new film, *Pirogov*. The film portrayed the life of a nineteenth-century Russian surgeon who, as a proud Russian patriot, did not kowtow to foreign medical experts and pioneered numerous surgical procedures. The film instantly gained the warm approval of the Party censors and was shown to great acclaim.

The State Museum of Western Art was closed, as were some university departments teaching Western philosophy and literature. A newly published book, *A History of European Philosophy*, was roundly condemned by the Politburo for undervaluing the contributions of Russian philosophers. Even Western classics from Rousseau to Dickens were no longer in vogue and were replaced by Russian writers.

Science, too, was not spared by Zhdanovshchina. A great Soviet physicist and a future Nobel-prize winner, Pyotr Kapitsa was accused of being a bourgeois scientist with contacts in the West. Two scientists, a husband and wife, were arrested and charged with betraying state secrets by sharing the results of their cancer research with Americans. New textbooks emphasized the idea of a Great Russia and informed students that Russians were first in all major scientific discoveries: from the airplane to the steamship, from the invention of the radio to electricity, and from the microscope to organic chemistry.

Zhdanov died in 1948, but Zhdanovshchina continued in different forms until Stalin's own death in 1953. In art and culture, it became known as the "struggle with formalism." In the sciences, its most notorious manifestation was the view of the Soviet agronomist Trofim Lysenko. He insisted that Mendel's genetic inheritance theory was reactionary, that genes and DNA did not exist, and that genetics was a false, bourgeois science. Lysenko's application of crude Marxist evolutionism to science appealed to the Soviet leadership and his belief in environmentally acquired inheritance became the new Soviet dogma with no room for dissent.

By the late 1940s, Zhdanovshchina had morphed into another ominous development, a charge of "cosmopolitanism." The label became a shortcut for condemning any intellectual who was deemed servile to Western influences and insufficiently patriotic. It also increasingly began to acquire anti-Semitic undertones; the phrase "rootless cosmopolitans" became a euphemism for Soviet Jews.

1947
Currency Reform

As the Cold War settled in, it looked like a struggle between two equally mighty superpowers, the US and USSR. The US economy was booming both during and after the war. The Soviet ecomomy was lying in ruins and continued to rely on forced labor and a war rationing system. Soviet agriculture was severely crippled by collectivization and war, and famine was widespread. The euphoria of victory could only last so long before more mundane issues of money and budgets had to be addressed in earnest.

The news of currency reform and the abolition of ration cards was announced to the public via the radio on the evening of December 14, 1947 and appeared in the newspapers the following day. The timing of the announcement was chosen so that people had no time to withdraw their savings. Practically overnight, the government seized large amounts of money and devalued the currency tenfold. The old ten-ruble notes were now replaced with a new one-ruble note. Bank accounts over 3,000 rubles, a large amount given the average annual salary of 7,000 rubles, were compensated at a less favorable exchange rate.

A blueprint for postwar reforms had been agreed upon in late 1943. The reasons for the reforms were obvious. The huge cost of the war had been financed by printing more money. The predictable result was inflation, and the equally predictable solution was to devalue the ruble. Yet fearful that the reform would be unpopular and lead to unrest, the Kremlin waited for two-and-a half-years after the war to implement it.

As always, the best way to mobilize people was to introduce the specter of an enemy. The reforms were needed, the government explained, to confiscate the money amassed by speculators. Concerned about its possible impact, Stalin personally edited the text of the Politburo resolution regarding the reforms. A copy of the resolution bears Stalin's handwritten correction, which added the promise that this would be the Soviet people's "final sacrifice."

The government's unease about the popular reaction to the reform was not without foundation. In November, while the reform was being prepared, rumors that something was about to happen spread like wildfire. The Secret Police reported to Stalin that people were withdrawing their savings and were flocking to stores to buy anything of value—furniture, furs, watches, jewelry, and food. Nonetheless, two weeks after the reform was announced, the old money was exchanged for new, ration cards were gone, and the state retail prices index had dropped to 83 percent of its previous level. Once again, the state had achieved its objective at the expense of its citizens— peoples' savings were confiscated and the consumer's purchasing power had declined eightfold.

As before, those who were hit the hardest by the reforms were peasants. Similar to others, peasants lost their savings and purchasing power, but they also suffered an additional loss because reduced state prices had pushed down the price of foodstuffs at city markets. Selling home-grown foods at markets had become the main source of income for many peasant families who could not rely on their poorly paid labor at the collective farms (*kolkhoz*). In fact, over a quarter of the country's entire agricultural output was raised on small plots allotted to peasants for their personal needs. The city markets remained a vivid testimony to the gross inefficiency of the kolkhoz system.

Those who benefited most from the reform were Party officials, their relatives, and friends. Having gotten a whiff of the upcoming reform, they put some of their money into jewelry and other valuable items, which they later resold at higher prices. They also broke up their savings accounts into smaller ones to keep them under the three-thousand-ruble limit. Some were arrested and charged with violating currency laws, but most enriched themselves with few consequences. The conclusion of one of the investigative reports spoke volumes: "a significant proportion of senior party and government officials have essentially escaped punishment."

In the end, the reform achieved its purpose of providing financial stability during the transition from a war economy to a postwar recovery. As in the past, it was achieved at the expense of average citizens, who found their savings and purchasing power greatly diminished. Contrary to Stalin's assurance, this was far from the "final sacrifice" made by the Soviet people.

1948
Rootless Cosmopolitans

On January 13, 1948, Soviet newspapers reported that Solomon Mikhoels, a prominent Jewish intellectual and head of the Soviet Jewish Anti-Fascist Committee, had been killed in a hit-and-run car accident. In fact, Mikhoels was murdered on Stalin's orders; his dead body was run over by a truck to make it look like an accident. The murder of Mikhoels marked the beginning of a vicious anti-Semitic campaign in the Soviet Union.

Shortly after Mikhoel's murder, the authorities closed the Moscow State Yiddish Theater, where Mikhoels had been the director, and disbanded the Jewish Anti-Fascist Committee. Most members of the Committee were prominent Jewish writers and poets, who were arrested, charged with treason, and sent to the camps.

One of them was the Yiddish poet Itzik Feffer. When, in June 1949, the famous American singer Paul Robeson arrived in Moscow to perform at a concert, he inquired after his old friend. Robeson and Feffer had met in New York in 1943 during a pro-Soviet fundraising rally chaired by Albert Einstein. In America, there were rumors that Jews were being arrested in Russia.

Robeson was told that Feffer was on vacation in the Crimea and would come to Moscow later. In the meantime, Feffer was taken out of the camp and quickly fattened up to appear normal. During their meeting, Feffer, who could not speak freely, motioned to Robeson indicating that he and others would be killed and pleaded for Robeson to speak out and save them. Robeson understood him, but chose to remain silent about Stalin's crimes. Eventually, all the arrested members of the Anti-Fascist Committee were shot on the same day, August 12, 1952.

What unleashed Stalin's anti-Semitism has always been a matter of some debate. Some have argued that Stalin had always been anti-Semitic. Others suggested that his growing anti-Semitism was a product of the war and Nazi propaganda and that he chose to ride the popular wave. It may also have been a by-product of Stalin's increasing emphasis on the country's Russian identity and his weariness of Soviet Jews' divided loyalties after the creation of the State of Israel in May 1948. Whatever it was, the tipping point was, as always, Stalin's paranoia and suspicion of any Soviet citizen who had contact with the West.

The Jewish Anti-Fascist Committee was founded during the war to establish relations with Jews in the West, to win them over to the Soviet

Itzik Feffer (left) and Solomon Mikhoels with Albert Einstein during their tour of the West in 1943 to raise funds for the Soviet war effort. Photo by Sovfoto/ UIG via Getty Images.

cause, and to raise money for the Soviet war effort. Mikhoels and other members of the Committee traveled around the world, particularly to New York, where they successfully raised funds for Moscow. Once the war was over, the Kremlin saw the same contacts by the Jewish organization as a source of dual loyalty or even espionage.

The Committee's compilation of *The Black Book of the Holocaust* documenting Nazi crimes against the Jews, and the publication of some documents in Yiddish were quickly censored. The Committee's work was contrary to the official Soviet line that the Holocaust had been a Western invention and that the Nazis committed crimes against all Soviet citizens. *The Black Book* was banned, and printed copies were confiscated and destroyed. Likewise, the Committee's role in supporting the emergence of the State of Israel had brought about accusations of Zionism. For Stalin, the organization that once served to help the war effort had become a nest of spies and traitors.

As in the past, the campaign against a specific group served as a convenient pretext for expanding the purge. No one was safe: professors and academics, scientists and engineers, even some of Stalin's old friends and comrades were suspects. The latter included Stalin's loyalists, the Soviet Foreign Minister Viacheslav Molotov and the Foreign Trade Minister Anastas Mikoyan.

In Molotov's case, the NKVD fabricated evidence that Molotov's Jewish wife, Polina Zhemchuzhina, was involved in anti-Soviet Jewish organizations. The fact that she had met with Israel's first ambassador to the USSR, Golda Meir, was enough to charge her with treason. Stalin demanded that Molotov divorce his wife. Molotov complied and, in a letter to Stalin, admitted his guilt in failing to prevent his wife's ties to "anti-Soviet Jewish nationalists, such as Michoels." But this "confession" was not enough. Stalin had made up his mind: both Molotov and Mikoyan lost their positions and Molotov's wife was sent to a labor camp.

In the following year, campaigns against rootless cosmopolitans became unabashedly anti-Semitic. In their efforts to expose cosmopolitans, several Soviet newspapers began to inform their readers that many well-known writers, poets, and critics were Jews hiding behind Russian-sounding pen names. The poet Svetlov turned out to be Sheidlin, the critic Kholodov was Meerovich, the writer Iakovlev was Kholtsman, and so the list went on. They were accused of "bourgeois nationalism," "kowtowing to the West," "serving as a tool of American imperialism," and having a "hatred of everything Russian and Soviet."

The latter charge was particularly revealing of the inextricable link between the growing anti-Semitic campaign and the growing overlap between Soviet and Russian identities. Since the founding of the Soviet Union in 1922, Stalin's nationality policy favored the rise of non-Russian ethnic identities. The official ideological line praised the uprisings of non-Russians as an example of anti-colonial struggle and condemned tsarist Russia as a prison of peoples. Right after the war, Stalin signaled a reversal of this policy when, on May 22, 1945, he offered a toast specifically to the Russian people as "the leading force among the peoples of the USSR."

He singled out the Russians as the one people responsible for winning the war, and he praised the Russian character as being capable of sacrifice for the sake of victory. It was ironic that the great champion of Russianness was an ethnic Georgian, who was often embarrassed about his heavily accented Russian.

Stalin's toast marked the beginning of an ideological pogrom that reversed the Marxist dogmas of the last two decades and equated the Soviet Union with Russia. One of the best examples was a renewed discussion at Moscow's Institute of History on how to evaluate Shamil's uprising, a thirty-year war by the North Caucasus highlanders against Russian conquest in the middle of the nineteenth century. Until that point, it had been considered as a progressive struggle by oppressed peoples against Russian imperial overlords. Now, the same uprising was deemed to be reactionary, and Shamil was branded an agent of British intelligence. Tsarist Russia was no longer a colonial empire, but a great power, whose civilizing influence had benefited peoples fortunate enough to become a part of the Russian Empire.

Both the Russo-centric and anti-Semitic trends continued under Stalin and, to a different degree, after his death. Stalin's anti-Semitic campaign reached its apogee in January 1953, when newspapers reported the discovery of a plot by Jewish doctors to kill Soviet leaders. In the atmosphere of a witch-hunt against Jews, many patients refused to be treated by Jewish doctors and denounced them. Jews were assaulted in the streets, insulted, and beaten. Many Jewish doctors were arrested and awaiting trial. Another wave of senseless bloodshed was prevented only by the dictator's own death on March 5, 1953.

1949
Atomic Project

On August 29, 1949, the Soviet Union successfully detonated its first atomic bomb and joined the nuclear age. The Soviet nuclear weapons program started almost by happenstance. In 1942, the Soviet nuclear physicist Georgy Flyorov noticed that scientific journals in the West had stopped publishing anything related to nuclear fission. There could be only one explanation, he told the Soviet authorities. Nuclear research must have become classified. Whether it was Flyorov's warning or the subsequent confirmation of his assessment by Soviet intelligence, on September 28, 1942, an order from the Kremlin instructed the Academy of Sciences to renew its research into the use of nuclear energy. The Academy's top physicist, Abram Ioffe, was charged with creating a special lab to explore nuclear fission and to report in six months on the possibility of developing a uranium bomb or uranium fuel. Underscoring the importance of the mission, Stalin appointed Viacheslav Molotov to supervise the project.

On February 11, 1943, the Academy created Laboratory no. 2, which became a top-secret research facility and the heart of the Soviet nuclear weapons program. Ioffe declined to become the head of the project because of his age and recommended, in his stead, a young bright physicist. His name was Igor Kurchatov, and he would become known as "the father" of the Soviet nuclear bomb.

Unhappy with the slow progress of the project, Stalin replaced Molotov with Beria. The project acquired further urgency after the bombing of Hiroshima in August 1945, and the government launched a crash program to build the bomb, deploying hundreds of scientists and engineers with an unlimited budget. On December 25, 1946, the Soviet physicists set in motion the first controlled nuclear chain reaction in Laboratory no. 2 in Moscow. It took until June 1948 to produce weapons-grade plutonium at the first Soviet reactor at Chelyabinsk–40, and another year to have a successful test of the first Soviet plutonium bomb. This was detonated on August 29, 1949 at the Semipalatinsk Test Site in Kazakhstan.

Soviet success in developing its nuclear weapons program came at a huge cost and sacrifice. Nuclear power required an enormous industrial base that did not exist in the USSR and had to be built to meet the needs of the atomic project. Yet progress was rapid. The speed of research and development was no doubt greatly helped by information supplied by Soviet intelligence. As early as 1945, Soviet spy rings, most notably those involving Klaus Fuchs and the Rosenbergs, were able to deliver the blueprint of the US atomic bomb to Moscow. This saved Soviet physicists a lot of time and effort that would otherwise have been spent trying to determine the size of a critical mass. Soviet spies continued to deliver information about the design and direction of atomic research in the US and Britain until 1950.

On August 12, 1953, less than a year after the US exploded the hydrogen bomb, the Soviets successfully tested their own H-bomb. The nuclear race was on.

6

End of Stalinism and Khrushchev's Revolution

1950
Expanding Communism in Asia

On February 14, 1950, the USSR and a barely five-month old People's Republic of China signed a Treaty of Friendship, Alliance, and Mutual Assistance. The Treaty marked the end of a difficult negotiation and the beginning of a complicated Sino-Soviet relationship.

While the civil war in China was still raging and the outcome was far from certain, Mao wanted to cement his partnership with Moscow and bolster his image through a personal meeting with Stalin. For the moment, however, the Soviet leader preferred to keep his distance. In July 1948, when Mao informed Stalin that he was ready to set out for Harbin and then fly to Moscow, he was once again rebuffed by the Kremlin. The message from Moscow advised Mao to delay his travel until November because Soviet leaders were about to leave for the countryside to supervise the grain harvest. The excuse for the delay was preposterous, and Mao was not pleased.

Stalin, unsure who would prevail in the Chinese civil war, wanted to keep his options open. In August 1945, Stalin and Mao's enemy, Chiang Kai-shek, had signed a Sino-Soviet Treaty that was very favorable to the USSR. That treaty stemmed from the Yalta agreements, where Winston Churchill and Franklin Roosevelt had agreed to reward Stalin with lands and rights that Russia lost in the Russo-Japanese War of 1905 in exchange for Stalin's commitment to enter the war against Japan.

Mao finally arrived in Moscow to meet Stalin on December 6, 1949, several months after his victory over Chiang Kai-shek. In their first meeting,

Mao behaved humbly and respectfully, deferring to his senior comrade, or "the main boss," as the Chinese officials called Stalin.

Yet Mao could not avoid raising an issue that was uncomfortable for Moscow—a reconsideration of the 1945 Sino-Soviet treaty. Stalin demurred, but agreed to discuss the issue later. In the end, he probably underestimated the persistence and shrewdness of his Chinese comrade. Like Stalin, Mao was both a Communist and a nationalist, and he could not accept the conditions of the previous treaty, which made Moscow look like an old colonial power. Stalin relented. On February 14, 1950, a new Sino-Soviet Treaty returned to China two ports, a part of the Chinese railway, and other lands and properties that had previously been given to the USSR. At the time it seemed that these concessions to Chinese comrades were worth the price of a strong bond between the two principal Communist countries.

Throughout 1949–50, the Moscow-installed leader of North Korea, Kim Il Sung, was pressing Stalin to support his plan of invading the south and unifying Korea under his rule. After Japan's defeat, the Korean peninsula was divided along the 38th parallel between the North and South Koreas. Initially refusing to commit, Stalin was finally convinced by Kim's assurances about the blitzkrieg. In April, Kim visited Moscow to discuss preparations, and on June 25, North Korean troops began the offensive.

The war did not go as planned. US troops, together with military contingents from other countries under the UN flag, counter-attacked and captured Pyongyang, the capital of North Korea. Only a full-scale Chinese intervention saved the North Korean regime and pushed back the US-led coalition. It looked like neither side could prevail in this war. Yet despite massive Korean and Chinese casualties, Stalin did not rush to conclude the armistice and preferred to bleed the Americans at the expense of Korean and Chinese lives. The armistice was finally signed in July 1953, several months after Stalin's death. The march of Communism through Asia would have to take a pause.

1951–52
The Dictator is Mad

During the last two years of Stalin's life, it was no longer possible to tell whether he continued to believe in conspiracies against him or was engaged in some kind of macabre fun by toying with the lives of the people around him. It seemed that in discovering plots, purging Party officials, and humiliating his old comrades, Stalin was feeding his insatiable need to confirm his greatness and enjoying his unlimited power. To those around Stalin, his behavior was becoming ever more erratic and no one, not even in his immediate circle, was safe from purge, arrest, and execution.

A series of purges in the late 1940s–early 1950s decimated top Party and government officials in the city of Leningrad. Initially, the spurious accusations involved embezzlement, but quickly developed into charges of forming "an anti-Leninist faction." Known as the "Leningrad Affair," the purge culminated in October 1950 with the executions of six government officials, including the city's mayor. Over 200 others received prison sentences ranging from ten to twenty-five years. Another 2,000 lost their jobs, were exiled with their families, or were sent to the camps. In 1952, the Museum of the Leningrad Siege was shut down after its staff came in for withering criticism by the Party commission sent from Moscow. The commission concluded that the Museum's exhibits did not adequately reflect the role of the great leader, Stalin. If Stalin did see the Leningrad Party branch as potential competition for Moscow, he certainly made sure that it was shut down.

As the pogrom of Leningraders was nearing its end, Stalin began another purge in a far-flung corner of his empire, his native Georgia. It became known as the "Mingrelian Affair" because it targeted an influential group within the Georgian Communist Party: the Mingrelians, a distinct sub-ethnic group. It is widely assumed that this purge was directed at Stalin's powerful deputy, Lavrentii Beria. Beria was of Mingrelian extraction and had installed and promoted his clansmen to key positions in Georgia. As in Leningrad, the initial accusations of abuse of power and patronage were followed by more serious charges of "anti-Soviet activity" and "espionage." Dozens of Georgia's leading officials were arrested, and thousands were deported.

The victims of these purges were commonly referred to as "repressed" and committed to the vast penal system that included prisons, labor camps, labor colonies, and special settlements. In the early 1950s, the Soviet empire of camps, or the Gulag archipelago, as famously described by Alexander Solzhenitsyn, included hundreds of camps with a total of anywhere between 8 and 15 million prisoners. The largest concentration of camps was situated in the remote parts of the Siberia and Kazakh steppes. Each camp could hold up to several hundred thousand prisoners.

At the time, the Gulag was the largest system of forced labor anywhere in the world. Prisoners were used in dangerous and labor-intensive industries, such as mining and logging. Long days in harsh conditions, with little attention to safety or sanitation, and a grossly inadequate diet translated into a high mortality rate and a sickly camp population. Shortly before Stalin's death, the Gulag system was burgeoning, and strikes and riots were becoming more common.

In the last months of his life, Stalin's paranoia was increasingly focused on Jews. At a meeting of top Party officials in October 1952, Stalin openly accused Molotov of being a Jewish sympathizer. A month later, Stalin organized the arrest and prompt execution of the Czech Communist Party leader Rudolf Slansky and fourteen senior members of his party. In a show trial in Prague, they were accused of being spies and found guilty of being Trotskyites, Titoists (from Josip Broz Tito, the leader of Yugoslavia), and Zionists.

Stalin's final bout of virulent anti-Semitism came to be known as the "Doctor's Plot." On January 13, 1953, headlines in the main Soviet newspapers announced the discovery of a plot by Jewish doctors to poison top Party, government, and military officials. Prominent Jewish physicians were arrested, forced to confess under torture, and were prepared for another show trial. After Stalin's death, those close to him recalled his incendiary anti-Semitic remarks threatening violence against Jews and his plan to deport them to Siberia.

On March 1, Stalin suffered a massive stroke. Four days later he was pronounced dead. A new, comprehensive, and unprecedented wave of terror—even by Stalinist standards—had been averted.

1953
The Dictator is Dead

The Great Leader, the Father of the People, the Greatest Genius of All Times and Peoples, the Lenin of Today, and Leader and Teacher of the Workers of the World, to mention only some of his titles, proved to be mortal after all. Many of those who had suffered repression and had lost their relatives in Stalin's purges quietly rejoiced over the welcome news. Yet for millions of people who faithfully believed everything they read in the papers, heard on the radio, and were told at their workplaces, this was a time of enormous grief and great uncertainty. The country was suddenly left rudderless. There was no succession mechanism, as Stalin had made sure that the idea of any heir apparent would be inconceivable.

At the same time, there was little, if any, confusion in Stalin's inner circle and among top Party officials. Once it became clear that Stalin was nearing his death, they calmly proceeded to take over his reign. On the day that Stalin died, Georgy Malenkov became the Premier of the USSR and, a few months later, the First Secretary of the Party; Molotov, who had been demoted and cast aside by Stalin a few years earlier, was reinstated as Foreign Minister; Beria remained the head of state security; and Nikita Khrushchev was charged with handling important administrative matters within the Party's Central Committee. These were the same four people who had offered eulogies at Stalin's funeral, and they emerged to become the principal leaders of the USSR.

The new leadership signaled a clear change, with a swift amnesty for Stalin's victims of terror and repression. Within two weeks those awaiting trial for the so-called "Doctors' Plot" or incarcerated for other political reasons were released. Four weeks after Stalin's death, a government decree was issued prohibiting torture and beatings and ordering torture chambers to be closed. In the following months, about 1 million innocent people who had been sent to camps for criticism of the state and its leader were set free.

The economic changes were equally sweeping. The new leadership curtailed the expansion of the Soviet military, stopped grandiose economic projects, and directed resources towards agriculture and housing. These new priorities brought quick and positive results.

To the Soviet people and the world, the new leaders presented themselves as a new type of collective leadership. But the veneer of harmonious decision-making hid from public view the shark-infested waters of the Kremlin's internal politics. As both witnesses and accomplices to Stalin's crimes, the new leaders only knew how to pursue their interests using Stalin's methods.

The first head to roll was that of the most feared man, Lavrentii Beria. As head of the ominous state security apparatus, he knew everything about his colleagues, who were convinced that it was only a matter of time before they would become his victims. In great secrecy and with the help of the military, the troika of Malenkov, Molotov, and Khrushchev plotted to remove Beria before he turned against them. On June 26, 1953, during a meeting in the Kremlin, Marshal Zhukov, together with several other top military commanders, burst into the room and placed Beria under arrest.

Beria was subsequently moved to a bunker of the Moscow military headquarters and two crack divisions were ordered to Moscow to ensure that no Secret Police troops loyal to Beria would attempt to free him. Ironically, Beria was charged with the same crimes as the thousands of people who were executed under his orders. He was found guilty of being a traitor and spy, and, together with six of his close associates, was shot on December 23, 1953.

In the following year, Khrushchev, now the First Secretary of the Party, was able to upstage Malenkov. Having secured the support of Molotov and others, he succeeded in having Malenkov demoted and his influence reduced. When, in 1955, Molotov disagreed with some of Khrushchev's policies, he turned against him, accusing him of being a member of the old guard. By mid-1956, the collective leadership was no more. Khrushchev, in his position as the First Secretary of the Communist Party, became the undisputable leader of the USSR.

1954
Nuclear War Exercise "Snowball"

When Stalin died, he left behind a country that was fully militarized in expectation of another world war. By 1949, the Soviet army had been reduced to 2.9 million troops, but in 1953 it ballooned to 5.8 million men under arms. Other numbers spoke for themselves: investments in the military rose by 60 percent in 1951 and 40 percent in 1952, while, at the same time, non-military investments grew 6 and 7 percent accordingly.

One of the very first policy reversals under the new Soviet leadership was to shrink the military budget and address the desperate needs of the civilian economy. Yet one part of the military continued to receive the ever-growing attention of the Soviet leaders and unlimited resources—the development of nuclear weapons. The Soviet army had more troops and heavy equipment than the US and NATO did in Europe. But the USSR fell far short of the US in the number and power of its nuclear weapons, and it believed that it was imperative to catch up at all costs.

For several years now, the Soviets had been testing the effects of radiation, but in the summer of 1954, the Soviet commanders decided to test the tactical use of nuclear weapons in a live military exercise, codenamed "Snowball." It is not clear whether the decision was made on purely military grounds or for internal political reasons intended to discredit Stalin's successor, Malenkov, who believed that a nuclear war was unwinnable.

On the morning of September 14, a Soviet bomber dropped a 40 kiloton nuclear bomb, twice as powerful as the one dropped on Hiroshima in 1945.

The bomb exploded 350 meters above the ground and 8 miles from the village of Totskoe in the Orenburg region bordering Kazakhstan. The location was chosen because of its similarity with the Fulda Gap in Germany, through which Soviet tank divisions were expected to launch their offensive in case of war with NATO.

The military exercise involved 45,000 Soviet troops who were positioned nearby with hundreds of planes, tanks, and personnel carriers. Marshal Zhukov personally supervised the Totskoe war game. With the nuclear mushroom cloud high above them, Soviet troops were ordered to launch their offensive. Most of the troops did not have any protective gear and were told that this was a regular military exercise with a mock nuclear explosion. It is believed that the troops were exposed to high levels of radiation throughout the day of the military exercise.

The local population was not warned about the nuclear explosion and only residents of two villages located four miles away from the epicenter of the explosion were temporarily evacuated. With no knowledge of what had happened, villagers were allowed to return a few days later and were surprised to find that tomatoes and other fruits were suddenly fully ripe. Other villagers went to collect wood from the damaged trees. Thousands of people who were treated in local hospitals for cancer and other illnesses were later surprised to find that their medical cards had simply vanished.

The nuclear war exercise "Snowball" was kept secret until after the collapse of the Soviet Union. Only in 1993, forty years after the event, did some of what happened at Totskoe become publicly known. The number of those who died from radiation and related illnesses remains unknown. Some of those who survived to tell their story recalled observing train cars loaded with coffins. Most people in the immediate vicinity and residents of several cities only eighty miles away from the epicenter never realized that they had been exposed to radiation. As always, human lives were secondary to Moscow's national prestige or the private ambitions of their leaders.

1955
Empire of Nations

Throughout 1955, Khrushchev, now clearly first among equals in the Soviet collective leadership, undertook several trips abroad. He and Foreign Minister Molotov had increasingly differed on foreign policy. Khrushchev

Khrushchev (center) visits Uzbekistan. Photo by TASS via Getty Images.

attended the summit of four great powers in Geneva and travelled to Yugoslavia and China. In December, Khrushchev and Prime Minister Nikolai Bulganin were on their way back to Moscow from India and made a short stop in the capital of Uzbekistan, Tashkent. It was the first time in nearly 100 years that high Russian officials had visited Central Asia.

The Uzbek leadership warmly welcomed the heads of Soviet government at the airport and then took them to a rally in the city. A huge crowd with portraits of the Soviet leaders and giant signs glorifying the Party and government greeted the guests from Moscow. Overwhelmed by this enthusiastic reception, Khrushchev reportedly turned to his associates and said: "Well, my friends, I will make a speech. I have to say something in front of these wonderful people."

He began his speech by saying "Greetings to you, my dear Tajiks," and then informed the crowd of the success of the Soviet mission to the neighboring peoples of India and Afghanistan. Then, suddenly changing the subject, Khrushchev proceeded: "You, Tajiks are good lads, you work well and have high yields of cotton. But your neighbors, the Uzbeks, are not doing as well. Some among their leadership resist the modern ways . . ."

At this point, recalls Nureddin Mukhitdinov, who at the time was the First Secretary of the Communist Party of Uzbekistan, everyone on stage froze. Mukhitdinov suggested that Bulganin tell Khrushchev that they were in Uzbekistan, and that he was speaking to Uzbeks. "Do it yourself" was Bulganin's response. Cautiously approaching the speaking Khrushchev, Mukhitdinov told him that the residents of Tashkent and all of Uzbekistan were listening with great attention. "What? Why was I not told before?" said Khrushchev, suddenly realizing his mistake. Then, without missing a beat, he continued: "Dear residents of Tashkent and Uzbekistan. I decided to criticize you publicly to see how you would react. And you, dear residents of Tashkent, understood my joke and listened carefully. I thank you for this!"

This episode was typical of both the ignorance of Soviet leadership about the peoples of Central Asia and Moscow's imperial approach to the Soviet periphery. Despite the official doctrine that proclaimed an "unbreakable friendship of the Soviet peoples," Moscow's policies towards the non-Russian peoples of the USSR differed little from the classic "divide and rule" attitude.

In the following years, the republics of Central Asia would receive greater attention from the Soviet leadership. In addition to being a major supplier of cotton to the entire country, the republics also were a convenient model of a successful socialist path for developing countries in Asia and Africa. In 1956, the government founded the Institute of Oriental Languages (presently the Institute of Countries of Asia and Africa) at Moscow State University. The Institute's specific task was forging professional Soviet cadres with expertise in the languages and cultures of developing countries. A year later, Nureddin Mukhitdinov was brought to Moscow to join the Party's Central Committee Presidium. In his new position, Mukhitdinov was charged with handling Soviet relations with countries in Asia and Africa. Supporting anti-colonial movements and spreading socialism to the developing world had now become one of the Kremlin's top priorities.

1956
End of Stalinism

On February 14, 1,430 delegates assembled in Moscow for a ten-day meeting of the 20th Congress of the Soviet Communist Party. The Congress convened every four years, and this was the first time it had since the death of Stalin.

Stalin, of course, had continued to be omnipresent in countless references and ubiquitous portraits that deified Lenin and Stalin, who "continued the great task of Marx and Engels."

As the delegates entered the hall of the Congress, many were bewildered to see that only one giant portrait was hanging above the stage, that of Lenin. No image of Stalin was to be found. The sense of unease among the delegates increased after Khrushchev, in his seven-hour-long speech, mentioned Stalin's name only once, and even then, only in passing. It became clear that it was no longer business as usual when member of the Presidium and Minister of Trade Anastas Mikoyan passionately condemned Stalin's excesses and referred to Stalin's "cult of personality."

Soviet leaders spent the following days in heated argument about whether and to what extent they should reveal Stalin's crimes. Stalin's close associates, Molotov, Voroshilov, and Kaganovich, opposed any move towards de-Stalinization, fearing the seismic repercussions of change and the prospect of their own accountability for Stalin's crimes. But after Khrushchev pushed back, they reached an uneasy compromise—Khrushchev would deliver a speech in a closed session of the congress and condemn Stalin's purges and mistakes, stopping short of the full and terrifying truth. On February 25, no journalists, guests or representatives of foreign Communist Parties were allowed into the Congress Hall, as Khrushchev dropped a bombshell that became known as the "Secret Speech."

It is hard to overestimate the significance of a speech that questioned the legacy of a man who, for nearly three decades, exercised total control over the country. Whether Khrushchev fully realized it at the time, his speech, with its detailed list of Stalin's crimes, set the country on a new course. The reign of terror was over, but not the opposition to what the old guard saw as a damaging and radical shift.

In June 1957, in a coup attempt organized by Stalin's loyalists Malenkov, Molotov, Bulganin, Kaganovich, Voroshilov, and several others, a majority of the Presidium's members voted to replace Khrushchev in his position as the First Secretary of the Communist Party. Khrushchev rejected their vote as illegal and insisted that only a larger meeting of the Central Committee's members had the power to replace him. When the Central Committee met in urgent session, Khrushchev successfully argued against those he denounced as an anti-Party group. Critical to Khrushchev's victory was the backing of Marshal Zhukov, who accused the opposition's members of being Stalin's accomplices and pledged the military's support for Khrushchev.

The coup failed, and Khrushchev ordered the removal of his old comrades from their positions of power. In disgrace, they were exiled to remote parts of the Soviet Union. A former Soviet Prime Minister, Malenkov was sent to Kazakhstan to become the director of a hydroelectric plant. A former First Deputy Prime Minister, Kaganovich was dispatched to head a small potassium factory in the Urals. But the ultimate humiliation was reserved for Molotov: a former Soviet Foreign Minister was to become the ambassador to Mongolia. Yet none of them were arrested, tortured, forced to confess their crimes, put on show trial, or ultimately executed, as so many were during Stalin's rule. The move away from the abyss of Stalinism was real and lasting.

1957
Sputnik

In March 1950, a group of US scientists decided to launch an International Geophysical Year to promote the exchange of ideas and discuss international scientific projects. The "year" ran from July 1, 1957 to December 31, 1958, as that was expected to be the period of maximum solar activity. In July 1955, the Eisenhower administration announced that the US contribution to the effort would consist of launching several small, Earth-orbiting satellites. Four days later, the Soviets announced that they, too, intended to launch a satellite in the near future. Within a month, Moscow had a special commission developing a program designed to beat the Americans. Washington may not have realized it yet, but the space race had just begun.

Focused on maintaining an edge in the military application of rocket science, the Eisenhower administration had little interest in a satellite launch and considered it a purely scientific affair. It proceeded cautiously, studying the legality of a satellite flight over Soviet territory and excluding the use of military rockets to avoid giving Moscow any pretext of accusing the United States of a provocation. As a result, the administration decided to use the untried Vanguard rocket, designed for research launches, rather than a tested Jupiter-C military rocket.

The Soviets had no such restraint and quickly understood the propaganda value of such a launch. In contrast to the lengthy legal and political process in the US, Moscow quickly prioritized the launch, devoted enormous resources to the project, and made the space program a closely guarded state secret. The initial design for a more ambitious satellite with several scientific instruments aboard proved to be too much of a challenge, so the Soviets moved towards developing the simplest satellite possible.

The original launch was scheduled for April 1958. But when it became known that the Americans were scheduled to give a paper titled "Satellite over the Planet" at the International Geophysical Year conference in Washington on October 6, 1957, the Soviets assumed that the Americans would launch their satellite a few days ahead of the gathering.

With a great sense of urgency, the Kremlin pressed its scientists to expedite the launch. On October 4, despite a touch-and-go launch with some nerve-wracking malfunctions, the Soviet rocket lifted off and placed the first artificial satellite into the earth's orbit. Sputnik ("satellite" in Russian) was a small ball about two feet in diameter and weighing less than 200 pounds. It was equipped with a radio transmitter which emitted distinct beeping sounds that quickly captured the attention of the entire world. The Soviet space mission was a success.

The Soviets had kept their intentions secret to the very end. On the day of the launch, the Soviet Embassy in Washington held a reception for the participants of the international conference aimed at coordinating the satellite launches. During the reception, the head of the American delegation suddenly announced that the *New York Times* had just informed him that a satellite had been sent into orbit. He congratulated his Soviet colleagues, who had broken into triumphant wide grins, when just moments earlier they had professed ignorance of any Soviet launch.

It was a wake-up call for the United States. President Dwight Eisenhower's response was to expedite the original project, still relying on nonmilitary rockets. On December 6, 1957, a rocket lifted off from Cape Canaveral, Florida, but two seconds later lost thrust and fell back ignominiously. Only after the Eisenhower administration switched back to a more reliable military rocket was the first American satellite launched into orbit on January 31, 1958. Named Explorer 1, it carried several scientific instruments and weighed just over 30 pounds.

Washington had always realized that the Cold War was more than a military competition. But before Sputnik, it had not quite grasped how much propaganda value lay in science and technology.

Sputnik changed that. In April 1958, Eisenhower recommended to Congress the establishment of a civilian agency for the nonmilitary use of space. Several months later, Congress, led by Lyndon Johnson, the Senate majority leader and future president, established the National Aeronautics and Space Administration (NASA). In the same year, it passed the National

Defense Education Act, which provided low-interest loans to students majoring in math and the sciences. The Cold War competition in science, civilian technology, and education was in full flight.

1958
Boris Pasternak

Five years after Stalin's death, Khrushchev's quiet revolution of de-Stalinization, or "the thaw", was moving in fits and starts. As the arrests and executions stopped and selective criticisms were permitted, many writers reached into their drawers for novels and stories that were waiting for post-Stalin times. The first to criticize Stalin's lawlessness was Ilya Ehrenburg's novel *The Thaw*, the namesake of the period of Khrushchev's reforms. It was published in the spring of 1954 and was initially welcomed. Then, in the fall of the same year, the Congress of the Soviet Writers censured the novel for an exceedingly negative view of Stalinism. The same happened to several other writers, who published works critical of Stalin. Soviet authorities were still groping for the boundaries of the fast-moving reforms.

Two steps forward and one step back was the typical formula of Soviet policies. Determined to reverse Moscow's strict control of the Communist Parties in satellite Eastern European countries, Khrushchev suddenly found himself facing an outright revolution in Hungary. After initially agreeing to withdraw Soviet troops, Moscow decided to crush the revolution and on November 4, 1956, ordered tanks into the Hungarian capital, Budapest, and other cities. During the following months several thousand Hungarians were killed, over 200,000 fled the country, and thousands of suspected sympathizers were arrested. Khrushchev's dilemma of how to change Stalin's course without losing control had no easy solution.

It was the fate of Boris Pasternak and his novel *Dr. Zhivago* that clearly showed the limits of the reforms. After working on the novel for almost twenty years, Pasternak submitted the manuscript to the literary journal *Novyi Mir* (*The New World*) in 1956. The editors initially accepted the manuscript, but several months later were forced to reject it under pressure from Party censors. The novel was condemned as anti-Soviet and counter-revolutionary. To the Party's cultural hacks, the novel pitted an individual against a society, contrary to the norms of socialist realism. It was one thing to criticize Stalin's abuse of power. It was quite another to have a novel's protagonist question the very cause of the Bolshevik revolution and the brutish society it bore.

Having little hope of publishing his novel at home, Pasternak handed the manuscript to an Italian journalist and had it smuggled out of the country. The manuscript ended up in the hands of a Milanese publisher and member of the Italian Communist Party, Giangiacomo Feltrinelli. Despite Soviet efforts to prevent the publication of *Dr. Zhivago*, Feltrinelli had the manuscript translated and published in 1957. It became an immediate success and was quickly translated into numerous languages. In October 1958, Pasternak was awarded the Nobel Prize for Literature.

Soviet authorities, embarrassed and furious, immediately condemned the Nobel Prize as "a provocation from hostile forces abroad." Pasternak was ousted from the Writers' Union, and Feltrinelli was expelled from the Italian Communist Party. Hounded by authorities, abandoned by his colleagues, and threatened with deportation from the USSR, Pasternak wrote to the Party's Central Committee pleading to be spared an exile. He explained that, for him, life outside of Russia equaled death and assured the Party that he could still be useful to Soviet literature. The condition for staying, however, was that he formally reject his Nobel Prize. He stayed and, a year and a half later, died a broken man without the honors he so richly deserved.

Despite its limits, Khrushchev's "thaw" introduced a decisive change into a society that was used to disposing of its citizens quickly and brutally. Pasternak was humiliated and hounded, he lost his writer's privileges and his reputation, but he was not arrested, tortured, or executed as "a spy and enemy of the people." This was progress!

1959
Census

In yet another sign that life was regaining a measure of normalcy, the government conducted the first post-Second World War census. The previous one had taken place in 1939. Stalin had refused to have a new census, rightly fearing that it would reveal precipitous population decline because of the war and the famine of the post-war years. The new census showed exactly that. The population of the USSR in January 1959 stood at almost 208.8 million, among them 117.5 million women and 94 million men. It was a stunning gender gap, with 23.5 million fewer men than women.

It looked as if in the twenty years between the 1939 and 1959 censuses, the population of the USSR had grown by 49 million. But the number was misleading. Most of the population growth had not come from an increase in the birth rate, but rather as a result of the USSR's territorial expansion during the war. Between 1939 and 1945, Moscow annexed large territories that included the Baltic states and parts of Finland, Poland, Germany, Romania, and Japan. The exact number of Soviet people who died in the Second World War is disputed, but most recent estimates put the number at 27 million. The 1959 census showed a huge demographic gap and stark disparity between the decreasing Slavic population and the growing non-Slavic population of Soviet Central Asia and the Caucasus.

Every census before 1959 offered powerful insights into the series of human calamities in the country. The Russian Empire's first and only comprehensive census was conducted in 1897. It showed the effects of the "tsar famine," a massive famine that struck Russia in 1891–1892. Caused by a combination of harsh weather conditions and government ineptitude, it affected nearly 20 million people with an estimated 400,000 deaths and long-term consequences of malnutrition and disease. Subsequent outbreaks of cholera carried away tens of thousands more lives.

The next census was planned for 1915, but the First World War, revolutions, and civil war intervened, so the next census did not take place until 1926. This counted 146 million people in the USSR and revealed the large population gap of millions who had perished due to the war, social upheaval, and famine.

The following three censuses were conducted during the 1930s, reflecting the turbulent and brutal years of Stalin's revolution from above. In 1934, the USSR census reported a population of 168 million people. Stalin was delighted with the results and hailed the progress and bright future of the Soviet people.

Yet three years later, the 1937 census revealed the large loss of human life. The results were quickly made a state secret and some of census' organizers were executed. It was later discovered that the 1937 census showed that the population in twelve regions of Russia had decreased by 40 million people and in five regions of Ukraine by 22 million. There was no doubt that this was the result of Stalin's repressions, purges, relentless industrialization, and famine caused by forcing the country's peasants into collective farms. Ukrainian peasants suffered the most. Nearly 4 million died from hunger and disease in what became known as the Holodomor (literally, death by hunger). Over 2 million people starved to death in Russia and nearly 2 million in Kazakhstan. It was no accident that in 1936 the government banned abortion to address a terrible demographic situation.

In 1939, Stalin authorized another census. This time the organizers made sure that numbers matched the Kremlin's expectations. The census counted 170 million people and supposedly showed the normal and healthy growth of the Soviet population. Twenty years later, a new and accurate census revealed the real numbers that once again spoke of immense human tragedy.

7

Between Reforms
and Dissent

1960
Virgin Lands

Khrushchev genuinely believed in the superiority of the socialist system. His foreign policy of seeking peaceful coexistence with the West was, in part, derived from his conviction that the Soviet economy would quickly outpace that of the US. Shortly after Stalin's death, Khrushchev turned his attention to the most troubled sector of the Soviet economy: agriculture. Khrushchev, who typically acted on impulse rather than patience and knowledge, decided that Soviet grain production should surpass the US by 1960.

A train departing to the Virgin Lands in Kazakhstan. A slogan on the train says: "Young hearts to you, the Virgin Lands." Photo by ITAR-TASS News Agency/Alamy Stock Photo.

A principal part of Khrushchev's agricultural plan involved the vast and rapid expansion of farmlands into previously uncultivated lands: the left bank of the Volga River, northern Kazakhstan, the northern Caucasus, and Western Siberia. The plan became known as the "Virgin Land Campaign" and lasted from 1953 to 1960.

The campaign was billed as an act of patriotism and romantic adventure. It relied on recruiting thousands of idealistic young men and women eager to resettle and improve Soviet agriculture. In the summer of 1954, the train stations of many Soviet cities were transformed by the joyful mood of thousands of young people, who sang and danced before boarding trains to exotic destinations. That summer, hundreds of trains festooned with Soviet slogans took some 300,000 members of the Young Communist League to new frontiers.

Inspired by the excellent harvest of 1954, the government decided to more than double the originally planned acreage of newly cultivated lands. Numbers spoke for themselves: 200,000 tractors belonging to 435 recently established state farms plowed nearly 30 million hectares of Virgin Lands. Khrushchev's plan seemed a great success. Yet a drought the following year put a damper on the plans for any further expansion, and grain output continued to fluctuate.

In 1960, Khrushchev decided to expand the Virgin Lands of northern Kazakhstan. The Kremlin organized several districts of northern Kazakhstan into a new administrative unit called the Virgin Land Territory and envisioned it as a new sixteenth republic of the USSR. Surprisingly, the idea ran into stiff resistance from Kazakh party bosses and had to be abandoned.

At the same time as Khrushchev was doubling down on his project in northern Kazakhstan, harvests from the Virgin Lands were some of the worst since the beginning of the campaign. Grain production had dropped substantially and never recovered.

The reasons for the eventual failure were many. The Virgin Lands expanded too quickly for the government to be able to provide the necessary labor and technology. The machinery broke down frequently, but mechanical shops were few. Mechanics, tractor drivers, and other experts were in short supply. A shortage of fertilizers failed to increase crop yield and lack of storage meant that 10-15 percent of the harvest was left in the fields to rot. The Kremlin's fast and furious approach also inflicted significant environmental damage. Poor infrastructure, living conditions, and persistent housing shortages soon turned the original enthusiasm of many young men and women into disappointment, and by 1960 many had returned home.

Khrushchev, however, did not give up easily. He renamed the Kazakh regional city Akmola as Tselinograd ("The Virgin Lands City" in Russian) and compared the achievements of the Virgin Land Campaign to those of the First Five-Year Plan, victory in the Second World War, and space exploration.

Yet the outcome of the Virgin Land Campaign was clear: the Soviets had failed to reach US levels of grain production, even though they had sowed a 50 percent larger acreage than the US and employed six times more labor. The Soviet collective farms could match neither American farmers' productivity, their level of mechanization, nor the capitalization of US agriculture.

In his speech in 1963, shortly before he was removed from power, Khrushchev had to concede that the Virgin Lands alone were not the solution to the challenges in Soviet agriculture. The Kremlin leaders who came after him were likewise stymied by failures of grain production. In the 1970s, instead of competing with the US, Moscow found a very different solution to its perennial grain shortages: ordering huge amounts of grain from the United States.

1961
Uncle Slava and the Berlin Wall

In 1961, the future Russian writer Viktor Erofeev was fourteen and was spending the summer at his parents' dacha near Moscow. Because his father was Stalin's personal translator from French and Molotov's top aide, the Erofeevs and their neighbors were no ordinary Soviet citizens. One of their neighbors was Uncle Slava, better known as Viacheslav Molotov, a former "right hand" to Stalin who was now spending his days in disgrace and semi-retirement. Incredibly, the curious teenager and the aging Molotov formed a bond. Once a week Molotov would stop by the Erofeevs, where the young Viktor and the former Soviet leader would listen together to the Russian broadcast of the Voice of America. Clearly, times had changed for Uncle Slava.

At that time, Khrushchev was at the pinnacle of his power and was basking in the glory of the newest Soviet achievement in space: the launching of the first human into orbit and the successful return of the cosmonaut, Yuri Gagarin, on April 12, 1961. Increasingly confident, Khrushchev unleashed a full-scale de-Stalinization campaign in October, during the 22nd Party

A part of the Berlin Wall in 1986. Photo by INTERFOTO/Alamy Stock Photo.

Congress. The new denunciations of Stalin were accompanied by the decision to remove his body from the Lenin Mausoleum, to rename the city of Stalingrad as Volgograd, and to strip Stalin's close associates, Molotov among them, from all official positions and membership of the Party. It was ironic that Khrushchev was condemning Stalin's cult of personality while at the same time creating his own.

While de-Stalinization seemed to be on course in the USSR, Khrushchev's policies were met with resistance from some quarters of the growing Communist world. China's leader, Mao, criticized Khrushchev for his revisionist policies and abandonment of the revolutionary spirit, and in Albania, Enver Hoxha refused to play along. But the most imminent and embarrassing threat came from Berlin, where millions of East Germans were voting with their feet by crossing into West Berlin and then moving further into West Germany.

The "economic miracle" that was taking place in West Germany was within easy reach for many who found their labor undervalued and their freedom curtailed in the socialist paradise of East Germany. Since the end of the blockade in 1948, 20 percent of the East German population–over 3 million people—consisting of mostly skilled workers and professionals left for the West, and the numbers kept growing. In July 1961 alone, some 30,000 people fled to West Berlin, followed by 18,400 people in the first twelve days of August.

To avert any further departures from East Germany, both Khrushchev and the East German leader Walter Ulbricht agreed to close the border by erecting a wall to separate East and West Berlin. Ulbricht signed the order on August 12, and at midnight the East German police and military were out in force, tearing up roads, blocking streets, and erecting barbed wire fences. This was an enormous project requiring the construction of a barrier around the ninety-seven-mile perimeter of West Berlin and a twenty-seven-mile wall within the city.

Practically overnight, city neighborhoods were cut in two, with neighbors and relatives finding themselves on opposite sides of the border. Suddenly, train lines terminated at stations in the middle of the city. The East German propaganda machine immediately went on the offensive, claiming that the barrier was needed to protect the population from hostile fascist elements from the West, officially referring to the Berlin Wall as an "Anti-Fascist Protection Wall." "Protection wall" it was, but unlike most walls which had historically been built to keep the enemy out, the Berlin Wall was built to keep its own people in.

The following summer, authorities built a second fence about 110 yards into East German territory. The houses between the two fences were razed, residents were resettled, the ground was covered with raked sand to detect footprints, and beds of nails were placed under balconies that hung over the zone. Thousands of border guards in 116 watchtowers and foot patrols with dogs were ordered to shoot escapees. Nearly 200 people were killed between 1961 and 1989 in what became known as "the death strip."

But the existing barriers never seemed quite satisfactory to the East German authorities. The Berlin Wall, as we knew it, was a fourth-generation wall built in 1975 from huge slabs of reinforced concrete 12 feet high and 3.9 feet wide. This formidable barrier became an enduring symbol of the Cold War, separating the ideological purity and one-party rule of the east from the freedom and prosperity of the west.

On November 9, 1989, as tens of thousands of East Germans broke through the Wall into forbidden West Berlin, the Wall fell and with it ended the Cold War. But in the summer of 1961, as the Wall was being built, Viktor Erofeev, who would become a dissident writer and mock the Soviet Union, and Viacheslav Molotov, who helped found it, were both listening to the Voice of America.

1962
The Novocherkassk Massacre

In speech after speech, Khrushchev promised to improve the standard of living of the Russian people by investing more into the consumer sector of the economy. Yet the official rosy pronouncements remained at odds with the worsening economic situation and shortages of such staples as bread, sugar, meat, and milk products. One of the popular jokes at the time ran as follows: "Where do you buy food these days?" one shopper asked another. "I am attaching my shopping bag to the radio," was the reply.

The Soviet economy was struggling to deal with increasing challenges from the rising cost of the arms race, the space program, and generous subsidies to fraternal socialist countries and those in the Third World on the path to socialism. Khrushchev's economic policies, often erratic and ill conceived, created more problems than they solved.

On January 1, 1961, the government introduced a major monetary reform. It deflated the value of the ruble ten-fold, while reducing the ratio of ruble to dollar and gold only by 4.4 times. The immediate impact reduced the purchasing power of Soviet consumers but lowered the cost of the government's purchases from abroad.

As the food shortages worsened, Secret Police reports warned of disgruntled crowds and possible disturbances. Indeed, food riots occurred in several towns and regions. The largest occurred on June 1, 1962, in Novocherkassk, a midsize industrial town in southern Russia. On that day, angry workers at a local Electric Locomotive Factory confronted the factory director with concerns about rising prices. For several months now, the regional authorities had been trying to raise productivity and cut the cost of production. Unable to do it by conventional means, the local Party leaders had resorted to the traditional Soviet ways: they increased production quotas, while at the same time requiring the workers to "volunteer" several hours of their labor without pay. The overall effect had reduced the workers' wages by about 30 percent. When on May 31 the government officially raised the price of meat by 30 percent and butter by 25 percent, factory workers had had enough.

On June 1, nearly 11,000 workers went on strike. Local authorities brought in police and military units with tanks who took up positions nearby. Some arrests followed. The next day, undeterred, crowds of workers, joined by some students, marched towards the city's Party headquarters to submit their demands. The reports differ on the details of what transpired next, but one thing is clear: ordered to open fire, the troops killed twenty-four people and wounded eighty-seven. An investigation conducted nearly three decades later suspected that KGB snipers had opened fire.

The following day, angry and undaunted crowds demanded the release of those arrested and talks with "those with blood on their hands." At noon, Khrushchev's confidant F.R. Kozlov, one of the senior Party members sent from Moscow to deal with the situation, addressed the workers on the radio. He promised to look into their grievances and blamed disturbances on local hooligans and riot organizers. It was only then, after the crowd had dispersed and the authorities had detained 240 people overnight, that the situation began to calm down.

In response to the riot, Soviet authorities delayed the price hike and made sure that the empty shelves of food stores were now full. At the same time, over 100 people were arrested and jailed. Fourteen were put on trial. Seven of them were sentenced to death and executed and others given long sentences in the Gulag. The bodies of those shot by troops were buried in unmarked graves. The whole incident was kept secret until 1992. At the time, only those brave enough to listen to the Voice of America heard the news of the bloody Novocherkassk massacre.

1963
The Thaw and its Limits

Khrushchev was finding it increasingly difficult to channel freedom of expression into the straitjacket of anti-Stalinism. The country was like a stuffy old room in desperate need of fresh air, but how much air no one knew. Leave the door wide open and a strong gust of wind will wreak havoc on everything in there; leave the door shut and the lack of air becomes oppressive.

The initial gust of fresh air came from literature and the arts. It all began with the publication of Alexander Solzhenitsyn's *One Day in the Life of Ivan Denisovich*, a short novel based on the author's own experience in Stalin's labor camps. It was the first description of life in Stalin's penal colonies and the cruel inhumanity of the Gulag.

The appearance of the novel in print was far from certain. On December 8, 1961, the manuscript arrived on the desk of Alexander Tvardovsky, the influential editor of the journal *Novyi Mir*. Tvardovsky immediately understood the significance of the novel, but he also knew that the censors would never approve it. It took almost a year of unsuccessful backroom maneuvers until the manuscript was finally brought to Khrushchev's attention.

One could never predict Khrushchev's reaction, but this was the last chance to have it published. Only a year earlier, Evgenii Evtushenko had published a poem decrying the absence of a memorial at Babii Yar, a notorious site in Kiev, where on two autumn days in 1941 the Nazis had massacred nearly 34,000 Jews. Khrushchev's reaction was to denounce the young poet as politically immature and ignorant. The brave editor of the *Literaturnaia gazeta* who had published the poem and who knew the risks involved in allowing it into print was fired. All those involved in pushing Solzhenitsyn's manuscript were well aware that their careers might be in danger.

According to one account, Khrushchev raised the issue with the members of the 22nd Party's Presidium and asked their opinion on whether to print the manuscript. When his question was met with dead silence, Khrushchev announced: "OK, this means we will print it." One month later, the novel appeared in the November issue of *Novyi Mir*, which immediately sold out.

Quite a different fate befell Vasilii Grossman's monumental novel *Life and Fate*. After Grossman submitted the manuscript to a publisher in 1961, the KGB raided his apartment and seized all copies of the novel, along with notebooks and typewriter ribbons. The Party's chief ideologist, Mikhail Suslov, considered the book to be more dangerous than *Dr. Zhivago* and swore that it would not be published for the next 200 years. Grossman's appeal to Khrushchev did not help. Luckily, Suslov was wrong. The book was published in 1988 to great acclaim but neither Suslov nor Grossman lived to see it.

This seesaw of opening debates on previously forbidden topics and shutting them down when they went astray continued until the end of Khrushchev's tenure. The first exhibition of avant-garde art in Moscow was another such example.

The Stalinist Soviet Union had no tolerance for any form of art that deviated from the officially approved socialist realism. A year after Stalin's death, three Moscow sculptors, Vladimir Lemport, Vadim Sidur (often referred to as the Soviet Henry Moore), and Nikolai Silis formed a workshop that launched a movement of "cellar non-conformism."

Unable to display avant-garde art openly, these sculptors supported themselves by continuing their work on grandiose Soviet monuments designed in the socialist realist style and intended to inspire patriotism. Like many Soviet writers who wrote "for the drawer," that is, confining to drawers work that had no chance of passing censorship, avant-garde artists, too, kept their art in the basement of their workshops hoping for a better day. Hence the "cellar non-conformism."

That day arrived in December 1962, when the first officially sanctioned show that included avant-garde art took place at Moscow's exhibition hall, the Manege. Khrushchev, together with other Party leaders, personally attended the exhibition. The artists were present, and, as it turned out, rightly nervous about the reaction from Soviet leaders. Khrushchev was outraged by what he called "degenerate" artworks that "distort the faces of the Soviet people," shouting that even his grandson could paint better and unleashing a long string of obscenities.

When Khrushchev threatened to deport the artists, the chief Soviet ideologist Mikhail Suslov, who was standing next to him, suggested that they should be strangled. Khrushchev concluded: "Soviet people do not need such art!" The exhibition was immediately closed, and the next day the official daily, *Pravda,* condemned "abstractionism and formalism" in art.

Khrushchev's volatile character and his half-hearted attempts to revitalize Soviet society resulted in chaotic policies. If it was a thaw, it failed to melt the thickness of decades-long Stalinist ice.

1964
Khrushchev's "Retirement"

In 1963, the Party began to resort to some of its old methods of cracking down on those espousing anti-socialist art forms. One of these was a future Nobel laureate in literature, Joseph Brodsky. His poetry was denounced as "pornographic and anti-Soviet." He was harassed, interrogated, and twice put into a mental institution. His arrest and trial in the following year were the clearest sign yet that Khrushchev's "thaw" was about to come to an end.

On February 18, 1964, Joseph Brodsky, a 24-year-old poet and translator, faced questions from a judge presiding over his trial in Leningrad. The charge was lack of a regular job, a crime of "social parasitism" that was punishable by a prison term or internal exile. Originally intended as a law against vagrancy, a charge of social parasitism proved to be a convenient way to crack down on anyone deviating from a socialist path. Brodsky was quickly found guilty of being *tuneiadets*, "a freeloader", and sentenced to a five-year banishment in Arkhangelsk, a city near the Arctic Circle.

Brodsky's trial marked the beginning of a crackdown on dissidents, those few who dared to question Soviet dogmas and were therefore accused of anti-Soviet activity. In addition to exile and the Gulag, the Soviet Secret Police, known since 1954 as the KGB, began to rely on another way to suppress dissent. Dissidents were now confined to a psychiatric institution with a diagnosis of "a delusion of reformism" or "a sluggish schizophrenia."

To many in the Soviet leadership, the trials of Brodsky and others were the result of Khrushchev's permissive policies, which had allowed too much room for anti-Soviet and anti-socialist ideas. Perhaps sensing the growing discontent in the Party over its loosened grip on culture and ideology, Khrushchev, too, engaged in more frequent denunciations of the intelligentsia as "cosmopolitans, formalists, and renegades" and abstract art as "a form of bourgeois ideology."

This was not enough. By 1964, grievances against Khrushchev were coming from many quarters. For the average Soviet citizen, Khrushchev's image was first and foremost identified with severe food shortages. Indeed, agriculture remained the Achilles heel of the Soviet system. For the first time, the Soviet government was compelled to make a large purchase of wheat from Canada and began negotiating similar purchases with the US and Australia. As Soviet consumers became more interested in their own wellbeing and less in a global proletarian revolution, Khrushchev was criticized for generous offers of aid to developing countries at the expense of his own.

For some time now, many Party officials had considered Khrushchev's policies to be erratic and blamed his de-Stalinization drive for allowing too much freedom. Some members of the Politburo could not forgive Khrushchev for caving in to American demands during the Cuban Missile Crisis or for weakening Moscow's grip on the Communist Parties across Europe.

Perhaps the most damning of all was the fact that a decade after denouncing Stalin's cult of personality, Khrushchev had now created his own and had emerged as the paramount leader of the USSR. Behind the official praises, toasts, and ceremonies, Khrushchev was disparagingly referred to as "Tsar Nikita" or, more maliciously, with reference to his short and stout statue, "the bald boar."

Of course, the very fact that people were able to deride their leader in private, if not in public, was a sign of tremendous change. No one had dared to say a critical word about Stalin even to their own best friends and relatives for fear of being denounced and sentenced to a minimum of three years in the Gulag—and often much more. The existential fear that had underpinned the Stalinist system was gone.

It was clear that Khrushchev's liberalization encouraged not only dissident voices in art and politics, but also gave rise to national movements in the Soviet republics, above all in Ukraine. When on May 24, 1964, a fire broke out in Ukraine's National Library, the perpetrator was quickly arrested, and in a speedy and secret trial found guilty. But lingering questions remained: What was the arsonist's motive and why did it take so long to extinguish a fire which destroyed some 600,000 rare books and manuscripts from Ukraine's pre-revolutionary history? To many, the incident looked like the heavy-handed work of the KGB, aiming to deprive Ukraine of its national heritage and identity.

True or not, the library fire in Kiev only invigorated a genuine Ukrainian intelligentsia and raised further alarm in Moscow about "the Ukrainian nationalist movement." The Party considered the rise of local nationalisms an existential threat to the territorial integrity of the USSR; that, too, was blamed on Khrushchev.

In this atmosphere, in October 1964, a small group of plotters, led by Leonid Brezhnev, Khrushchev's first deputy, protégé, and heir-apparent, staged a coup. Shortly before, Khrushchev was warned of a possible plot but chose to ignore it. When on October 12 he received a call summoning him from his vacation residence on the Black Sea coast to a meeting in Moscow to discuss the state of agriculture, the coup was set in motion. At the Central Committee meeting two days later, the Party's chief ideologue, Mikhail Suslov, took four hours to read a long list of charges. The next day, members of the Central Committee voted unanimously to accept Khrushchev's "voluntary" resignation. On October 16, a press release announced to the Soviet people and the world that Nikita Khrushchev had been relieved of all his responsibilities "because of his advanced age and declining health."

By all accounts, Khrushchev refused to put up a fight and took credit for the changed country, where his colleagues were able to insist on his resignation without fear of retribution. Until his death in 1971, he lived peacefully at his summerhouse near Moscow. This, too, was a sign of the seismic change initiated by Khrushchev. Previously, no Russian tsar or Soviet leader had left the pinnacle of power alive.

1965
Soviet State Capitalism

A coup against Khrushchev brought back a sense of collective leadership under three men: Leonid Brezhnev as the General Secretary of the Communist Party, Aleksei Kosygin, the Prime Minister, and Anastas Mikoyan, the President with a largely ceremonial post. Early on, the new leadership made its priorities clear: to replace Khrushchev's single-handedness with a collective decision-making process, to reform the economy, and to stifle dissent.

The top priority was the economy. Ideas about how to revive the moribund Soviet economy had already been circulating for several years. Between 1962–65, a number of articles addressing the issues of economic reform were published in the Party newspaper, *Pravda*. Most articles concerned themselves with ways of raising economic productivity, suggesting a decentralized approach and reliance on computerized planning. The notions that were previously roundly condemned as the pillars of rotten capitalism—profitability, bonuses, housing, competitive wages, and cost-efficiency—had suddenly found their way onto the pages of Soviet newspapers and journals.

A discussion of the economic reforms began in earnest on September 9, 1962, when *Pravda* published an article titled "Plan, Profit, and Bonus." The author, Professor Evsei Liberman, suggested giving more power to individual enterprises, creating material incentives for profitability, and rewarding workers and managers for increased productivity. This was the first bold attempt to challenge the existing principles of the Soviet economy. In the context of a heavily centralized economy still based on the Stalinist model, which relied on public enthusiasm to increase productivity, the new ideas were nothing short of revolutionary.

On September 27, 1965, Prime Minister Aleksei Kosygin initiated the reforms in his report to the Party's Central Committee. Unlike most members of the Central Committee, who had reached their pinnacle of power through the Party ranks, Kosygin was a technocrat, and thus well suited to pitch economic reforms to his colleagues.

Kosygin's reform project of reducing the role of central planning, allowing greater autonomy to the state enterprises, and loosening price controls received full support at the Party's 23rd Congress in March–April 1966. And yet, the implementation of the reforms was muddled. The unwieldy Party bureaucracy saw the reforms as a threat to its own privileges in a system that some Soviet dissidents called "economic absolutism."

The 1965 reforms did produce some positive changes in the economy, but were mired in delays and contradictory objectives. The result was a hybrid economic system, where profit and social considerations had to coexist with and be managed by massive bureaucracy. Officially considered a socialist economy, it had, in fact, become a peculiar form of Soviet state capitalism.

1966–67
Crushing Dissent

Khrushchev's Thaw, uneven and short-lived as it was, brought about irreversible change. Criticism of Stalinism in arts and literature rapidly grew into a dissident movement that questioned some fundamentals of the Soviet system. This group of dissidents became known as the "sixtiers," identified by a decade during which they matured into an important political movement. They were the intellectual elite, a small sliver of Soviet society, yet their voices were heard far and wide and had an unmistakable impact both within and outside the country.

Moscow inevitably viewed the dissidents as a dangerous challenge to the Soviet regime. The Party's first target was the writers. The Brodsky trial in 1964 was intended to send a signal to those who chose to defy socialist norms in literature and lifestyle. It was a blatant attempt to silence Brodsky for his poetry, yet he was charged and convicted for being a freeloader, a man who refused to have a steady job. By contrast, almost exactly two years later, in February 1966, two young Soviet writers, Iulii Daniel and Andrei Siniavsky, were put on trial for publishing their satirical writing abroad. They were charged with "anti-Soviet agitation and propaganda with the purpose of undermining the Soviet state and society," convicted in a closed trial, and sentenced respectively to five and thirteen years in a labor camp with a strict regime.

It seemed that the authorities were poised to revive the show trials of the Stalinist era. But the times had changed. Hundreds of intellectuals in Europe and the US, including dozens of world-famous writers such as Italo Calvino, Graham Greene, and Arthur Miller, signed letters of protest. More surprisingly, sixty-three members of the USSR Union of Writers also signed a letter appealing to the government to have Daniel and Siniavsky released. Twenty-three prominent members of the Soviet intelligentsia, including the renowned nuclear physicist Andrei Sakharov, signed a letter protesting the revival of Stalinism. Despite the authorities' efforts to jam the airwaves, a small but growing number of Soviet citizens took to their shortwave radios to hear the alternative news broadcast by the BBC, Radio Liberty, and the Voice of America.

Determined to squash the fruits of Khrushchev's liberalization, the Communist old guard relied on, among other things, the support of a retrograde intelligentsia. The most recognizable name among them was that of Mikhail Sholokhov, who had just been awarded the Nobel Prize in literature. Speaking at the 23rd Party Congress in March 1966, Sholokhov called the dissident writers "werewolves." He argued that their sentencing was too lenient and that if this had happened in the revolutionary 1920s, they would have been shot. Sholokhov's sentiments were typical among many of those who longed for a return to Stalinism.

Yet to turn around a ship that for more than a decade had been awkwardly sailing into the open sea was no easy matter. By the mid-1960s, the rusty ship of socialist realism had more than one leak. In 1963, Mikhail Bakhtin published his *Problems of Dostoyevsky's Poetics*, which augured for a new approach to literary criticism and made him famous among Western scholars. In 1964, Grigorii Kozintsev directed *Hamlet*, a film based on Boris Pasternak's translation of Shakespeare with a score by Dmitri Shostakovich. The film won a Special Prize at the Venice Film Festival, and Sir Laurence Olivier praised the leading actor, Innokentii Smoktunovskii, as being the best Hamlet ever. The following year, another Soviet film won several prizes at international festivals. This hauntingly beautiful film by Sergei Paradzhanov, *The Shadows of the Forgotten Ancestors,* was a Ukrainian ballad set in the Carpathian Mountains. Later, in the same year, a newly founded theater of satire led by a popular comedian, Arkady Raikin, toured England and performed satirical sketches to much acclaim from British audiences.

Herein lay the Soviet leadership's dilemma. The same art that broke through the confining boundaries of accepted norms and dogmas, and that therefore had to be suppressed, was the same art that won prizes and praise in the West and raised the status of the USSR on the global artistic stage. The Party ideologues chose to tolerate some of the new art and carefully managed the boundaries of acceptable social criticism.

But a more formidable challenge to the Soviet regime came from elsewhere—increasingly assertive national elites that began to formulate dissident ideas challenging the dominance of Russian culture and Moscow's central rule. The Party saw the rise of national cultures and sentiments in constituent republics as an existential threat to the political structure of the USSR. On this issue, it brooked no compromise.

A wave of repression against the national elites was particularly pronounced in Ukraine, where hundreds of Ukrainian intellectuals were arrested between 1965 and 1968. The common charges were writing and spreading subversive literature in the Ukrainian language, questioning Soviet national policies, and undermining "the eternal friendship" between the Russian and Ukrainian peoples.

The official Soviet press simply labeled the accused as "nationalists." Among the most prominent was Ivan Dziuba, a Ukrainian literary critic, whose treatise *Internationalism or Russification?* was both a defense of Ukrainian national culture and a direct attack on Russian chauvinism. Dziuba was arrested, charged with disseminating anti-Soviet nationalist ideas, and sentenced to five years of jail and five years of exile.

The trials, however, instead of suppressing the dissident movement, had the opposite effect. Hundreds of Soviet intellectuals protested the closed trials, curiously under the slogan: "Respect the Soviet Constitution." The dissidents' approach was to challenge the regime within the legitimate bounds of Soviet society. After all, the Soviet Constitution enshrined the right to demonstrate and protest. Suddenly, the constitution and Soviet laws that, until now, had been seen as smoke and mirrors had to be taken seriously.

The authorities responded by diagnosing those who demanded human rights and criticized Soviet society as suffering from "social schizophrenia" or "pathological honesty." They were confined to psychiatric institutions, fed depressants, and treated as mentally ill individuals. Among the most famous and early victims of such psychiatric abuse was Alexander Esenin-Volpin, a dissident mathematician who was hospitalized in 1968.

But the numbers of those who refused to remain silent kept growing. Later that year, ninety-eight Soviet mathematicians signed a letter asking for Esenin-Volpin's release. At the same time, a letter signed by 139 intellectuals protested political trials as contrary to Soviet law.

Challenges to the status quo came from different quarters. In November 1967, a group known as the Berdiaevtsy went on trial in Leningrad. They were followers of the Russian philosopher Nikolai Berdiaev, who had been expelled from Russia in 1922. Berdiaev was a Christian universalist and a Russian patriot, and his followers chose to confront the godless Soviet regime as devout Russian Orthodox Christians. In the same year, following the Six-Day War in the Middle East and Moscow's ensuing vehement anti-Zionist propaganda, Soviet Jews began to turn to Zionism in yet another challenge to the regime.

Fifty years after the Bolshevik revolution, the Soviet regime found itself embattled on many fronts: from Soviet writers and artists, national elites, religious groups, and increasingly human rights advocates from a broad swath of Soviet intelligentsia. The cracks within the system were becoming more visible, and even workers—the ideological backbone of the Soviet system—were increasingly conscious of the mismatch between government rhetoric and everyday life.

1968
The Sakharov Manifesto

In the spring of 1968, as Western democracies were in the midst of the anti-war movement, race riots, and student protests, in Moscow, a soft-spoken 47-year-old man was writing an essay warning of the dangers of a thermonuclear war, environmental degradation, demographic explosion, hunger, and dehumanization. The man's name was Andrei Sakharov, the world-renowned physicist and father of the Soviet hydrogen bomb. His essay, *Reflections on Progress, Peaceful Coexistence, and Intellectual Freedom*, became the manifesto of the human rights movement in the country. Its author became the most visible proponent of democracy and humanism in the USSR.

Sakharov's manifesto called for a complete and thorough de-Stalinization of Soviet society, respect for the Constitution, and the introduction of democratic freedoms. He envisioned a future of peaceful coexistence, disarmament, and the eventual convergence of free market democracies and socialist societies. Later, he would repudiate his theories of convergence and symmetry, which viewed both the USA and USSR as equally oppressive, bureaucratic states. Instead, Sakharov concluded that comparing the two was like comparing a normal cell (the US) with a cancerous one (the USSR).

When a copy of Sakharov's manifesto, typed by hand and secretly distributed within the country, also appeared in the Western press, the Kremlin decided that Sakharov's stature as a world-renowned physicist could no longer outweigh his subversive activity. He was barred from any military-related research, watched, harassed, and hounded. Finally, in 1980, unable to stop his dissident activity, the KGB ordered his arrest and exiled him to the provincial Russian city of Gorky (today Nizhny Novgorod).

While the KGB was nervously watching the rise of the dissident movement in the Soviet Union, an even greater challenge had emerged outside the country, in the neighboring Warsaw Pact country of Czechoslovakia. The Prague Spring, as it became known, began in January 1968 with the election of a reformer, Alexander Dubček, to the post of the First Secretary of the Communist Party. In the following months, Dubček supported attempts to decentralize the economy and opened the society to basic freedoms of expression and speech. A sudden end of censorship brought about debates about a pluralist society, the creation of new parties, free elections, and a competitive economy—everything that the Kremlin deemed "anti-socialist tendencies." In reality, Dubček believed in socialism with a human face and had never entertained the idea of reintroducing private property or withdrawing from the Warsaw Pact Treaty. But even these mild reforms were viewed as a threat in Moscow.

On August 21, 1968, Soviet troops, joined by the troops of four other Warsaw Pact nations, invaded Czechoslovakia. The brave and peaceful resistance by many Czechoslovaks could do little in the face of the 600,000-strong foreign soldiers with several thousand tanks. Dubček was arrested, taken to Moscow, and eventually dismissed from his job. Within a year, the opposition groups had been suppressed, reformist officials removed, and censorship restored. This was the end of the Prague Spring and of the stillborn idea of socialism with a human face.

To the Soviet people and the world, the invasion was presented as an act of "fraternal assistance" and "international duty" in response to the "invitation" of the Czechoslovak government and Party officials. Such unimaginative mendacity could fool few people in the West, where protests against the Soviet invasion took place in many cities. Even the friendly Communist parties in Italy, France, and other European countries had no choice but to condemn the Soviet invasion.

In the Soviet Union, however, the government touted its own version of events and claimed that it had saved the brotherly Czechoslovak people from an imminent invasion by NATO troops. Throughout the country, the Party quickly organized meetings under the slogan "Hands off Czechoslovakia." Many of the people who participated in patriotic meetings in the daytime also tuned their shortwave radios to the Voice of America or Radio Liberty by night. Only seven brave people assembled in Red Square to express their support for the free and independent Czechoslovakia. They were quickly rounded up by the KGB, beaten, arrested, put on trial, and sentenced to various terms.

For Sakharov, the Soviet invasion of Czechoslovakia and the authorities' brutal reaction to the small demonstration in Moscow left no doubt that the Soviet Union could not tolerate even a modicum of openness and that socialism and democracy were simply incompatible. From now on, he was at war with the entire Soviet socialist system.

1969
The Soviet Dr. Seuss

From the Kremlin's point of view, the summer of 1969 was an ideological disaster. Eight years after launching the first man into space and turning it into a huge propaganda victory, the Soviet government helplessly watched on as the Americans successfully landed on the moon. Hundreds of millions of people around the world listened and watched as two US astronauts explored the moon's surface.

One of those who closely followed the mission to the moon was a popular Soviet writer, Kornei Chukovsky. A few months before his death, he left this entry in his diary:

> I am completely absorbed by the American mission to the Moon. Our internationalists who talked so much about the international significance of space flights are full of envy and hatred towards great American heroes, and they imparted the same feelings to the people. At a time when 'my breast aches with tender love' [Walt Whitman, *Pioneers*] for these people, Lida's [Chukovsky's daughter] housemaid, Marusia said: "I wish they had died on the way." The authorities convinced children that Americans were sending humans to the Moon because of their inhumanity and callousness: while we are sending tools and machines, the lowly Americans are sending live human beings! In a word, these poor sectarians do not even wish to be a part of humanity. Besides, they forgot that they were boasting that they would be first to land on the Moon.

For Chukovsky, the crude Soviet propagandists who blamed the cruelty of capitalism for sending men to the moon were despicable "lying conmen."

A serious literary critic and a gifted children's writer, a sort of Russian Dr. Seuss, Chukovsky, who mostly became known for his lighthearted and playful children's books, was frequently criticized for a lack of ideological content in his stories. In 1928, Lenin's wife Nadezhda Krupskaia attacked Chukovsky's fantasy fairy-tale *The Crocodile* as meaningless nonsense that should not be read by children. Throughout the 1930s, Chukovsky's books were banned, and he and his family were brought to ruin. Desperate and hounded by the authorities, Chukovsky was forced to sign a confession letter in which he renounced his previous work, admitted to damage caused by his children's tales, and promised henceforth to write in the spirit of socialism.

In 1944, he again came under criticism for subverting the "great task of bringing up children in the spirit of socialist patriotism." Ten years later, his short children's poem about a gregarious fly was condemned by one critic as "not appropriate for our mission of bringing up children in the spirit of friendship, unity, and mutual help." It was not until after Stalin's death that Chukovsky became Russia's most popular children's writer, and his books sold millions of copies.

In the late 1960s, Chukovsky had an idea for a book that would explain the Bible to children. This was a serious challenge in an atheist state. Somehow, the authorities agreed, on the condition that neither the word God nor Jews would be mentioned in the book.

The book was published in 1968 under the title *The Babylonian Tower and Other Ancient Tales*. Instead of God, the book referred to the "Magician Jehovah." Even then, its shelf life was very short, as some powerful guardians of Soviet morality were shocked by the appearance of a book that seemed to

The cover of Kornei Chukovsky's children's book, *An Awesome Cockroach*.

have slipped through the cracks of the atheist foundation of the Soviet state. The authorities quickly confiscated and destroyed all copies. The book was republished in 1990, a year before the Soviet Union fell apart.

For writers like Chukovsky, life in the stifling world of Soviet propaganda, ideological censorship, and the vulgarity of the official culture was a painful and demoralizing experience. On March 24, 1969, while hospitalized, he wrote in his diary:

> Here in the hospital, I realized particularly clearly how the authorities use radio, TV, and newspapers to spread among millions of people primitive and vile songs, so that people will not be aware of Akhmatova, Blok, and Mandelshtam. The masseurs and nurses can quote the most vulgar songs, but no one knows Pushkin, Baratynsky, Zhukovsky, Fet—no one.... The entire semi-educated Russia swims in this ocean of vulgarity, and those who know and love poetry form just a tiny pond. One can predict in advance what they have to say on any topic. They are not people, but pieces of furniture, a set of armchairs and chairs ... with a uniform, official way of thinking, bright individuals have become a greatest rarity ...

Bravely, Chukovsky signed numerous letters in support of political dissidents and persecuted fellow writers. His summerhouse at the writers' village of Peredelkino, near Moscow, was always open to many Soviet writers and poets who fell afoul of Soviet cultural dogmas. One of the frequent visitors was Alexander Solzhenitsyn, with whom Chukovsky formed a particularly close and warm friendship.

8

Stagnation

1970
Solzhenitsyn's Nobel Prize

Among dissident Soviet writers, Alexander Solzhenitsyn occupied a special place. His first work, *One Day in the Life of Ivan Denisovich* (1962), marked an inflection point away from Stalinist culture, and Solzhenitsyn's name became synonymous with uncompromising truth. Yet between 1962 and 1990, Solzhenitsyn was allowed to publish only a few short stories, as the new leadership that came to replace the ousted Khrushchev considered his work too raw and inflammatory. The KGB was watching him and once raided his apartment, seizing parts of the manuscript *The First Circle*, which he later rewrote and published in 1968. Despite continuous harassment by the KGB and censure by the official Union of Writers, which finally expelled him in 1969, Solzhenitsyn continued to write. His manuscripts were smuggled out of the country and published in the West: *Cancer Ward* in 1968 and *August 1914* in 1971.

At the same time, he was feverishly writing what would become his best-known work, a three-volume epic history of the convict labor camp system in the USSR. It took him a decade to write the book that some consider among the most influential works of the twentieth century. He worked in secret, never able to have the entire manuscript in front of him at once for fear of a sudden KGB raid. *The Gulag Archipelago* appeared in the West in 1973.

But even before the publication of his most famous work, in 1970 Solzhenitsyn was awarded the Nobel Prize in Literature for "the ethical force with which he has pursued the indispensable traditions of Russian literature." This "ethical force" came from Solzhenitsyn's own bitter experience. In the last months of the Second World War, in which he served as an artillery captain, he witnessed the horrendous crimes of Soviet soldiers against German civilians, in particular the massive number of gang rapes of German women. Disturbed by the cruelty, drunkenness, and poor prosecution of the war by the Soviet command, he wrote a private letter to a friend in which he indirectly criticized Stalin. The letter was read by censors before it could reach the addressee, and Solzhenitsyn was arrested, charged with anti-Soviet propaganda, and sentenced to eight years in a labor camp. It was only after eight years in the Gulag camps and three years of internal exile that he was finally freed and rehabilitated under Khrushchev's broad amnesty in 1956.

Fearing that he would be stripped of Soviet citizenship and not allowed back into the country at a time when his wife was expecting their first child, Solzhenitsyn decided against attending the Nobel ceremony in Stockholm. The Swedish government proposed to hand him the prize at the Swedish embassy in Moscow but, unwilling to antagonize the Soviets, suggested a small and private ceremony. Solzhenitsyn was appalled by this cowardly behavior and rejected the suggestion that he called "an insult to the Nobel Prize itself."

For the next four years before his expulsion from the USSR in 1974, Solzhenitsyn was subjected to relentless harassment by the KGB. In 1971, an attempt to poison him with ricin failed, but made him very sick for some time. Even after his expulsion from the country, KGB heads approved launching a special operation codenamed "Spider", to discredit Solzhenitsyn. They concocted a fake memoir by Solzhenitsyn's first wife, composed a fake anti-Semitic essay, which they claimed he had written, sent intimidating letters, and tried to infiltrate his intimate circles. The full extent of the KGB operation against him may never be known because 105 volumes of material from the KGB archives related to Solzhenitsyn were burned in 1990. Who ordered the destruction of the Spider files remains unknown.

In April 1972, the Swedish Academy again planned to hand Solzhenitsyn the Nobel Prize in Moscow. This time it was to be delivered personally by the Permanent Secretary of the Swedish Academy, Karl Ragnar Gierow. But when Gierow was refused a visa to the USSR, this plan too came to naught. Frustrated and angry, Solzhenitsyn decided to have his Nobel lecture smuggled out of the country. He photographed the lecture on several negatives and passed them, in secret, to his trusted courier, a Swedish correspondent in Moscow, Stig Fredrikson, who smuggled the negatives to Finland in the back of his transistor radio.

The speech was published in the West in August 1972 and became a sensation. In his distinctive voice, this unbreakable man delivered a darkly poetical lecture from behind the Iron Curtain. It was filled with the raw human pain of someone who had witnessed the horrors of Stalin's camps and survived. It was also optimistic and hopeful in its belief that the beauty of art and literature would prevail over human depravity. And it was uncompromising in its commitment to exposing lies and speaking the truth.

Solzhenitsyn and Sakharov became two giants of the Soviet dissident movement. Both were persecuted by the authorities and eventually exiled: Solzhenitsyn was deported to Germany in 1974, and Sakharov was sent into internal exile to Gorky in 1980. Both had profound respect for each other yet had very different visions of the future. Sakharov's cosmopolitan, universalist, human-rights vision based on the Western democratic model contrasted with Solzhenitsyn's belief in the spiritual renewal of individual nations and a Christian vision of the world. In the following years, Solzhenitsyn would continue to denounce the Soviet regime, chastising the flaws and weaknesses of Western democracies and criticizing Russian nationalists for their anti-Semitism and Western liberals for their permissiveness. To the end, Solzhenitsyn remained a lonely Russian prophet, an incorruptible, towering figure who remained committed to writing and speaking the truth.

1971
A Soviet Bob Dylan

In February 1970, the authorities removed Alexander Tvardovskii from his post of Editor-in-Chief of the journal *Novyi Mir*. Tvardovskii, who had made the brave decision to publish Solzhenitsyn in 1962, became a symbol of cultural change; his journal became a reliable barometer of the limits of official tolerance. Tvardovskii's removal was a heavy blow to the aspirations of the anti-Stalinist Soviet intelligentsia and a bad omen of the return of stringent Soviet norms.

Yet if the Soviet ideological watchdogs were winning the battle, they were losing the war. Despite a formidable arsenal of sticks and carrots, it was no longer possible to enforce the strict boundaries of Soviet culture. What began with one literary journal had now spread to theaters, film, music, and the visual arts.

Vladimir Vysotsky. Photo by SPUTNIK/Alamy Stock Photo.

In the world of Soviet theater, one theater came to play the same role as *Novyi Mir*. Founded in 1964 by Yuri Liubimov, the Taganka Theater eschewed the stale Soviet repertoire in favor of novel and imaginative productions of both classics and new plays. In 1971, Liubimov staged *Hamlet,* casting Vladimir Vysotsky in the main role. Vysotsky was already famous for being a charismatic film actor, musician, and the handsome husband of the French actress Marina Vlady. Their Soviet-era international romance was endlessly fascinating to the Soviet public. Even the head of the French Communist Party, Georges Marchais, had interceded on behalf of the star couple to the Soviet leader, Leonid Brezhnev.

Vysotsky's Hamlet was an intellectual loner, a tragic and isolated individual empowered by his moral force to rise against the authorities. The theme of "a superfluous man," a man who is discarded by society because he refuses to conform to its oppressive and senseless rules, was all-too-typical in classic Russian literature. But such loners were not supposed to populate the wholesome Soviet culture of irreducible optimism and a bright future. No wonder that censors saw the play as subversive, and officials in the Main Administration of the Theaters and the Ministry of Culture demanded changes. Yet the play proved to be such a success that official criticism was muted. For years, *Hamlet* remained the most popular play in Moscow and coveted tickets to Taganka were impossible to come by.

Shortly before the start of the play, Vysotsky walked onto the stage with a guitar, quietly singing a song about Hamlet. It was his seven-string guitar, inimitable guttural voice, and the hundreds of songs that he had written and performed that had made him the country's most famous unofficial pop star. Vysotsky's songs tapped into the anxious minds of the post-war Soviet generation. Instead of singing about a bright future for young men and women in the lands of socialism, Vysotsky sang about unsung heroes, broken lives, and the suffocating banalities of everyday life. His songs ranged from satirical to lyrical, from critical to patriotic, and though rarely openly anti-Soviet, they were far from endorsing the Soviet way of life.

Despite, or because of, his enormous success, the authorities never stopped hounding Vysotsky: barring him from film roles, fining him for concerts they deemed illegal, paying little for his regular concerts, and subjecting his songs to withering criticism in the press.

Vysotsky followed in the footsteps of several songwriters and performers, who, like him, were harassed by the authorities. The first in the post-war USSR to redefine the traditional Russian romance was Alexander Galich, who began to compose and perform his songs in the late 1950s. Galich's melodies were simple, his voice prosaic, but his lyrics were a sharp and powerful denunciation of the Soviet regime. Eventually, he lost his privileges, was expelled from professional organizations, and deported to the West in 1974.

More popular than Galich was Bulat Okudzhava, whose sad and gentle songs were a departure from typical Soviet themes, but who was nonetheless acceptable to Soviet authorities. While Vysotsky considered Okudzhava to be his inspiration, he stood apart from both Galich and Okudzhava, who were in some ways the voice of the Soviet intelligentsia. Vysotsky's unique performance and deep voice, his breadth of themes and powerful lyrics, struck a deep chord with many listeners. He was a Soviet Bob Dylan, a singer whose art resonated particularly strongly with the youth and whose popularity in the Soviet Union matched that of the Beatles.

Until his death on July 25, 1980, from a combination of drugs and alcohol, Vysotsky remained unrecognized by official Soviet culture. Yet he became a cult figure and a hero to his admirers; tens of thousands came to say goodbye on the day of his funeral, turning it into the largest unauthorized gathering in the history of the Soviet capital.

In 1971, Vysotsky composed one of his signature songs, "Fastidious Horses". Like many of his songs, it lacked a conventional theme and could not be reduced to a simple message. It was about a poet-singer who drives horses along the edge of the precipice. He tries to slow them down, he feels that death is near, but the horses will not stop, and he just wants another brief moment at the edge of the precipice.

"But the horses I was given, stubborn and so unforgiving, if I can't complete the life I'm living, I wish I could finish the song I'm singing" were the words of the song's last verse. They might also have been Vysotsky's last words. He, too, desperately tried to survive on the edge of the Soviet precipice but was finally carried over that edge by his unbridled talent.

1972
Nixon's Détente and the Great Grain Robbery

On May 29, 1972, the people of the Ukrainian capital of Kiev woke up in disbelief. Overnight, residents of dozens of old houses in one city neighborhood had been moved, their houses had been demolished, and trees and bushes had been planted in their stead. In other neighborhoods, the streets were unusually clean, with freshly painted houses. A new, tall fence had been erected to hide a decrepit structure that could not be easily removed. The reason for these miraculous changes came later that day. The President of the United States, Richard Nixon, had arrived in Kiev for a two-day official visit. The streets that had undergone this sudden transformation formed part of Nixon's travel route. Naturally, the Kiev that Richard Nixon was meant to see was yet another Potemkin village.

Why did Nixon spend only one short day in Russia's famed second city, Leningrad, and choose to spend more time in Kiev? It is likely that US officials had correctly gauged the growing national sentiment in Ukraine and wanted to use the visit to bolster Ukrainian national identity.

In Kiev, Nixon was greeted by Volodymyr Shcherbytskyi, who only four days previously had been appointed the head of the Ukrainian Communist Party. Officially, his predecessor, Petro Shelest, had been transferred to another position, but in reality he had been forced to step down because of his encouragement of Ukrainian culture and identity. If Nixon's visit, the first by an American President to the capital of Ukraine, was intended to play on the ethnic tensions in the USSR, it was a shrewd and successful move.

Nixon arrived in Kiev following a four-day summit with Kremlin leaders. Both Brezhnev and Nixon had strong incentives to reach a deal that had previously eluded them. Nixon was in the middle of his reelection campaign, much of it predicated on his success in foreign affairs and winding down the war in Vietnam. The Kremlin was very keen to avoid isolation following the sudden US-Chinese rapprochement and Nixon's recent summit with Mao. The result was the signing of several groundbreaking treaties, most importantly the Anti-Ballistic Missile Treaty (ABM) and the first Strategic Arms Limitations Treaty (SALT I).

In a communiqué issued on the last day of the summit, both parties broadly committed to further limitation of missile threats, reducing the risk of a nuclear war, improved trade and cooperation in science and space, recognizing the borders of European states, and addressing multiple other issues in the spirit of cooperation. The summit brought a dramatic change in US–Soviet relations and augured the beginning of détente, the process of reducing Cold War tensions between the two major antagonists.

By the time Air Force One took off from Kiev airport on its way to Tehran, Nixon's next stop, the image of the US president had been transformed from an enemy to a friend. Typical posters with the words "Hands Off Vietnam" or "No to Nuclear War" written across a sullen and ominous-looking Nixon were quickly replaced by new ones of a smiling Nixon and the words "Trade, Not War." During the Watergate hearings, the Kremlin would maintain that Nixon had been persecuted because of his friendship with the USSR.

Trade was indeed one of the linchpins of détente. Moscow hoped to achieve access to US goods and obtain the "most favored nation" (MFN) status that would dramatically reduce tariffs, while Washington believed that Moscow's dependence on trade with the US was the best way to gain leverage over the Kremlin.

At the center of the new commercial ties was a grain deal. The USSR was experiencing increasing shortages of cereals and was willing to purchase large shipments of grain from the US. But no one knew how much grain Moscow was willing to buy that year, and after the contract was signed in July 1972, the US was in for a big surprise. Moscow had decided on the immediate purchase of several years' worth of allotments—10 million tons of mostly wheat and corn. The event became known as the Great Grain Robbery, as the US government had unwittingly sold grain at subsidized prices, which then caused a huge spike in the price of cereals in the US and worldwide. For the next two decades, Moscow continued to rely on large purchases of American grain.

Nixon's détente was a significant international breakthrough, but it was not universally welcomed. Soviet dissidents denounced the détente as a capitulation to Moscow, which continued to deny the Soviet people the most elementary of freedoms. Andrei Sakharov argued that that there could be no international peace and security without basic respect for human rights within the country.

Critics of the Soviet regime had a point. As the brainchild of Nixon's National Security Advisor, Henry Kissinger, détente was based on the premise of accepting a geopolitical status quo and refraining from criticism of Soviet internal policies. Indeed, during the Moscow summit, Nixon's team did not discuss any thorny issues, such as the mistreatment of dissidents, disregard for human rights, and prohibition on travel and emigration.

Soviet leaders clearly interpreted the summit as carte blanche approval for their internal policies. In August 1972, the authorities introduced a special education tax on potential emigrants, a tax that was fifty times the average salary and made the application for an exit visa virtually untenable for most people. While the tax applied to any emigrant, it was clearly directed at one particular group, as the authorities attempted to stamp out the incipient Zionist movement among Soviet Jews and their immigration to Israel.

Help arrived from one man in Washington, the US Democratic Senator Henry "Scoop" Jackson. No friend of Moscow, Jackson believed that Nixon's détente was made on the backs of those who opposed an oppressive totalitarian system. Jackson was convinced that if the Soviet people had the opportunity to emigrate, they would do so in large numbers and discredit the Soviet regime by voting with their feet.

In October 1972, Jackson introduced an amendment to the 1972 Trade Reform Act that would bar the Soviet Union and other Communist countries from receiving MFN status unless they allowed freedom of movement. After the Senate overwhelmingly voted in favor of the amendment, it was then co-sponsored by Democratic Congressman Charles Vanik of Ohio and introduced in the House. It took months of negotiations and debate before the Trade Act, accompanied by the Jackson-Vanik amendment that specifically called for the right to emigration with no education or any other emigration tax, was finally signed into law by President Gerald Ford on January 3, 1975.

While the Soviet authorities refused to provide any assurances on emigration and vowed to ignore the amendment, the education tax was dropped in 1973 and emigration from the USSR continued. Despite all the barriers to emigration and the thousands of *refusniks*, who were denied exit visas on the spurious grounds of having once had "access to state secrets," a quarter of a million Jews and tens of thousands of Germans, Armenians, and Greeks left the USSR throughout the 1970s. People, indeed, were voting with their feet.

1973
Friendship of Peoples

The vast majority of the Soviet people remained confined within Soviet borders with no option to emigrate. For all its enormous diversity and tireless proclamations of "the brotherly friendship of peoples," the USSR was neither a happy socialist melting pot nor a brotherly Soviet mosaic. In April 1973, members of the Politburo convened to discuss "the national question," (i.e., issues related to ethnic tensions within the country).

The main concern was the rise of nationalist sentiment in Ukraine. The head of the KGB, Yuri Andropov, reported about a group of Ukrainian nationalists and their recent manifesto against Russification, while one of the Party's chief ideologues, Boris Ponamarev, commented on the unprecedented and "unacceptable Ukrainianization" of Ukraine. Replacing the Ukrainian leader a little less than a year previously had done little to assuage the Kremlin's unease.

No less disconcerting was the rise of nationalism in Armenia and its growing tension with Azerbaijan over the Azeri regions of Karabakh and Nakhichevan, which Armenians considered a part of their historical patrimony. The Politburo's statement acknowledged "the existence of the national question" in some parts of the USSR, but not a word was said about an increasingly virulent and widespread anti-Semitism.

Nor did the Politburo address the issue of the Slavic majority's typical condescending treatment of non-Slavs in the ethno-territorial regions of the USSR. Traditionally, to manage ethnic relations within ethno-territorial units, the Party relied on a balance of power by appointing a titular ethnic cadre to the position of the First Secretary of the Communist Party and an ethnic Russian as the Second Secretary. To the local titular elites, however, there was never any doubt that it was the Second Secretary who had a direct line to Moscow, and that the word "Soviet policies" really meant those of the Russians.

Ethnic tensions were not a new issue. Despite, or perhaps because of, the official policies promoting non-Russian ethnic minorities, everyday Russian chauvinism and prejudice towards non-Russians was common. A wave of Russian patriotism inspired by Moscow during the Second World War was quickly transformed into Russian nationalism after the war.

During the following decades, the Party promoted the idea of the Russian people as first among the brotherly Soviet peoples. Gradually, the Russian language began to replace other national languages. A turning point came in

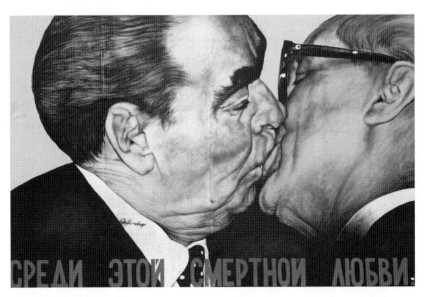

The Soviet leader, Leonid Brezhnev, and the East German leader, Erich Honecker, greeting each other. Photo by Universal History Archive/UIG via Getty Images.

1971, with the 24th Communist Party Congress launching the idea of uniting all the peoples of the USSR into one common identity, "the Soviet people," with one common language, Russian. For many non-Russian elites, this was a clear signal of Moscow's plan of "Russification", which would diminish their power and deprive indigenous peoples of their language and identity.

The national question emerged in force on yet another front. In the early 1970s, a large number of Soviet army officers were ready to retire. Many of them had spent decades serving in distant parts of the USSR or in occupied Eastern European countries. Long disconnected from their places of birth and bolstered by sizable pensions and subsidies, they chose to retire in attractive parts of the Soviet Union. Many Russian officers settled in the Crimea, a beautiful peninsula in the Black Sea and one of the few beach vacation destinations in the entire country. In 1956, the Crimea had officially become a part of Ukraine and because of a continuous ban on the return of deported Crimean Tatars, it became further Russified with the arrival of more Russian speakers.

Another large group of retired Russian officers came to settle in the Baltic republics of Estonia, Latvia, and Lithuania, tipping the ethnic balance among these small non-Russian peoples. The first sign of trouble came in the summer of 1972, with the publication of a letter from seventeen Latvian

Communists. The letter, addressed to Party officials, was a desperate cry against growing Russification. After professing their loyalty to the cause of Communism, these prominent Latvian Communists charged Russian Party officials in Latvia with using "Marxism-Leninism as a cover for a Great Russian chauvinism." Their list of grievances was long: a mass influx of Slavic settlers was the direct result of Moscow's policy of erasing Latvian identity; the Russian language had become prevalent in schools; streets with Latvian names had been renamed after Russian political leaders; the mass media promoted Russian culture; theaters and orchestras were forced to switch to a Russian repertoire; Latvian national culture and customs had been undermined by the Russians; and last, but not least, the entire leadership of the republic consisted of Russians, who could not speak a word of Latvian.

Curiously, the authors of the letter also addressed the plight of Jews in the USSR, condemning the fact that 3.5 million Soviet Jews had no opportunity to learn about their own culture and language, there were no theaters or clubs, and there was only one newspaper and one magazine in their native language. The letter denounced gross violations of the Marxist-Leninist national policies and the harm that Russification was doing to the cause of Communism throughout the world.

Despite the Kremlin's statements to the contrary, the national question in the country remained the single most critical issue that remained unresolved until the demise of the USSR in 1991.

1974
Cult of Personality

On December 31, 1973, following a long-established tradition, Soviet people received official congratulations for the occasion of the coming New Year. This time, however, the greetings were issued in the name of the General Secretary of the Communist Party, Leonid Ilyich Brezhnev, alone and did not include the usual reference to the Presidium of the Supreme Council, the Central Committee of the Communist Party, and the Soviet government. For those concerned that the General Secretary had developed the same cult of personality as his predecessors, no further proof was needed.

The image of Brezhnev had become omnipresent in newspapers, TV news, documentaries, books, and films. He could be seen kissing visiting leaders from comradely Communist parties, giving speeches at meetings, sending greetings

Brezhnev receiving a parade with four gold stars of the Hero of the Soviet Union pinned to his chest. Photo by AFP/Getty Images.

to the participants of international conferences and workers who exceeded their quotas, and making toasts at Kremlin receptions. He was particularly fond of medals and awards, and received over 100 Soviet decorations for his service to the Motherland. Brezhnev's typical portrait showed him with four Hero of the Soviet Union stars, the highest Soviet award. Brezhnev and Marshal Zhukov were the only people to have received four stars.

Brezhnev's dominance in the media coincided with his visibly deteriorating health. Years of heavy consumption of alcohol, cigarettes, and sleeping pills were taking their toll, and in 1974 he suffered several minor strokes. Brezhnev was becoming the butt of dozens of Soviet jokes as his speech slurred, and he appeared increasingly confused. Yet Soviet leaders had no tradition of resigning their top posts, and Brezhnev labored on, appearing frequently on TV and making arbitrary decisions about matters large and small.

One such small matter became a perfect illustration of the absurdities of Soviet life and the country's political system. It concerned the publication of a book by a Kazakh writer, Olzhas Suleimenov. Titled *Az i Ia*, a word-play on *Asia*, the book was an amateurish attempt to show the influence of nomadic steppe culture and language on the famous Russian epic, *The Tale of Igor's Campaign*. Soviet censors deemed the book the work of a revisionist author who was promoting Kazakh nationalist ideas.

The controversy reached the highest levels of the Party. The chief of the Kazakhstan Communist Party and a full member of the Politburo, Dinmukhamed Kunaev, personally intervened in defense of the book. But the Party's chief ideologue, Mikhail Suslov, was against its publication. Just as with Khrushchev, who had to decide the fate of Solzhenitsyn's first novel, it fell upon Brezhnev to settle the issue.

According to some stories, a few days after Brezhnev was given a copy of the manuscript, Suslov approached him and inquired, "So what do you think? Is there anything [subversive] there?" To which Brezhnev allegedly responded, "there is not a fucking thing there." That was taken as a sign of approval and a final word on the issue. The book was published in 1975 and continued to be a subject of debate among Soviet scholars. At a time when the Soviet leadership was preoccupied with weeding out subversion and maintaining ideological purity, the Soviet economy entered a tailspin.

1975
Consumer Crisis

The gap between the soaring ideological pronouncements and bleak economic reality had become so obvious that even Brezhnev could no longer close his eyes to reality. On more than one occasion, he derided the use of the ideological bromides that the Party hacks repeated in their speeches. Yet Brezhnev did little to reduce the weight of such ideological pronouncements or to shift the focus away from the military-industrial complex that was eating up most of the budget.

Ideology and propaganda were the glue that kept the society together by both trumpeting the threat from the West and announcing the inevitable triumph of socialism all over the world. The worn-out clichés promised "a collapse of imperialism" and "an uncompromising ideological struggle that will lead us to victory." Lest the forced resignation of President Nixon, which stood in sharp contrast to the infallibility of Soviet leaders, be seen as a dangerous sign of democracy, the Soviet media described the event as the sign of "a deep crisis of bourgeois society and the moral disintegration of the ruling class."

But no amount of ideological rhetoric could hide the deep flaws within the Soviet economic and political system. Ordinary citizens were craving consumer goods that the Soviet economy was incapable of delivering. The housing shortage remained acute: many continued to dwell in communal apartments, where several families shared a kitchen and bathroom, and young married adults were forced to live with their parents. Ownership of goods such as cars, dishwashers, and washing machines was rare. One example may suffice to illustrate the unbridgeable consumer divide between the US and USSR. By the mid-1970s, over 90 percent of US households had a washing machine; the Soviet Union had fewer than 1 million washing machines for the entire population of 250 million people.

The Ninth Five-Year Plan (1971–1975) proved to be a failure by almost any measure, yet the picture presented to the Soviet public was that of a victorious march forward. Soviet leaders boasted that their country produced more steel and pig iron than the US, forgetting to mention that only 40 percent of Soviet steel was of comparable quality to that of the US. The daily news reported record grain harvests but failed to mention that many crops were rotting in the open fields because of a lack of storage facilities, and that a crisis was only averted thanks to large purchases of grain from the US and Canada.

A contrast in quality between the products of Soviet industry and those of Western counterparts was particularly visible in the consumer sector. The more Soviet citizens were exposed to western goods—shoes and shirts, colorful publications and electronics, packaged foods and music records—the more they realized how extraordinarily shoddy Soviet-made products were.

Even worse than the demoralizing influence of Western goods and culture were the constant food shortages throughout the country. Meat was often rationed, bread was sold out by the early afternoon, and it was not unusual for potatoes and herring, two staples of the Soviet diet, to arrive in the store rotten and old. Soviet citizens were long accustomed to queuing for what were considered exotic foods, such as bananas and oranges or rare items like toilet paper. Now, people had to queue for basic items—eggs, chicken, fish— sometimes leaving in deep frustration when, after several hours, they reached the counter only to hear the saleswoman announcing that the item was completely sold out.

Perhaps the most common words in the vocabulary of Soviet people became "deficit," which referred to any product in great demand and short supply, and "blat," a connection to someone who could provide a "deficit" product in exchange for some valuable service or a bribe. With Party officials having access to special, well-stocked stores that were off-limits to ordinary citizens, it was no wonder that corruption and misuse of the office were widespread.

Several things buffered the Soviet economy from total collapse. Year after year, the Soviet government dispatched soldiers, students, and civilians to spend weeks and sometimes months helping to harvest crops and perform other agricultural activities. Even more important was Moscow's growing reliance on the export of oil and gas, as prices had quadrupled after the 1973 Arab oil embargo. This reliance on free labor and the energy sector helped to prop up the increasingly inefficient and failing Soviet economy, as the USSR entered a period of deep stagnation.

1976
Dissenters into Defectors

On a warm July day in 1976, the Soviet chess grandmaster, Viktor Korchnoi, who had just won an international tournament in Amsterdam, surrendered to Dutch authorities and asked for political asylum. Moscow was livid. Despite all the careful considerations of who might be allowed to travel abroad and the elaborate security arrangements that put every Soviet citizen under constant KGB surveillance, Kremlin leaders had to live through this major international embarrassment. Korchnoi was among the three strongest chess players in the world, together with Bobby Fisher and Anatoly Karpov, and his defection was a huge blow to a Soviet regime ever-more sensitive about its image abroad.

Korchnoi was not the first nor would he be the last to defect in search of freedom and opportunities in the West. In June 1961, a young and brilliant Soviet ballet dancer, Rudolf Nureyev, chose not to return home from Paris; thirteen years later, the equally brilliant ballet dancer, Mikhail Baryshnikov, defected while his company was on tour in Canada. By the end of the 1970s, scores of Soviet defectors included ballet dancers, musicians, and athletes. The most visible among them was an iconic figure-skating couple, the Olympic and World champions Liudmila Belousova and Oleg Protopopov, who asked for asylum in Switzerland in 1979. The Soviet ideologues found themselves particularly hard pressed to explain how and why these Soviet sports heroes, so famous and beloved by the Soviet people, could "betray and abandon their Motherland."

It is clear, in retrospect, that by the mid-1970s, Soviet authorities were fighting a losing battle. The economy was unable to meet the basic demands of Soviet consumers, let alone compete with the West. As the Iron Curtain was becoming increasingly permeable, more western goods were making their way into the USSR, underscoring the shocking inferiority of Soviet consumer goods. The socialist rhetoric that was capable of inspiring citizens a decade ago was now ringing ever-more-hollow, as the gap between the haves (the Party officials) and have-nots (ordinary citizens) became more visible.

All along, the Party had to fend off challenges from a growing dissident movement that it inadvertently helped to legalize by signing the Helsinki Accords on August 1, 1975. The Accords, signed by all major European states, the US and Canada, recognized the territorial integrity of the European states and pledged improved cooperation between the West and Soviet bloc countries. The Kremlin was delighted that the West accepted the post-Second World War boundaries, which legitimized the Soviet annexation of eastern Poland and the Baltics.

The Accords also mentioned "respect for human rights and fundamental freedoms, including freedom of thought, conscience, religion and belief," issues that Moscow believed were the usual empty talk and could be safely ignored. Much to the Kremlin's surprise, human rights activists resolved to turn Moscow's legal commitments on paper into a real guarantee of respect for basic freedoms in the USSR. In 1976, Yuri Orlov formed the Moscow Helsinki Watch Group to catalog and publicize Soviet violations of human rights. Within several months, similar Helsinki Watch Groups had been formed in Ukraine, Lithuania, Georgia, and Armenia.

Pursuing détente internationally was proving to be a double-edged sword, as it also emboldened the dissident movement at home. In 1975, the man who gave Moscow its hydrogen bomb received a peace prize that bore the name of the man who gave the world dynamite. The news that Andrei Sakharov had been awarded the Nobel Peace Prize prompted the head of the KGB, Yuri Andropov, to declare Sakharov "Domestic Enemy Number One" and to crack down on critics of the Soviet regime.

1977
Bombings in Moscow and Repression

On January 8, 1977, several bombs exploded in Moscow. The largest exploded in a subway train car, killing and maiming dozens. Within half an hour, two more bombs exploded in two grocery stores. No one claimed responsibility. Several days later, three Armenian men were arrested and charged with terrorism. In the following three weeks, they were tried in a closed court, found guilty of terrorism inspired by Armenian nationalism, sentenced to death, and executed on January 30. One Soviet newspaper, *Izvestiia*, had briefly mentioned the event, while in Armenia the authorities imposed a news blackout.

Andrei Sakharov and other dissidents accused the government of provocation and the execution of innocent men. The matter indeed was murky. Some of the accused had an alibi, and their quick trial and execution raised suspicions. What was particularly worrisome was that a Soviet journalist, Viktor Lui, who worked as the Moscow correspondent of the British newspaper, the *Evening News*, but who in fact was a KGB agent, suggested in his article that the bombings might have been the work of Soviet dissidents. Lui, as he became known in the 1990s, was taking his orders directly from the head of the KGB, Yuri Andropov. For Sakharov and other dissidents, Lui's article was a clear sign that the KGB was probing the reaction to a possible harsh crackdown down on the Soviet human rights movement.

Sakharov and members of several Helsinki Watch Groups wrote urgent letters condemning the bombings and expressing their belief in a nonviolent approach. Sakharov went further and suggested that "the bombing of the subway and the tragic death of innocent people was a new and most dangerous provocation of the repressive state agencies." He also connected this incident with the suspicious deaths of several dissidents who had been beaten and murdered by groups of thugs in recent months. The fact that the KGB was engaged in murders of selective dissidents was not much of a secret. Two decades later, it was confirmed that as early as 1974, the KGB had formed a special unit for political assassinations at home; similar assassinations abroad had been a long-established practice.

One may never know whether the bombings were indeed engineered by the KGB, but there are reasons to believe that Sakharov's letter, which was published in the West, might have compelled the KGB operatives to abandon their original plan of blaming the terrorist acts on dissidents. Regardless, shortly after the event, Andropov resolved to proceed with a wide-ranging crackdown on the Soviet dissident movement. He firmly believed that the human rights movement was yet another "imperialist plot to undermine the Soviet state," therefore the Helsinki Watch Groups had to be dismantled.

On February 10, 1977, the head of the Moscow Helsinki Group, Yuri Orlov, was arrested and put on trial. Orlov's crime was cataloging Soviet human rights violations. He was charged "with disseminating anti-Soviet propaganda" and sentenced to seven years in a labor camp and five years of internal exile. A similar fate befell other leaders of the dissident movement: they were arrested, tried, and sentenced to long terms in prison and labor camps. The lucky ones were stripped of their citizenship and deported to the West. Others were confined to psychiatric hospitals under false diagnoses, a practice pioneered by Andropov as early as 1969.

In addition, the KGB deployed the usual tools of systematic intimidation and harassment: letters threatening to target dissidents and their families, insinuations of sexual misconduct, false rumors, job discrimination, and, when necessary, political assassination by poison, arranged car accidents, and violent street attacks. It is no surprise that only a few brave souls chose to openly oppose the regime.

It is likely that the Soviet human rights movement would have been decimated if not for the reaction from the West. And the reaction was swift. Dozens of letters of protest signed by thousands of scientists, human rights and religious leaders, writers, artists, intellectuals, and other people from different walks of life arrived at the Kremlin. Even more important was the commitment on the part of the newly elected US President Jimmy Carter to make human rights a cornerstone of US foreign policy. If the détente and Soviet purchases of grain from the US and Canada were to continue, Moscow had to restrain its assault on dissidents, soften the terms of their imprisonment, and allow greater emigration from the country. For the time being, the KGB had to slow down a wave of repressions and Sakharov, "domestic enemy No. 1," was spared arrest or exile.

1978
USSR, Less Than the Sum of its Parts

On April 14, 1978, after several days of sporadic protests, tens of thousands of people took to the streets of Georgia's capital, Tbilisi. They rallied to protest a proposed change to the Georgian Constitution to replace a clause that guaranteed the official use of the Georgian language with a new clause that stipulated the predominance of Russian. To many Georgians, the push to expand the use of Russian in local schools and media and a proposed change to their Constitution were unacceptable signs of Moscow's attempts to Russify their homeland.

Georgians had always been fiercely protective of their identity, and their renewed suspicions of Moscow's assimilationist designs were reignited after October 7, 1977, when the Soviet authorities adopted a new Constitution. Superseding the Stalin Constitution of 1936, the Brezhnev Constitution declared the end of the class struggle, the formation of a mature socialist society, and the emergence of a new national identity. In the Party's vision, existing ethnic and national differences between the peoples of the USSR were to be replaced by one Soviet identity; Russians and Ukrainians, Kazakhs and Estonians, Uzbeks and Georgians—all were to merge into a single Soviet people.

If this was supposed to be the Party's response to the rise of nationalist movements around the country, it proved to be wishful thinking. For most non-Russians, "Soviet" was synonymous with "Russian." A typical joke went like this: when a Georgian man on the train from Tbilisi to Moscow was asked where he was traveling, his reply was "To the Soviet Union." In fact, many among the non-Russian elites and commoners alike saw Moscow's new approach as an unambiguous attempt to erase their national heritage and to impose a hegemony of Russian language and culture. In Georgia, this sentiment brought people onto the streets.

As tens of thousands marched towards the central square, they were blocked by police and military units. Only quick and decisive action by Georgia's First Secretary of the Communist Party, Eduard Shevardnadze, prevented the repetition of the bloody anti-Moscow uprising in March 1956 when hundreds of Georgians were killed and injured. Shevardnadze was able to convince a reluctant Kremlin to retain the previous clause of the Constitution, which guaranteed the official status of the Georgian language, and bloodshed was avoided. The crowds began to disperse only after Shevardnadze personally assured the demonstrators that Georgian would remain the only official language of the republic.

The demonstration in Tbilisi raised both alarm and jubilant cheers. The Kremlin chose to exercise caution, and Georgia's neighbors, Armenia and Azerbaijan, were also allowed to retain their republics' titular languages. Georgians, of course, celebrated Moscow's concession as a victory. But not everyone was happy. The Abkhaz ethnic minority tucked along the Black Sea coast into an autonomous region within Georgia saw the new development as proof of Georgia's growing nationalism. The Abkhaz had long chafed under Tbilisi's rule and resented their status as second-class citizens. They demanded that Moscow protect them from Georgian hegemony and include their region in the Russian Federation. Moscow refused their demands of secession from Georgia but supported their claim for greater cultural and linguistic autonomy.

If the Georgians were concerned about Moscow's intentions to undermine their Georgian identity, the Abkhaz, in turn, had concerns about the hegemony of Georgian language and culture. Georgia was only one example of the USSR's complex national challenges surrounding hierarchy and identity. In the end, it fell to Moscow to handle multiple nationalist sentiments across the country, a challenge that would eventually bring down the Soviet Union in 1991.

1979
Afghanistan: A Soviet Vietnam

The early days of February 1979 brought more bad news to President Carter's White House. In Iran, the interim government of Shahpour Bakhtiar collapsed, and the Islamic revolutionaries of Ayatollah Khomeini seized power. At the same time, the US ambassador Adolph Dubs was kidnapped in neighboring Afghanistan and killed during a failed rescue mission. Despite the US plea to negotiate with the hostage takers, the Afghan police followed the directives of their Soviet advisors and stormed the hotel where Dubs was being kept hostage. The suspicious circumstances of Ambassador Adolph Dubs' death were never explained and pointed to some sort of collusion between the Soviet and Afghan regimes.

An Afghan mujahideen with an American Stinger missile.

But worse was yet to come. On November 4, Islamic militants took over the US embassy in Tehran, where for the next 444 days they would hold 52 Americans hostage. Iran, a former staunch ally, had become a bitter enemy. To add insult to injury, Moscow launched a full-scale military invasion to install a puppet regime in Afghanistan. On Christmas Eve, 30,000 Soviet troops were ordered in and within several days their numbers had grown to 100,000.

The Kremlin had concluded that the Carter administration was weak and ineffective, and the détente could be dispensed with. At the time, nobody could foresee that the invasion would turn into a drawn-out Soviet–Afghan War, which would end nine years later with the humiliating withdrawal of Soviet troops.

The trouble in Afghanistan began in April 1978, with Moscow's engineered coup against the Afghan President Daoud Khan. Khan, who had tried to strike an independent course from Moscow, was assassinated and replaced by a pro-Moscow, Marxist-Leninist Party figurehead. The new government launched a Five-Year Plan of secularization and modernization that immediately antagonized traditional Muslim segments of the population. The brutal purges of the opposition led to the executions of tens of thousands, raising concerns even in Moscow. As tribal insurgency spread across the country, the government further splintered into rival factions.

Twenty-five out of twenty-eight of Afghanistan's provinces rose against the government.

It was at this point that the KGB chief, Yuri Andropov, convinced other Politburo members of the need for Soviet intervention. The invasion began on December 24, and within three days, Soviet troops had occupied the capital, Kabul, seized the Presidential Palace, killed President Hafizullah Amin, and installed another Moscow loyalist, Babrak Karmal.

This proved to be the easy part. Karmal had no popular support. Instead of quelling the uprising, the Soviet invasion only fueled it further, turning it into a Holy War led by the Islamic guerillas, the mujahideens. The new government's control was limited to the urban centers, extending to no more than 20 percent of the country.

For the next nine years, Soviet troops were engaged in battles with an enemy that fought in small groups, was highly mobile, resilient, motivated, and took full advantage of the challenging mountainous terrain. Despite the Soviet deployment of the Air Force and heavy weapons, the mujahideens proved to be an elusive target. They received the support of the civilian population, crossed into safe havens in Pakistan, and most importantly were trained and equipped by the US, some Muslim countries, and China. In 1986, the CIA provided the mujahideens with the shoulder-fired "Stinger" missile which brought down numerous Soviet aircraft and changed the course of the war.

The Soviet tactic of the iron fist relied on intimidation, punishment, and destruction. To deny the mujahideens civilian support, Soviet troops bombed villages and razed them to the ground, burned crops, killed livestock, captured and tortured civilians, engaged in mass executions and rape, and used chemical weapons in dozens of known cases.

This tactic quickly proved to be counterproductive, as it depopulated large areas of the country and drove more men into the ranks of the mujahideens. By the end of the war, one-third of Afghanistan's pre-war population, about 5.5 million people, were in exile in Pakistan and Iran. An estimated 2 million Afghans had died in the war and hundreds of thousands had been maimed or wounded. By the end of the war, Afghanistan was lying in ruins. A fragile secular nation-state before the war, it now collapsed into tribal and Islamic identities, with people divided, dispersed, and heavily armed.

Yet the Afghans felt victorious as they watched how, in February 1989, the demoralized Soviet army left their country humiliated and defeated. The numbers spoke for themselves: nearly 30,000 Soviet military personnel killed, 54,000 wounded, several hundreds of thousands felled by various illnesses and drug addiction. What began as a triumphant invasion in December 1979 ended in February 1989 as a Soviet Vietnam.

The Afghan debacle caused some soul-searching among the moribund Soviet leadership. After the Second World War, the Kremlin's carefully constructed image of the invincible Soviet army and its glorious victory over Nazi Germany had become fundamental to the Soviet national character. As such, Afghanistan was more than a military defeat. It was a blow to the very heart of Soviet identity.

9

Paradise Lost

1980
The Moscow Olympics

After the first week of seemingly flawless operation, Moscow's invasion of Afghanistan came under heavy criticism from many corners, above all the US. Soviet leaders seriously underestimated the reaction of the White House, which was already embattled by the hostage crisis in Tehran. On January 20, 1980, President Jimmy Carter issued an ultimatum to the Soviet leadership—withdraw from Afghanistan within one month or face a boycott of the Moscow Summer Olympics.

The opening ceremony of the Summer Olympic Games in Moscow. Photo by Angelo Cozzi/Archivio Angelo Cozzi/Mondadori Portfolio via Getty Images.

The Kremlin was incensed. This was the first time that the Olympic Games were to take place in a socialist country, and Moscow planned on using the Games as a giant propaganda platform both at home and abroad. The boycott threatened to undermine the Kremlin's principal goal of projecting the image of a happy Soviet society as a model of success for the future of the world.

Moscow's immediate reaction was to condemn the ultimatum and to crack down on dissidents at home. On January 22, two days after the threat of the boycott by the US and its allies, Andrei Sakharov was arrested on the streets of Moscow and sent into internal exile. The head of the KGB, Yuri Andropov, had finally acted on his long-conceived plan to neutralize "Public Enemy no. 1."

For the next six years, the top Soviet nuclear physicist and the winner of the Nobel Peace Prize would be confined to a small apartment on the outskirts of the industrial city of Gorky. No foreigners were allowed into the city, and many of Sakharov's friends and relatives were denied visits. He was kept under constant surveillance, harassed, threatened, and roughly handled by the KGB. Provocations were numerous, but so were Sakharov's hunger strikes protesting abuses by the authorities.

The Kremlin's concern over the dissidents' attempt to tarnish the Soviet image during the Games was apparent early on. In June 1977, the KGB formed a special department charged with preventing "subversive actions by hostile elements before and during the Summer Olympic Games in Moscow." Dozens of human rights activists were arrested on the eve of the Games. Other activists together with criminals, prostitutes, vagrants, and alcoholics were sent outside the boundary of the Moscow region, popularly referred to as the "beyond 101-kilometer mark," for the duration of the Games. The known criminal bosses were warned against taking advantage of the influx of foreigners. And of course, tens of thousands of plain-clothes police were deployed in and around the Games. Some foreign athletes observed that even before the gates of the stadium were officially open, it was already one-third full of "spectators."

Long before the Olympics, Leonid Brezhnev had expressed concern over the projected costs and raised the question of whether the Soviet economy could ever recover after such an expense. Indeed, the Moscow Olympic Games became a major national project, siphoning off resources from the rest of the country. The construction of the facilities for the Games required mass mobilization. Large parts of old Moscow, with its traditional nineteenth-century houses, were demolished to make way for high-rises to accommodate Olympic athletes.

For the duration of the Games, Moscow was the perfect version of a Potemkin village. The streets were clean and not crowded—non-Moscow residents were not allowed into the city—college students were sent out to work in the fields and construction sites around the country, and high-school students were dispatched to summer camps. Traffic moved in an orderly fashion because only vehicles associated with the Olympics were allowed. Stores were fully stocked, and Muscovites could suddenly purchase toilet paper and other items that were usually in short supply. For two weeks in late July and early August, Moscow had become the socialist paradise it was meant to be and never was.

When the Games opened on July 19, teams from over fifty countries were absent because of the US-led boycott. Other countries sent smaller delegations or marched under the Olympic flag rather than their national ones. The Moscow Olympics had the lowest number of participating countries since the 1956 Melbourne Olympics in Australia. The Moscow Olympic Games were greatly diminished because of the boycott, and Soviet prestige suffered a blow. Détente seemed to be in tatters.

1981
Trouble in Poland

On December 13, 1981, Polish troops were ordered out of their barracks and onto the streets of the cities and towns of Poland. The commander of the Polish army, General Wojciech Jaruzelski, whom Moscow had effectively appointed as head of state only two months previously, had declared a state of martial law that would last until July 1983.

A storm had been brewing in Poland for several years. The economy was in steep decline and dissatisfaction with the Communist Party and its policies was rising. Another hike in food prices in August 1980 proved to be the last straw, and workers at the Gdansk Shipyard and elsewhere went on strike. Several weeks later, led by the electrician Lech Walesa, the Gdansk shipyard workers formed the first independent trade union. They named it Solidarity (Solidarnosc) and within a year it had almost 10 million members. The stage was set for imminent conflict.

The trouble in Poland was not just a matter of the shrinking economy. It was also directly related to an event of extraordinary national pride and significance—the election in October 1978 of the Polish Cardinal Karol Jozef Wojtyla as the first non-Italian pope in four-and-a-half centuries. John Paul II, as he was now known, arrived in his native Poland in June 1979. In his sermons, he spoke of human rights and freedom of consciousness and boldly called for change. For the Poles, always intensely proud of their Catholic and national identity, the words of John Paul II pitting religion and human rights against atheist Communists were a call for resistance and mobilization.

Moscow was alarmed. The situation in Poland seemed to have been spiraling out of control and was endangering Moscow's grip on its East European satellites. If the previous uprisings in Hungary in 1956 and Czechoslovakia in 1968 were the work of moderate reformers seeking to modify the existing socialist regime, Poland's popular movement was deeply nationalist, anti-communist, and relied on mass support. Inspired by the Polish pope, unrest in Poland was a direct challenge to Moscow.

As the clouds were gathering over Poland, shocking news hit the world: on May 13, 1981, a Turkish militant shot and critically wounded the pope in Rome's St. Peter's Square. After several hours of surgery, John Paul II's life was saved. The assailant was arrested and remained in jail until 2010. Years of investigation pointed to a plot that involved right-wing Turkish groups, the Turkish mafia, and Bulgarian officials. Even though no direct link has ever been established, there is little doubt that the plot was hatched in the bowels of the Soviet security services.

If Moscow hoped that the attempted assassination of the pope would intimidate the Solidarity movement, it was wrong. Declassified notes of Politburo meetings show numerous phone conversations and consultations between Soviet and Polish leaders. As Moscow called for more forceful measures, the respective chiefs of the East German and Soviet militaries met in secret to discuss military options. The KGB chief Andropov warned that, unless contained, the turmoil in Poland could have an impact on many in the western part of Belarus, whose citizens listened to Polish radio, and on the anti-Soviet demonstrators in Georgia.

By late summer 1981, the Kremlin's demands that Warsaw contain the crisis became more urgent. In October, Moscow replaced the First Secretary of the Polish Communist Party, Stanislaw Kania, with General Jaruzelski, who immediately started to prepare for martial law. The Politburo considered, but rejected, a scenario that would have repeated the Soviet invasions of Hungary and Czechoslovakia decades earlier. With over 100,000 Soviet troops tied up in an Afghan war, Moscow had little appetite for dispatching more troops to occupy Poland.

Jaruzelski was ready to introduce martial law but warned Moscow that this would require a large aid package to compensate for the expected loss of credit from the West. Suddenly, the Politburo's main concern was whether the Soviet Union could afford to provide this amount of aid. "Not without dipping into reserves and not without an expense to the Soviet consumer" was the response of the Soviet Ministry of Economics. Yet, as was typical of the Soviet leadership, political considerations trumped those of the economy, and martial law in Poland came into effect. With this, the Soviet Union came a step closer to becoming a state that was both economically insolvent and politically bankrupt.

1982
Brezhnev's Death

1982 was a year of death. In January, the long-time Politburo insider and Soviet chief ideologue, Mikhail Suslov, died. As the year drew to a close, on November 10, the General Secretary of the Communist Party and the country's leader, Leonid Brezhnev, finally succumbed to a heart attack. With Brezhnev's death, the Soviet system reached a dead end.

Brezhnev's health had been in steady decline for many years. At least since 1973 and until his death, he had had many health issues that were kept secret from the public. He suffered his first heart attack in 1975 and was eventually fitted with a pacemaker. He had several minor strokes that, by the late 1970s, had made his gait shaky and his speech slurred. In addition, he suffered from insomnia, acute arteriosclerosis, and several other ailments. In his last years, he also developed an addiction to a combination of alcohol and sleeping pills that was taking a severe toll on his health.

In many ways, Brezhnev's health was the mirror image of the social system over which he presided. Throughout the 1970s, the Soviet economy had declined across a broad measure of indicators. The state of agriculture was nearly catastrophic, heavy industry continued to churn out products of inferior quality, the consumer sector was grossly underinvested and underperforming, and new technology such as computers remained virtually unknown. In 1982, non-automated labor in the Soviet industry stood at a stunning 40 percent.

Just like Brezhnev's health issues, the true state of the Soviet economy was a closely guarded secret. And like Brezhnev's deteriorating health, which could no longer be disguised from the public, the general malaise of the Soviet system had also been laid bare. Unable to acknowledge, discuss, or rectify the issues openly, the Kremlin preferred to continue in its familiar mode of denial. The Soviet leadership failed to realize that the growing gap between official pronouncements and public perception had been steadily eroding any remaining faith in the Soviet system.

Never having been subject to elections and unaccountable to the public, Brezhnev, like most other Soviet leaders before and after him, remained on the job until his death. Frail and unable to enunciate words properly, Brezhnev continued his duties to the end, giving speeches and reviewing an annual parade from the top of the Mausoleum only three days before his death.

Even though Khrushchev's removal was justified in large measure by his cult of personality, over his eighteen years in office, Brezhnev had built an even more powerful cult around himself. Unlike Khrushchev, with his combustive personality and lack of manners, Brezhnev maintained the aura of a collective decision-making process, which more often than not hid his ultimate authority over the sycophantic members of the Politburo. No official event could take place without the bestowal of lavish praises upon Comrade Brezhnev. Multiple volumes of his collected speeches and writings were published; even the history of the Second World War was rewritten to emphasize his heroic deeds. By the end of his life, Brezhnev was the most decorated Soviet leader and only the second person after the famed Marshal Zhukov to be awarded the highest order of the country, the Hero of the Soviet Union, four times.

Two days after Brezhnev's death, the Politburo elected one of its own to become the next General Secretary of the Central Committee of the Communist Party. The chosen leader was the 68-year-old head of the KGB, Yuri Andropov. The choice of Andropov was the clearest indication yet of the KGB's pervasive influence and control of Soviet society. A pragmatic believer in the Soviet cause and a ruthless executioner, Andropov quickly concluded that the Soviet system had become corrupt and inefficient. His short tenure in office was marked by harsh disciplinary measures.

Andropov also realized that there was an urgent need for a generational change among the top Party brass. In 1982, the median age of the Politburo members was 70. It was at this time that Andropov put his full support behind the Politburo's youngest member, Mikhail Gorbachev.

1983
The Missile Debate

By 1983, the Soviet intelligence network in the West had grown to unprecedented levels. Despite numerous warnings and mostly discreet expulsions of Soviet spies, Moscow refused to scale down its aggressive intelligence operations. In 1983, the West resorted to a coordinated effort to cleanse itself of Soviet spies, expelling 135 Soviets from 21 countries. France alone expelled 47 Soviet officials, and even the neutral Swiss shut down the Soviet news agency Novosti and expelled its bureau chief.

The magnitude and intensity of the Soviet intelligence gathering was in part driven by the realization that the Soviet economy and military were falling behind, thus stealing Western civilian and military technologies had become ever more important. There was also another reason for this unprecedented level of Soviet intelligence operations—subverting NATO's plans to deploy the US Pershing II missiles in Western Europe. Such deployment would have neutralized the previous deployment of the Soviet SS-20 missiles, which gave Moscow a clear nuclear advantage.

Since 1977, Moscow had been deploying intermediate-range nuclear missiles, SS-20s, which placed the whole of Western Europe within striking

A peace march against nuclear war in London. Photo by Keystone/Getty Images.

range. By 1983, 300 of them had been deployed. In an early response to the deployment, President Carter announced that the US would deploy the same kind of missile in Western Europe. It was a modernized version of the Pershing missile: the Pershing II. Using solid fuel, the Pershing II was more mobile, powerful, and precise than previous types and could reach Moscow within six to eight minutes.

To counter the US and NATO plan, the Kremlin launched a major campaign against the deployment of the Pershing II missiles. Throughout the early 1980s, the Kremlin's mass propaganda aimed to discredit the US using typical rhetoric: condemning US imperialism and expansionism and its military-industrial complex, while presenting itself as a supporter of peace and security in Europe.

Less well-known was Soviet intelligence's infiltration and manipulation of peace protests in the West. Tens of thousands marched through Western European cities demanding the abandonment of the deployment of the Pershing II. The demonstrations were particularly numerous in Germany, where, in the aftermath of the Second World War, anti-war sentiment was particularly strong. The protests ranged from peaceful marches to break-ins at US military bases, roadblocks near the installation sites, and attempts to damage the equipment related to missile deployment. According to some sources, Moscow spent hundreds of millions of dollars to secretly fund various peace movement organizations. Many Christian organizations, student associations, and peace groups joined hands with supporters of the Communist parties under the seductive slogans of "a nuclear freeze" and "stopping the arms race," unaware that they were also doing Moscow's bidding.

In the end, Moscow's campaign failed. The US president Ronald Reagan, the British Prime Minister Margaret Thatcher, and the German Chancellor Helmut Kohl did not waiver. Most of the German public, the main target of the Soviet propaganda campaign, had also come to believe that "it was better to have a Pershing in the garden than an SS-20 on the roof." In November 1983, the first deployment of the Pershing II missiles began in Germany.

Throughout the early 1980s, the US hoped to negotiate with the Soviets for the removal of the intermediate-range missiles from Europe. Washington promised to abandon the deployment of the Pershing II if Moscow agreed to remove the SS-20s. In a celebrated walk in the woods, the US negotiator Paul Nitze and his Soviet counterpart Yuli Kvitsinsky worked out a possible blueprint for a treaty, but the Kremlin refused to compromise.

Indeed, it seemed that Andropov's USSR was aggressively building up towards a possible military confrontation. As early as 1981, Andropov established Vympel, a special unit within the KGB whose members were deployed in the West with the goal of sabotage, the destruction of infrastructure, and the assassination of foreign leaders. Weapons caches were being hidden in the West for this purpose. At the same time, fear that the US might launch the first strike prompted the establishment of the Soviet intelligence operation RYAN, whose agents in the West were charged with collecting any missile-related information.

Moscow's aggressiveness and paranoia were reinforced by Ronald Reagan's blunt denunciation of the USSR as "an evil empire" and his call for creating a US missile-defense system, known as the Strategic Defense Initiative. On September 1, a Soviet pilot shot down a Korean Airlines Boeing 747, killing all 269 passengers and crew on board. Moscow initially denied making the fatal mistake and then called the incident a provocation by the US. Only three weeks later, one of the Soviet nuclear early-warning systems indicated an incoming US missile followed by several more. Stanislav Petrov, the Soviet officer on duty at the command center, concluded that the system had malfunctioned and did not report the incident to his superiors. His correct judgment and brave decision may well have saved the world from a catastrophic nuclear exchange.

By the end of this year, the Cold War had reached its peak. The Kremlin increasingly resorted to threats of using nuclear weapons. Not since the Cuban Missile Crisis did the world stand so close to the brink of a nuclear war.

1984
Iron Maiden Behind the Iron Curtain

Fans of *1984,* George Orwell's political satire of a totalitarian state, had long been comparing the book, written thirty-six years earlier, to contemporary Soviet society. To many, the words "Soviet" and "Orwellian" had become virtually synonymous. By the early 1980s, socialist rhetoric rang hollow to most Soviet people; few continued to believe in the great promise of Communism.

This was particularly true for the younger generation in Soviet-bloc countries. The influence of Western pop and material culture, fashion, and goods proved to be a greater threat to socialist mores than any weapons system or missiles. Young men and women behind the rusty and decaying Iron Curtain were much more interested in blue jeans and the Beatles than in Marxist ideological dogmas.

The gap between official anti-Western rhetoric and young peoples' infatuation with the West had never been so great. Shoddy Soviet products could not compete with Western brand names, and stodgy Soviet culture was no match for jazz and rock music. Certain brand names had become objects of adulation: Levi Strauss jeans, the Beatles, Miles Davis, and ABBA, to name but a few. Most people did not understand the lyrics. Rather, it was the music itself and the song titles that sounded magical: "Back in the USSR" or "Born in the USA." The fact that the 1968 Beatles' song "Back in the USSR" was a parody of the Beach Boys and that Bruce Springsteen's "Born in the USA" was a melancholy song about post-Vietnam small-town America was completely lost on the Soviet audience, who remained spellbound by a few recognizable English words and wistful melodies.

The government's attempts to ban or control Western cultural influences proved futile. The influx of jeans and records was unstoppable, and the Soviet regime's economic and moral order seemed increasingly wanting. With the Kremlin unable to resist Western influences within its own borders, the governments of other Soviet-bloc countries were more able to accommodate the pull of Western culture.

In August 1984, the first Western band to perform behind the Iron Curtain was an English heavy metal band appropriately named Iron Maiden. The band's first stop was Warsaw, where more than 6,000 people crammed into a local sports arena. For the enthralled Polish audience, this was an incredible spectacle of rock music and pyrotechnics. Even Polish soldiers, hundreds of whom were stationed to keep order, took off their shirts and threw their hats up in ecstasy. Iron Maiden toured through several Polish cities and then continued into Hungary and Yugoslavia. Two years later, Billy Joel became the first Western rock musician to tour the USSR, where a frozen Soviet audience took a while to warm up to the appropriate emotions of rock concerts. The Iron Curtain was crumbling.

What made matters worse was the crisis among top Soviet leadership. In early 1983, Andropov suffered total kidney failure. He was hospitalized in August and remained in the hospital until his death in February 1984. His successor, Konstantin Chernenko, was already terminally ill and died in March 1985, thirteen months after Andropov. It fell upon a Soviet leader from the younger generation to address the country's mounting challenges. His name was Mikhail Gorbachev.

1985
Vodka

"In the beginning was a word, and that word was vodka," wrote the Russian writer Viktor Erofeev in his jocular book *The Russian Apocalypses*. By 1985, vodka had indeed become a measure of the Soviet apocalypse. The record per capita consumption of alcohol in the USSR was unchallenged by any other country. An average Soviet adult drank half a liter of vodka every two days. When one factors in the much lower rate of alcohol consumption in the Muslim regions of the USSR, the level of drinking among the Soviet Slavic population is truly staggering.

Heavy drinking was the norm and drunkards were a common site. With an average family spending 15–20 percent of its disposable income on alcohol, drinking and alcoholism had become a central part of Soviet life. Alcohol abuse was a major health issue and was responsible for a high level of mortality. In addition, many alcoholics who were unable to afford vodka resorted to drinking anything that contained alcohol: cologne, brake fluid, undiluted alcohol used for industrial purposes, etc., resulting in thousands of deaths from alcohol poisoning.

Absenteeism or working in an intoxicated state severely affected productivity; some estimates in the early 1980s put the cost to the Soviet economy at no less than 10 percent of GNP. Heavy drinking was also related to a rise in criminal activity and had a serious effect on family life. In short, alcoholism and drinking in the USSR were a major social malaise with far-reaching consequences.

The Soviet state had a full monopoly on the production and sale of liquor. It might have seemed easy to address the issue by reducing sales or raising prices. The trouble was that vodka constituted 25 percent of all sales taxes and 28 percent of all foodstuffs sold in the USSR. The beleaguered Soviet economy could hardly afford to dispense with one of its principal sources of revenue, so the drunken nation carried on in an intoxicated stupor.

It was a measure of how serious a crisis alcoholism had become when, in May 1985, barely two months after assuming leadership in the Party, the new General Secretary, Mikhail Gorbachev, launched an Anti-Alcohol Campaign. The resolution passed by the Politburo was called "Concerning Measures in Overcoming Drunkenness and Alcoholism," and it ushered in new stringent policies. The official drinking age was raised from 18 to 21, the sale of liquor was not permitted before 2 pm, and restaurants could no longer serve hard liquor. The government simultaneously cut the production of liquor by approximately 40 percent and raised prices by 25 percent. Heavy fines were imposed to punish those charged with public drunkenness and those tempted by moonshining. The local authorities were instructed to encourage a healthy lifestyle by building more recreational facilities and providing better treatment for alcoholics. All in all, these were the toughest and most wide-ranging measures adopted since the Soviet prohibition campaign of 1919–1925.

The Anti-Alcohol Campaign was a success. It significantly reduced the rate of alcohol consumption and dramatically improved the mortality rate. Yet it remained deeply unpopular. In 1989, a combination of political pressure and fiscal need forced the government to repeal the laws of the Anti-Alcohol Campaign. Levels of alcohol abuse returned to normal and the mortality rate shot back up. However, the government was now confronted by a myriad of other, no less urgent problems, which had been unleashed by Gorbachev's reforms.

1986
Chernobyl

A year after he became the General Secretary of the Communist Party, Gorbachev launched a reformist project that he sketched out in his speech at the 27th Party Congress in February–March 1986. It was a bold vision of structural changes to the Soviet system and an attempt to reinvigorate a bankrupt socialist model. Gorbachev's reforms became widely known under two Russian words: *perestroika* (restructuring) and *glasnost* (openness). Whether Gorbachev and his reformers realized it, they were inextricably linking the prospect of economic and political reforms with greater freedoms and tolerance for criticism.

This new concept of openness was suddenly put to an early test when at 1:23 am on April 26, the worst disaster in the history of the nuclear industry occurred at a Soviet nuclear plant near the Ukrainian town of Chernobyl. Flaws in the reactor's design, combined with several human errors, produced a huge explosion and an open-air fire of the graphite core in reactor no. 4.

As the phones rang in the Ukrainian capital of Kiev and in Moscow, Soviet authorities quickly fell into their usual pattern of cover up and denial. Soviet citizens had no knowledge that a dozen or so nuclear-related accidents had taken place in the USSR in previous years. Now, too, the government hoped to avoid any publicity.

Reactor No. 4 after the explosion at the Chernobyl nuclear power station.
Photo by Valentin Obodzinsky/MCT/MCT via Getty Images.

But the world in and around the USSR had changed. While the fire continued to rage at the reactor and the winds carried radioactive material northwest, Moscow remained silent. Two days later, more than fifty-five hours after the explosion, Swedish authorities discovered heightened levels of radiation with a source pointing towards a place in Ukraine, 680 miles south of Sweden. When the Swedes requested information, Moscow denied that any accident had taken place. It took another twelve hours before the Soviet news channel briefly announced that a minor accident had occurred but everything was under control.

By this time, news of a serious accident had begun to spread around the world and filter back into the USSR via the Voice of America, the BBC, and Radio Liberty. At this time, when dozens of first responders were already dead, the government began to admit that the accident was serious and had killed two people, but claimed that there was nothing to worry about. With shifting winds bringing radiation back to Ukraine and neighboring Belarus, the authorities continued to deny the magnitude of the accident and deliberately misinformed the public. With high levels of radiation in and around Chernobyl, the authorities did nothing to stop the usual May 1 parades, when hundreds of thousands of people marched in the streets to celebrate International Workers' Day. Usually the jubilant and often intoxicated crowds would reach the city's main thoroughfare where high Party officials would greet them from the reviewing stands. This time, the stands were empty because the officials, well informed about the dangers of being outside, had left the city.

It was only on May 6, more than ten days after the nuclear accident, that news broadcasts in Kiev and other towns advised the public to stay indoors, close windows, and take other precautions. Panic ensued. Desperate parents tried to send their children as far away as possible. Crowds stormed train stations to get a seat on the few available trains. Weeks after the disaster, the Kremlin continued to mislead the public and deny any responsibility. Years later, after the collapse of the USSR, documents from KGB archives revealed that the authorities were aware of numerous technical problems, code violations, and the shoddy construction that had plagued the Chernobyl plant from the very first days of operation.

By remaining silent, denying the disaster, and misleading the public during the crisis, Gorbachev had miserably failed his own test of openness. While claiming the mantle of a reformer, he issued typically bland Soviet statements that appeared to continue the well-worn tradition of Soviet mendacity. The Chernobyl disaster occurred at the worst possible moment for Gorbachev's reforms. At a time when he needed to rally the Soviet people and win their trust, the incident at Chernobyl had further eroded public faith in the government and Soviet system.

For many in the USSR, Chernobyl was a turning point that produced a great deal of resentment towards the Party bosses. People have never forgotten how government officials evacuated their own children and relatives immediately after the nuclear accident, while failing to inform the public of basic precautions that had to be taken early on. By 1991, the resentment in Ukraine turned its full force against the Ukrainian Communist Party and particularly against Moscow. Many years later, Gorbachev admitted that the Chernobyl accident, in terms of economic and social cost, was perhaps the real reason for the fall of the USSR.

1987
Health Care and Medicine

The political fallout from Chernobyl convinced Gorbachev and his allies that reforms were not only irreversible but should also be accelerated. At the heart of the reforms was the principle of openness, which in the Soviet context meant confronting problems instead of denying them and providing truthful information instead of lies and propaganda. At the time, however, few people understood that a campaign of openness in an Orwellian society based on mendacity and secrecy was the surest way to dismantle the entire state.

With ideological taboos crumbling, the emboldened media and individuals focused on previously ignored social and economic problems. All of a sudden, Soviet society, which until now had been heralded as a model for a progressive world, was revealed to be a dismal failure. Among many issues that required immediate attention was Soviet health care and medicine.

In February 1987, Gorbachev appointed a new Minister of Health, Evgeny Chazov, a well-known and respected cardiologist who was in charge of the Ministry's Fourth Directorate responsible for providing medical services to the Party leadership. Chazov's task was to bring the Soviet health system, which had been rotting for decades, up to a reasonable standard. Top Party officials were well aware that Soviet socialized medicine was beset with problems, but as long as they and their families enjoyed access to special hospitals and the best doctors, the issue was swept under the rug.

Chazov had to tackle a dismal situation. Many hospitals were dilapidated and lacked modern medical equipment. Basic medicine and medical instruments were in critically short supply. In 1987 alone, with an estimated need for 3.5 billion syringes, the government made plans to produce 100 million, but by the end of the year was only able to make a mere 7.8 million. At the same time, the most basic drugs and even toothpaste disappeared from stores for weeks and months.

The problem with medical personnel was no less acute. Many doctors were grossly incompetent and lacked basic knowledge and skills, while nurses were often untrained. Even worse was the pervasive corruption in a healthcare system that was meant to be universal and free. Those who could offer bribes would be assured of reasonable medical attention, surgery, and access to much-needed drugs. A small bribe could secure a doctor's note that would allow one to take a few days off sick. A large bribe could ensure a diagnosis that would defer or prevent a young man from being drafted into the military. Doctors became one of the highest-paid professions because of a lively black market.

The result was a healthcare system that was in a catastrophic state. The average life expectancy dropped to 69 years with a particularly high mortality rate of 64 for men. Its infant mortality rate placed the USSR in the 35th spot among other countries. Chazov immediately fired several top officials in the Ministry of Health and ordered a review of Soviet physicians' qualifications. The results were shocking. Ten percent of doctors were not aware that cancer was treatable and 40 percent of medical school graduates could not read a cardiogram. Thousands of doctors were either fired or had their licenses temporarily suspended.

Despite serious efforts to address the crisis in the Soviet health system, the problems were just too overwhelming and costs were too high. The health-related consequences of the Chernobyl disaster and the AIDS epidemic were making a bad situation worse. By the time the Soviet leadership began to comprehend fully the social cost of healthcare—poor public health, low productivity and life expectancy, and high infant mortality—the dwindling state budget could not cope with the challenge.

1988
The Old Guard Strikes Back

The Gorbachev reforms highlighted numerous failures of the Soviet system, but there was no adequate time or resources to provide immediate remedies.

The process of *perestroika,* which literally meant re-construction, was still in its demolition phase.

Against the background of a deteriorating economy, an unaffordable arms race, and vocal criticisms of the government, some top Party officials began to question the nature and pace of reforms. The hardliners, led by the Party Secretary Egor Ligachev, were uneasy about so much change taking place so rapidly. The impatient reformers, by contrast, wanted to accelerate perestroika. One of the most ardent reformers was Boris Yeltsin, only recently elected to the Politburo. Known for his directness, Yeltsin openly criticized the leadership for delays and procrastination, something that would have been impossible a few years before. Mikhail Gorbachev represented a middle course between the reformers and the hardliners.

By early 1988, the hardliners began to assert themselves and successfully maneuvered to remove Yeltsin from the Politburo. Their next attack came in the form of a letter written by a chemistry instructor at the Leningrad Technological Institute, Nina Andreeva.

The long letter, published in the newspaper *Soviet Russia* on March 13, was titled "I Cannot Give Up My Principles." A dogmatic communist, Andreeva bemoaned the questioning of traditional Marxist concepts, criticisms of Stalin and Lenin, new works of art and literature, rock music, and the general erosion of ideological education among the young. She infused her hardcore Communist principles with the ideas of Russian nationalism, castigating reformers as "left-wing socialists" and "militant cosmopolitans," the latter being the usual code name for Jews. In short, this was a full-blown anti-perestroika manifesto, and it was most certainly written and published with the help of ideological hardliners at the top.

The following day, March 14, Ligachev met with key newspaper editors and expressed his approval of the article; it was immediately reprinted in all major newspapers. The Andreeva affair certainly had all the elements of an ideological, if not a political, coup.

Yet the reformers proved to be more resilient than the hardliners expected. Gorbachev, who at the time was on an official five-day visit to Yugoslavia, returned to Moscow. A few days later, on March 23, he convened a long and grueling meeting with top Party officials to discuss Andreeva's letter. After Gorbachev made clear his view that the letter was an attempt to scuttle the reforms, no one, except Ligachev, dared to disagree. It was also a measure of Gorbachev's *glasnost* policies that Ligachev faced no consequences and retained his post.

The task of answering the Andreeva letter fell upon "the father of glasnost," a member of the Politburo and Gorbachev's close advisor, Alexander Yakovlev.

On April 5, the Party newspaper *Pravda* published Yakovlev's response to Nina Andreeva. Titled "Principles of Restructuring: The Revolutionary Nature of Thinking and Acting," it was a forceful defense of reform, transparency, democracy, freedom, and a more efficient economy. However, Yakovlev maintained that a change did not mean abandoning socialist ideas.

It was clear that in the minds of the reformers *perestroika* was a set of changes intended to humanize and improve socialist society. It was the Soviet version of socialism with a human face that Czechoslovak officials had tried to introduce twenty years earlier and which was brutally crushed by Soviet tanks. What Gorbachev did not realize was that he was twenty years too late, and that socialism with or without a human face could no longer be revived.

1989
The Beginning of the End

Having pushed back against his Party hardliners, Gorbachev proceeded with another part of his reforms, introducing a measure of democracy into the election process. Previous national and regional elections were a sham, with Party candidates invariably elected to their posts because they faced no competition. Gorbachev wanted to invigorate the Soviet system by making it more competitive and allowing some non-Party members into its legislative body.

For this reason, the old Supreme Soviet was replaced by a new body: the Congress of People's Deputies, consisting of 2,250 delegates. One-third of the seats were reserved for members of the Communist Party, but two-thirds were open to a contest. Of course, even in openly elected seats, the Party-endorsed candidates had numerous advantages. Yet when the election took place in March 1989, there were big surprises: 300 candidates, or about 16 percent of the new legislative body, won over the candidates endorsed by the Party. Among those who lost were five Central Committee members, one member of the Politburo, and thirty-five regional Party bosses.

The names of some non-Party delegates were easily recognizable, such as the legendary weightlifter Yuri Vlasov, the famous hockey player Anatoly Firsov, and other Soviet celebrities. Among the newly elected delegates was also Andrei Sakharov, the champion of human rights, whose stellar integrity had survived the denunciations and persecutions of the Soviet regime. Other names were as yet little known to the wider public. The most noticeable setback for the Kremlin was the return of Boris Yeltsin, who trounced his Communist Party opponent, collecting 89 percent of the vote in his electoral district in Moscow.

The election of March 1989 was unprecedented in the history of the USSR. As the first partially free national election since 1917, it introduced a new cohort of delegates, who used the national stage to launch further criticisms of the Party and expose the country's social ills. Gorbachev touted the new election as a victory for his reforms and a successful effort to democratize the Soviet political system. The hardliners, unnerved by new freedoms and unaccustomed to the notion of a political opposition, were not amused.

The old Communist guard had reason to worry. Championed by Andrei Sakharov, several opposition groups had united with one common goal—to change the Constitution, which enshrined the leading role of the Communist Party in the society, and thus remove the Communists from power. But Sakharov, whose health had been badly undermined by the years of house arrests and exile, died on December 14, 1989. It fell to Yeltsin to lead the first united Soviet opposition.

In September, while visiting the Johnson Space Center in Houston, Yeltsin made an unscheduled visit to a neighboring medium-sized supermarket, Randalls. By all accounts, Yeltsin left the store heartsick. The contrast between the abundance of products in a run-of-the-mill American grocery store and the shortages and long lines for food and basic goods in the USSR was simply overwhelming. Even the elite Soviet stores, accessible only to top Party officials, paled by comparison.

Later, in his memoirs, Yeltsin admitted that the visit to the store left him "sick with despair for the Soviet people." Yeltsin's close aid, Anatoly Sukhanov, recalled that Yeltsin confessed a "pain for all of us, for our country so rich, so talented, and so exhausted by incessant experiments." This was the moment, noted Sukhanov, when Yeltsin parted with any Communist illusions.

In some ways, Yeltsin's experience at the Houston grocery store became emblematic of his future leadership of Russia. For him, like many other Soviet citizens, Communism was synonymous with everyday shortages, therefore an abundance of goods meant the end of Communism. Yeltsin never understood the insidious nature of the Communist Party and never took serious steps to confront and purge its influence from society. Herein lay the seeds of Putinism and the future restoration of Soviet practices that would eventually erase Yeltsin's own achievements.

Part III

The Democratic Experiment

10

The Rise and Fall of Russian Democracy

1990
Soviet Nationalisms and Ethnic Wars

Allowing more vocal criticisms of Soviet society also meant opening old wounds and airing unaddressed historical grievances between the USSR's different peoples. Emerging in the 1920s from the ruins of the Russian Empire, the USSR was founded as a federation of peoples residing within their own ethno-territorial boundaries. The official federative principles, where dozens of ethnic and national groups supposedly coexisted in peace and friendship, were, in fact, hiding deep historical animosities between different peoples chafing under Moscow's rule.

Initial reforms quickly exposed the fragile constitutional structure of the USSR. In December 1986, hoping to stem corruption and nepotism in Kazakhstan, Gorbachev broke with the tradition of having an ethnic Kazakh in charge of the Communist Party and replaced the outgoing Kazakh Party leader with an ethnic Russian from Moscow. In response, thousands of Kazakhs took to the streets. The merits of Moscow's decision aside, the event triggered a deep-seated Kazakh resentment towards Russian rule.

Much more serious nationalist tensions broke out in the south Caucasus in February 1988. Armenians, squeezed between Turkey in the west and Azerbaijan in the east, saw themselves as victims of both the 1915 genocide, in which they lost nearly 1 million people, and the loss of their native land. One particular enclave, Nagorno-Karabakh, populated mostly by Armenians but awarded by Stalin to Azerbaijan in the 1920s, became a focal point of Armenian national revival. While the movement to unite Nagorno-Karabakh with Armenia was peaceful, rumors of atrocities against the Azeris there stirred a wave of violence against Armenians residing in Azerbaijan. The pogrom in the Azeri city of Sumgait claimed an unknown number of Armenian lives and saw rape, torture, and mass destruction. The local police remained passive, and Soviet troops arrived too late to stop the pogrom.

In January 1990, a far larger and more violent pogrom took place in Azerbaijan's capital, Baku. Once again, the police did nothing, and Soviet troops intervened belatedly. Whether the pogrom broke out spontaneously or, as some suggested, was staged by KGB provocateurs to discredit Gorbachev and his reforms, may never be known.

Together with inter-ethnic violence, a growing chorus of Soviet republics was demanding outright independence from Moscow. Initially, Moscow met this clamor for national sovereignty with force. On April 19, 1989, Soviet troops were deployed to disperse demonstrators in Georgia's capital, Tbilisi. Twenty demonstrators were reported dead and hundreds were wounded. Moscow's intimidation notwithstanding, new opposition parties that made the issue of national sovereignty their main platform mushroomed throughout the Soviet republics.

With the collapse of the Berlin Wall on November 9, 1989, the rippling effects of the East European peaceful revolution reached the Soviet Baltic republics. In March 1990, in a culmination of several years of struggle to restore Lithuanian sovereignty, the parliament of the republic officially declared Lithuania's secession from the USSR. Many in the Kremlin concluded that a policy of openness went too far.

A month later, after failing to dissuade Lithuanian authorities to withdraw their declaration, Moscow announced an economic blockade of the republic. In the following two months, Moscow stopped delivering petroleum and basic goods, but, despite widespread shortages, the Lithuanians stood firm. In January 1991, Moscow made one more attempt to reverse the course of the independence movement in Lithuania. Hatched and orchestrated by the KGB, a military coup in which troops killed fourteen and injured several hundred Lithuanians received no support from the public and was doomed to fail. The Soviet Union was disintegrating, and all the Kremlin's plans to save the country proved to be too little too late.

1991
Death of the Empire

In the first months of 1991, a wave of referenda surged through several Soviet republics. A referendum was something unknown to Soviet citizens. It was a great and welcome novelty to have one's opinion registered in confidence and to know that it would matter. The result was virtually unanimous support for declaring national independence from Moscow.

Gorbachev's reforms intended to break the monopoly of the Communist Party and make it more competitive by introducing a measure of political pluralism. Instead, political reforms led to the emergence of anti-Moscow and pro-independence parties in the legislatures of the Soviet republics. Sincere, if naïve, Gorbachev hoped for a new union treaty that would create a true federation of independent states. But decades of violence and mistrust were not easily overcome. The time for moderation was over; it was time for a revolution.

Throughout 1990, the Kremlin was able to prevent a full and formal cession of several Soviet republics, including Russia, which adopted declarations of independence. But when, in April 1991, Georgia's Supreme Council unanimously adopted a declaration of independence and formally broke away from the Soviet Union, Moscow was powerless to stop it. It now looked inevitable that others would follow suit, and that a new union treaty might have been no more than a pipe dream.

Concerned with the possibility of a violent breakup of the nuclear-armed USSR, Washington and London decided to lend their support to Gorbachev's efforts to keep the union together. After visiting Moscow, President George H. W. Bush arrived in the Ukrainian capital of Kiev on August 1, 1991 to warn against a declaration of independence and what he called "suicidal nationalism." His speech, which was later dubbed the "Chicken Kiev speech," showed that Washington was tone deaf to the realities on the ground. The speech caused dismay in Ukraine, where a recent referendum had made clear that there was overwhelming support for Ukraine's independence.

What made matters worse was the fact that the unraveling of the Soviet state was also taking place against the background of an economic disaster. Bringing changes to an economy that, for decades, had remained distorted by total state control inevitably led to some mistakes and setbacks. For example, the government abolished the state monopoly on foreign trade at the same time as it continued to subsidize prices within the country. Newly emerging entrepreneurs quickly took advantage of the situation by purchasing goods inside the country and selling them at a huge profit abroad. The unintended consequences of the economic reforms brought about the worst stereotypes of socialism and capitalism: empty store shelves on the one hand and lavishly spending Russian nouveau riche on the other.

Gorbachev was under assault from all sides. Yeltsin and other reformers pushed for more radical reforms, while the old guard insisted on curtailing them. Fearing the collapse of the USSR and ensuing chaos, a group of hardliners hatched a plot to remove Gorbachev and to restore the old order. The plotters struck on August 19, a day before the scheduled signing of the New Union Treaty, which was designed to create a genuine federation of independent states.

The plotters, led by the KGB chief Vladimir Kriuchkov, formed a committee that included the chiefs of the security agencies and the army. Their first move was to put Gorbachev under house arrest, cut off his communications channels, and declare a state of emergency. It was the last, desperate gasp of the old regime, and it did not work. In Moscow and other cities people took to the streets to defend their newly won freedoms, and the military refused to open fire on the crowds. Three stormy days later, the plotters were arrested, and Gorbachev was restored to power. Instead of saving the USSR, the organizers of the coup helped to drive the final nail into the country's coffin.

In the days following the failed coup, events unfolded at great speed. Gorbachev dissolved the Central Committee of the Communist Party and resigned his position as General Secretary. One republic after another declared independence and when on December 1, 90 percent of Ukrainians voted for an unequivocal secession, the fate of the USSR was sealed. By mid December, Gorbachev was a president without a country. He officially resigned his presidency on December 25, the Soviet flag was lowered, and the Russian one raised. The USSR was no more.

1992
Another Revolution

New Year's Eve 1991 signaled the end of one era and the beginning of another. But what new era would come to replace 74 years of Soviet rule? As the legal successor to the USSR, Russia inherited its privileges as well as its burdens. The challenge of creating a new country out of the sclerotic and finally deceased Soviet Empire was formidable and unprecedented. The most daunting task was a fundamental restructuring of the economy.

Never before had the largest country in the world had to make a transition from a centrally planned and state-owned economy dominated by military production to a market economy run by private businesses. Examples of former socialist countries in Eastern Europe who were in the middle of their own reforms were not terribly helpful. After all, their economies were much smaller and their historical experience with socialism significantly shorter.

How was one to privatize land with thousands of deadweight collective farms or turn huge industrial enterprises into productive businesses? To provide for millions of workers and engineers whose numbers far exceeded Russia's industrial capacity? To turn Soviet salaried managers into business entrepreneurs? These were some of the economic and social challenges that had to be resolved, and there was no blueprint to follow. At the time, there were only two options: a rapid but painful economic restructuring, known as shock therapy, or gradual reforms that might soften the blow but would take longer to implement. Some Russian leaders saw it in more dramatic terms as a choice between ruthless, radical reforms and the introduction of marshal law and strict rationing.

With the economy in free fall, the Yeltsin government chose the shock therapy approach. Disregarding the opposition from parliament, President Yeltsin appointed Yegor Gaidar as Finance Minister and architect of the reforms. Gaidar deregulated prices, shut down inefficient industries, and initiated a voucher program to give everyone a share in the newly privatized industries. The initial impact of shock therapy was brutal and not everything worked the way it was intended.

Price deregulation alleviated the chronic shortages that were typical of Soviet times. While store shelves were now full of food and goods, few could afford to purchase them. Lifting price controls had also created hyperinflation, which practically wiped out peoples' savings.

Hundreds of factories that relied on state subsidies and produced shoddy goods were unable to compete in the new environment and had to close their doors. With millions of workers out on the streets, many turned to peddling or other means of survival. Former factory managers had become bank tellers, former engineers taxi drivers, and former scientists private tutors. Those who could emigrated. By some estimates, the economic situation was worse than during the Great Depression of the 1930s.

Perhaps the biggest long-term failure was a voucher program to privatize state industries. Every citizen was entitled to, and received, a share in government properties scheduled for privatization. But desperate poverty and deep skepticism about government promises led most people to sell their shares to whoever was willing to buy them. Those who did buy them in a systematic and organized way were those few entrepreneurs who, in the preceding years, had used their connections within the Party to accumulate small fortunes. Now was the time to turn small fortunes into big ones.

This was the time when Russia's new robber barons came to control industries mostly centered around natural resources. A rapid rise of Russian billionaires, who soon turned into powerful oligarchs, stood in sharp contrast to the stark poverty of the rest of the population. Today, Russia remains a country with one of the world's largest gaps between the haves and the have-nots.

By the end of 1992, the Russian economy had shrunk by 14.5 percent. It was only a matter of time before popular anger with the nouveau riche and policies that seemed to benefit them would turn the tide against the Yeltsin government.

1993
Constitutional Crisis

By December 1992, President Yeltsin and the Parliament were at war. Dominated by the Communists and other anti-reform parties, the Parliament refused to confirm Yegor Gaidar as Russia's Prime Minister. It demanded government subsidies for failing industries and altogether scuttling the reforms. It also charged that Yeltsin attempted to change the Constitution to expand his presidential powers. Furious, Yeltsin denounced the Parliament and suggested that the matter be put to a referendum: support the President and the path of the reforms or support the Parliament and abandon the reforms.

With a referendum scheduled for April, the Parliament continued to block one government initiative after another and initiated impeachment proceedings against Yeltsin. When impeachment failed and a majority of the voters in the referendum expressed confidence in the President and his government, Yeltsin offered to draft a new constitution with expanded presidential powers and a restructured Parliament. Once again, the Parliament refused to consider the changes.

In the following months, the President and Parliament remained at loggerheads. The Parliament ignored the President's decrees and was issuing

Russia's Parliament hit by tank shells in the coup of August 1993. Photo by ITAR-TASS News Agency/Alamy Stock Photo.

its own. The situation had worsened when Yeltsin's own Vice President, Alexander Rutskoi, took the side of the Parliament. When on September 1 Yeltsin attempted to dismiss Rutskoi on corruption charges, the Parliament referred the matter to the Constitutional Court. It ruled that Yeltsin's move was unconstitutional and that the President could be impeached.

Yeltsin upped the ante by dissolving the Parliament and announcing new elections in December 1993. The Speaker of the Parliament, Ruslan Khasbulatov, responded by hastily convening the Parliament to have Yeltsin impeached and Rutskoi appointed President along with the appointment of key defense and security ministers. There were now two Presidents in Russia and dual power was a reality.

The situation threatened to develop into a civil war; on October 3, Yeltsin declared a state of emergency in Moscow. Hundreds of well-armed supporters barricaded themselves inside the White House, as the seat of the Parliament was known. Rutskoi and Khasbulatov called upon the people to march on City Hall and the main TV station. An armed confrontation near the TV station between troops loyal to Yeltsin and supporters of the Parliament left sixty-two people dead and left the TV station badly damaged.

The time for a compromise was over, and Yeltsin ordered heavily armed troops with tanks to surround the White House. Declaring that the Parliament and its supporters were an armed band of fascist-communist rebels who had risen against the Russian state, Yeltsin ordered a siege of the White House. The siege began in the morning of October 4 with tank shells slamming into the building. By the end of the day, the building had been seized and the rebellious leaders had been arrested.

Yeltsin's victory was bittersweet. On December 12, a new Constitution that greatly expanded the power of the presidency and restructured the Parliament was approved in a referendum. Yet the newly elected Parliament, which was now renamed the Duma after an assembly in imperial Russia, was once again dominated by the hardliners.

The most disturbing and surprising development was the rise of the ultranationalist, neo-fascist party of Vladimir Zhirinovsky, which garnered 23 percent of the vote. Even the unpopular Communists received 12.4 percent of the vote, just behind the 15.5 percent of a pro-Yeltsin reformist party. It took only two months before the Duma passed an amnesty for all those involved in the mass disturbances of the previous months. Rutskoi and Khasbulatov were released from prison and, by early 1995, all criminal proceedings against them had been dismissed.

Yeltsin succeeded in creating a powerful presidency and pushing through his economic reforms. Yet the price of victory was high: he would forever be a hostage to the interests of the military and security agencies who had supported him.

1994
Corruption and the First Chechen War

With challenges on many fronts, Yeltsin had little appetite for another confrontation with the new hardline Duma. As a result, the Russian government never initiated the lustration of high officials responsible for historic crimes against the people, the way it was done in Eastern Europe. Nor did it establish a Truth and Reconciliation Commission, the kind created in post-apartheid South Africa. Instead, many former Communists and KGB officers made the smooth transition into entrepreneurs and politicians. Clearly, the 1993 constitutional crisis failed to put Russia on a historically radical path.

No one understood this better than Russia's literary giant and self-styled prophet, Alexander Solzhenitsyn. Arriving in Russia on May 28, 1994 after twenty years of exile, Solzhenitsyn blasted both reformers and ultranationalists in a fiery speech. Yet he reserved his most righteous anger for the Communists. He called on Russia to face up to the crimes of the Soviet regime and engage in spiritual cleansing before reconciling.

His passionate words, however, fell on the deaf ears of his compatriots, most of whom were either preoccupied with survival in harsh economic conditions or were busy enriching themselves by siphoning off money in corrupt government ploys.

In this transitional legal and political climate, moral depravity and corruption quickly reached new heights. Billionaires were born, criminal syndicates rose, and anyone in a position to enrich himself by stealing or misappropriating state assets hastened to do so. Not surprisingly, the rise of new fortunes was closely mirrored by an alarming rise in contract killings and the murder of investigative journalists.

One particular murder had all the signs of a skilled and professional assassination. On October 17, a military correspondent for the Russian newspaper *Moskovskii Komsomolets*, Dmitrii Kholodov, was blown up when he opened a booby-trapped briefcase that was supposed to contain

Chechen capital, Groznyi, during the First Chechen War. Photo by Georges DeKeerle/Sygma via Getty Images.

incriminating material. Kholodov was about to publish a report on huge corruption schemes in the Russian military that personally involved the Defense Minister, Pavel Grachev.

One month later, Moscow ordered a military intervention in Chechnya, a rebellious republic in the North Caucasus which had declared independence from Russia. Relations with Chechnya and its leader, Dzhohar Dudaev, had been tense for some time, and Moscow might have run out of patience. But critics suggested that the decision to resort to military confrontation might have been intended to distract public attention from corruption scandals in Russian military.

On November 26, the Moscow-supported Chechen opposition launched the first serious attack on the Chechen capital, Groznyi. These Chechens were joined by Russian "volunteers" who happened to be on "vacation" from their regular military units. They also happened "to vacation" with armored vehicles and tanks and were supported by the Russian Air Force and heavy artillery from across the border.

The assault failed and dozens of Russians were captured. Moscow stubbornly refused the Chechen leadership's offer to exchange or return captives and insisted that no regular Russian soldiers had taken part in the campaign. Instead, Yeltsin ordered a heavy aerial bombardment of the city followed by a full-scale military invasion several weeks later. To their credit, several of Yeltsin's advisors resigned in protest and some Russian commanders refused to participate in the war. The military operation proved to be another disaster, with many poorly trained Russian troops captured or killed and dozens of tanks and other vehicles destroyed.

And then, on New Year's Eve, came another infamous assault on Groznyi. It was poorly planned and executed, and rumors swelled that the assault was ordered by Yeltsin and Grachev in the midst of a drunken stupor. Whatever the case, sending dozens of tanks into the streets of Groznyi proved to be a complete military failure. Having no maps of the city and no firm objective, the tank units were quickly ambushed and destroyed by small mobile groups of Chechens.

Despite heavy casualties, the Russians continued their assault and were in control of the city by the spring of 1995. What followed was a cycle of mutual brutality, war crimes against civilians, hostage-taking, ambushes, and counter-attacks that slowly bled Russians into a stalemate.

The First Chechen War ended in August 1996 with Moscow and Chechen leaders signing an accord that would cease hostilities and see Russian troops withdrawn. The war had claimed over 100,000 civilian lives, many of them ethnic Russian residents of Groznyi, with an unknown number of Chechens killed and missing. Russia's casualties were heavy: between 7,000 and 14,000 soldiers dead, 3,000 missing in action, and 52,000 wounded. The city of Groznyi lay in ruins, its population on the brink of starvation, and its destruction comparable to that of Dresden in the Second World War.

1995–96 Elections

Amid the continuing privatization of state assets, half-hearted legal and political reforms, the continuing war in Chechnya, and the country's geopolitical retreat, the Russian public further soured on Yeltsin and his government. When a new election of the Duma took place on December 17, 1995, the results were shocking. The Party of United Democrats, led by Yeltsin's top reformer Yegor Gaidar, suffered a crushing defeat, collecting less than 4 percent of the vote and keeping nine out of ninety-six seats. By far the biggest winner was the Communist Party, with 22 percent of the vote, followed by Zhirinovsky's ultranationalist party, with 12 percent. Yeltsin's only consolation was that a newly founded pro-government party, Our Home Russia, ended up with 10 percent of the vote.

The results of the Duma elections were calamitous for the Yeltsin government. People made it clear that they were tired of liberal reforms and corruption, had little trust in the government, and were willing to return the Communists to power only five years after the end of the USSR. The omens for the presidential election that were to take place in six months were inauspicious.

In January 1996, Yeltsin's popularity polled at 8 percent, fifth among eleven presidential candidates. It seemed all but assured that the leader of the Communist Party, Gennadii Ziuganov, would be Russia's next president. The future of Russia was at stake. But so were the vast fortunes of the new oligarchs, who decided to put aside their differences and create a united front to support Yeltsin.

When on March 15, the Communist-dominated Duma passed a resolution denouncing Yeltsin's 1991 agreement with Ukraine and Belarus as illegal, the full specter of the restoration of the USSR under the Communists became real. The oligarchs flooded Yeltsin's campaign with money. Most of the mass media—owned either by the oligarchs or the state—unleashed a propaganda campaign against the Communists. The campaign was sophisticated and effective in portraying a potential Communist Party victory as a return to the Gulag system and a loss of hard-won freedoms.

At the same time, having its own concerns about the Communists' return, the US engineered a $10.2 billion loan granted to Russia by the IMF. Its arrival could not have been more timely, allowing Moscow to pay back salaries and pensions. The Yeltsin campaign also resorted to dirty tricks against opponents and would later be accused of rigging votes in some regions.

Despite all this, the election on June 16 did not produce a clear winner, and a second round between Yeltsin and Ziuganov was scheduled for July 3. In the meantime, Yeltsin suffered a heart attack, but that was not revealed to the public. His images were doctored, and interviews were staged to create an impression of his campaign activity. When the votes were counted on July 3, Yeltsin received 50.4 percent of the vote to Ziuganov's 40.7 percent.

The oligarchs could exhale, the West was relieved, and millions of Russians, who believed in a new democratic Russia, rejoiced. But democracy it was not. The election was unfair and set a dangerous precedent for the future. It was only a matter of time before a conservative majority was to assert its power.

1997
Russian Fascism

During the time of *glasnost* in the late 1980s, when a new freedom to criticize the Communist Party and government was associated with greater democracy, few noticed the emergence of darker forces, whose criticism of the Communist rule came from the far-right corner of ultra-nationalism. In the fall of 1987, several groups that had been initially formed as the Societies for the Promotion of Russian History and Culture morphed into a National Patriotic Front named Pamiat (Memory). The Front's agenda was to seek "a national and spiritual revival of the Russian people" based on Orthodox Christianity, spirituality, and national character. Many believed that the KGB had a strong hand in founding Pamiat.

Within a year, the Front began to split into several smaller groups with the same name: Pamiat. Despite a bitter rivalry between different factions, they were all united by the common ideology of Russian ultranationalism, sweeping xenophobia, and virulent anti-Semitism. Some were National Bolsheviks, who venerated the legacy of Stalin, others argued for the resurrection of the Orthodox Christian empire of the tsars, and all believed that the world was in danger from International Zionism and the masonic West. At one point, the leaders of Pamiat accused President Yeltsin of being the puppet of a Jewish coterie and warned that he would end up like other Zionist-supported dictators, "Napoleon and Hitler among them."

Apparent contradictions, lack of veracity, and bizarre conspiracy theories did not bother the faithful. One of them was Alexander Dugin, who joined Pamiat in 1988 and became the intellectual father of modern Russian fascism. In 1997, he published an article, "Fascism—Borderless and Red," in which he proclaimed the arrival of "a genuine, fascist fascism" in Russia. Dugin's vision combined nostalgia for Stalin and the USSR with deep social and religious conservatism. Russia was to be the bulwark against American hegemony and the liberal West.

Dugin spelled out his ideas further in a book that he published the same year and which, since then, has become the textbook for the Kremlin's rulers, *The Foundations of Geopolitics*. The basic premise was simple and predictably anti-Western: the US and NATO were the main enemies who were trying to contain Russia by creating a *cordon sanitaire* out of the former Soviet republics. Dugin's solution was to reestablish the USSR, enter diplomatic alliances with Japan, Iran, and Germany, and push the US out of the continent. His call for the formation of a geopolitical "axis" with Germany and Japan to divide Europe and Asia was only one of his many admiring references to the policies of the Nazis and Imperial Japan.

To this concoction of anti-Americanism, nationalism, and neo-Nazism, Dugin added the idea of Eurasianism, which had made its debut in 1920s Russian émigré circles. In Dugin's vision, Russia was destined to emerge as a Eurasian empire with a messianic mission to save the world from insidious Western liberalism antithetical to Russian values. Dugin believed that Russia was unique in its combination of nationalism and empire, for without an empire "Russians would lose their identity and disappear as a nation."

Dugin's ideas were a prescription for Russian revanchism, and they fell on the fertile ground of bitterness, discontent, and nostalgia for the USSR's former greatness. At a time when many Russians associated new freedoms with chaos and venality, and the demise of the USSR with a loss of power and prestige, Dugin agitated for Russians to rise from their knees to recover the glory of the olden days.

The book quickly became a bestseller and was adopted as the primer in Russia's military academies. Several reprints followed and Dugin's ideas spread like a virus. As Russians were searching for a new national identity, Dugin's passionate vision of a Great Russia with its unique national destiny inspired and seduced many. "Geopolitics" had become a mantra overshadowing concerns about economic prosperity, civil society, and the rule of law. A growing chorus of conservative forces were allying themselves with Dugin's ideas. Russia was returning to a familiar historical ground, where its weaknesses were turned into virtues and its backwardness into Russia's special destiny.

1998
Return of the KGB

Yeltsin and his reformers were in trouble. Yeltsin was seriously ill and drinking heavily, and his behavior was becoming increasingly erratic. The Duma, dominated by the nationalist hardliners, opposed any significant reform proposed by the government. The fragile economy that was only beginning a modest recovery was hit by sliding oil prices, and the first signs of trouble were coming from financial markets in Asia.

A fiscal crisis in the summer of 1998 sent the Russian economy into a tailspin. In the US, "it was the summer when a president's penis was on everyone's mind," observed the American writer Philip Roth, referring to the Monica Lewinsky scandal, but in Russia people went hungry. The ruble collapsed, inflation reached 84 percent, and the worst harvest in forty-five years resulted in severe food shortages throughout the country. Only urgent supplies of agricultural products from the West, mostly the US, saved Russia from collapse. The fact that much of the aid was either free or given on very favorable terms did not reduce the anger and frustration directed at liberal reformers and the West.

Under pressure, Yeltsin began to reshuffle his government. In July he appointed a new head of the FSB (a new renamed KGB), a former KGB lieutenant-colonel, Vladimir Putin. In September, after the Duma twice refused to confirm Yeltsin's choice for prime minister, he was compelled to nominate a professional spy and the former head of Russia's Foreign Intelligence Service, Yevgeny Primakov. Russian security services, which traditionally operated behind the scene, were now assuming a higher and bolder profile.

One woman adamantly opposed the return of the old, unreconstructed security agencies. Galina Starovoitova, a professor of social anthropology who turned to politics in the turbulent 1990s, had tirelessly argued for purging and reforming the former Secret Police. Five times she presented the Duma with a draft of a law dictating major restructuring of the security apparatus, and each time it was rejected.

An ardent reformer, she was elected to the Duma in 1995 and three years later became the leader of the Democratic Russia Party. She voted against the appointment of the spy master Yevgeny Primakov to Prime Minister, and her strong opposition to the FSB's role in society became a plank in her party's platform.

As an expert on non-Russian minorities in Russia, she proved to be a valuable advisor to Yeltsin on delicate and violence-fraught issues of inter-ethnic relations in the Russian Federation. However, once Yeltsin became a hostage to the nationalist hardliners and security agencies, her advice was no longer sought. She remained one of the few committed liberal democrats and that put her squarely at odds with most members of the Duma.

On November 13, the Duma debated, but refused to condemn, the hateful anti-Semitic speech by Albert Makashov, an ultra nationalist deputy from the Communist faction. Starovoitova condemned Makashov and scolded the Duma members. One week later, as she entered her apartment building in St. Petersburg, she was gunned down with three bullets to her head.

It took seven years to convict two hitmen for the murder of Starovoitova. The hit organizer, Yuri Kolchin, turned out to be a professionally trained assassin formerly employed by the Russian intelligence service. Little surprise that the court was not able to find out who ordered and paid for the murder.

The murder of Galina Starovoitova was a turning point that marked the end of Yeltsin's democratic reforms and the emergence of an alliance of sinister forces in post-Soviet Russia. Her call to purge the ranks of the security services and hold them responsible for their past crimes crossed the line for many former KGB men, who had made a smooth transition into new Russia's crime- and graft-ridden economy. And her unflinching condemnation of Russian ultra nationalists earned her the ire of Communists and other hard-liners. Whether her murder was organized by the red-brown groups of nationalists or the gray assassins of the FSB did not matter. At this point, the interests of the security services and those of the ultra right coalesced. Between the Communist red and the Nationalist brown, the gray of the FSB had become a primary color.

1999
Prime Minister Putin

By the end of the year, the FSB coup put state security agencies in full control of the government. To what extent the head of the FSB, Vladimir Putin, took advantage of the new developments and to what extent he actually engineered them remains murky.

Throughout the year, the Prime Minister's office remained a revolving door, but one that was open only to those with security service credentials. In May, Yeltsin fired Primakov, a former chief spymaster, who lasted barely eight

An apartment building in Volgodonsk, Russia after a series of unexplained bombings across the country.

months. He replaced Primakov with Sergei Stepashin, who had previously held positions as the head of security services, Minister of Justice, and Minister of Internal Affairs, that is, the head of Russia's police force. Three months later, Stepashin too was gone. On August 16, Yeltsin appointed the current head of the FSB, Vladimir Putin, to be Russia's new Prime Minister.

These kaleidoscopic changes reflected an ongoing struggle between different power brokers—the oligarchs, who had little taste for ideology but a big appetite for corrupt business deals, and the security agencies, whose political and business ambitions fit neatly into their agenda of restoring Russia's greatness. Putin seemed to offer a middle path between protecting the oligarchs' wealth and rebuilding the Russian state.

Putin's appointment came at a time of growing Russian resentment of the West and nostalgia for Soviet might. To the average Russian, it seemed that the West was adding the insult of endless humiliations to the injury of economic hardships. There was the Bosnian war (1992–95), where NATO's intervention forced Russia's traditional friends, the Serbs, to conclude an uneasy peace in Bosnia. Then there was the Kosovo War (1998–99), where a NATO bombing campaign again compelled the Serbs to agree to Kosovo's independence in June 1999.

Russians felt angry, powerless and humiliated. The fact that in both Yugoslav wars, NATO had intervened reluctantly and belatedly, and only to stop Serb atrocities, rape, genocide, and ethnic cleansing in Bosnia and Kosovo, was lost on most Russians. NATO's expansion a few months earlier to include the USSR's former satellites, Poland, the Czech Republic, and Hungary was seen as yet another ignominy.

When in April 2005 Putin infamously referred to the collapse of the USSR as "the greatest geopolitical catastrophe of the 20th century," he was speaking for many in Russia, who were appalled that the country's breakup had left millions of ethnic Russians outside Russia's borders. Russians, who used to be the dominant group in the Soviet Union, but who had suddenly become second-class citizens in neighboring countries, found it hard to swallow.

Battered on many fronts, Russian nationalism found its first outlet within Russia itself, in the ever-troublesome Chechnya, which had become a center of Islamic radicalism in Russia. In August, several local warlords led a large and well-armed group of Chechens and other Islamic fighters into neighboring Dagestan. Their goal was to establish an Islamic state and declare jihad against Russia.

In contrast to his predecessors, Putin refused to seek any compromise and ordered a full-scale assault on the villages occupied by Islamic fighters. Several weeks of merciless air campaigns razed villages to the ground and killed scores of civilians, yet most of the Chechen fighters were able to escape. It was then that a strange sequence of apartment bombings unfolded in Russia.

On September 4, a car bomb exploded near an apartment building in the Dagestani town of Buinaksk. In the following days, two apartment buildings were blown up in Moscow and one in Volgodonsk. A total of 293 people were killed with hundreds more wounded. Several bombs were found and defused, and in one case the three men who were caught red-handed while setting the explosives proved to be FSB agents. Moscow blamed the Chechens, even though they consistently denied any responsibility, and multiple investigations by journalists and human rights groups pointed to the FSB's involvement.

The apartment bombings served Moscow as a pretext for starting a full-scale war against Chechnya. Were the bombings—Putin's equivalent of the Reichstag fire—intended to generate support for a new war in Chechnya and ensure his Presidency? We may never know, but many with intimate knowledge of these events claimed that they were. Most of those who were involved in the investigations or had some inside knowledge were either assassinated or died in mysterious circumstances. One way or another, Putin's road to the President's office was paved with the blood of thousands of innocent civilians.

Epilogue
2000
President Putin

"Leadership, any leadership" was a common refrain among Russians who believed that Russia was sliding further into chaos. They soon got their wish.

On December 31, 1999, Yeltsin suddenly announced his resignation automatically making the sitting Prime Minister, Vladimir Putin, the Acting President. It was a deal that was both simple and ruthless. Battered by investigations into his "family's" graft and embezzlement, Yeltsin was compelled to step aside to make room for a new president, who in return vowed to protect him from any criminal charges. Indeed, hours later, Putin signed his first presidential decree granting Yeltsin and his family immunity from any criminal and administrative investigation.

With snap elections to be held in three months, Putin undertook his first presidential trip to war-torn Chechnya, where Russian troops were making costly but steady gains. Projecting the image of a strong and uncompromising leader ready to restore Russia's dignity and power was critical for Putin's presidential campaign. When elections were held on March 26, Putin won with 53 percent of the vote.

To most people, Putin was a welcome change from Yeltsin, whose poor health and drunken revelries had become a source of great embarrassment. Putin's meteoric rise to the presidency, which at first sight appeared improbable, was far from accidental. Throughout 1999, Russia's polling agencies were busy trying to "cast" a favorable image of a new president. One poll stood out: when asked which film character would make the best president, the responders chose three: the legendary Second World War hero depicted in many films, Marshal Zhukov, the tough detective from a crime thriller, Gleb Zhiglov, and the Soviet spy who penetrated the Nazi's Gestapo in a widely admired TV series, Max Stierlitz.

Yeltsin's handing over of power to his Prime Minister and now Acting President, Vladimir Putin, in the only peaceful transfer of power in Russian history. Photo by AFP/AFP/Getty Images.

The latter choice of an intelligent, quiet, and decisive man on a dangerous mission for his country proved to be the most popular. Operation "Successor," as the Kremlin spin doctors dubbed it, had settled on a perfect match, Vladimir Putin, a former KGB officer, who had lived and worked in Germany. On the day of the election, one of Russia's weekly magazines appeared with the headline "Stierlitz—Our President."

Putin might have been elected as Stierlitz, but to some his actions were more reminiscent of Stierlitz' superiors in the Gestapo. On May 11, four days after his inauguration, Putin ordered a raid on the corporate offices of Media MOST, a large holding company of print, radio, and TV media. The pretext was unpaid taxes; however, the real reason was to silence an independent media company that was aggressively pursuing investigations into the recent bombings of the apartment buildings and high-level corruption in the presidential administration.

A raid by men wearing black masks and wielding guns was not entirely new to the MOST owner, Vladimir Gusinsky. In 1994, he drew the Kremlin's ire for his media's independent coverage of the Chechen War. In December 1994, his offices were ransacked, he was threatened, and he left Russia. Yet several months later, he was able to return to Moscow, and his media empire retained its independence.

This time it was different. The Kremlin was determined not only to tame Media MOST, but to turn it into a government mouthpiece, in the process reaping a handsome profit. On June 13, Gusinsky was arrested and sent to a notorious Moscow jail. An offer from the Kremlin quickly followed: freedom, in exchange for selling Media MOST to the government-founded Gazprom group. The price was set by Gazprom at $300 million, whereas the actual price was $1.1 billion. Several weeks later, in July, Gusinsky signed an agreement that sold his company for $300 million, the criminal case against him was dropped, and he was allowed to leave the country.

There was another reason why Putin chose to crush Gusinsky's media first. One particular show, the Dolls, was a popular, biting satire of Russian politicians, but when it mocked Putin and refused to tone down its criticisms after a warning from the presidential administration, the Kremlin took steps to shut it down. It was an early sign of new censorship and Putin's own sensitivity about his image.

In retrospect, the signs of what was to come were numerous and came early. In 1999, soon after Putin was appointed to the position of Prime Minister, he spoke to FSB officers gathered to mark the anniversary of the foundation of the Soviet Secret Police: "The intelligence operatives planted inside the Russian government have successfully completed the first stage of the operation." It was supposed to be a joke, but it was not.

Later that year, on December 20, Prime Minister Putin came to Lubyanka, the headquarters of the FSB, to unveil a restored memorial plaque to Yuri Andropov, which had been dismantled in August 1991. Andropov, of course, was Putin's former boss and the long-term head of the KGB, notorious for his methods of suppressing dissidents, including the use of psychiatric institutions.

Yeltsin was the first to recognize that reforming the KGB would prove to be a tall order, and that Russia's political police, while presently inactive, could be easily revived. He did not relish transferring power to a KGB man, but helpless, ill, and cornered, he had little choice.

During his first year in office, Putin rapidly consolidated his power. By August, despite overwhelming evidence, criminal investigations involving top government officials including Putin's own graft and embezzlement during his years in St. Petersburg were dropped. Main witnesses were silenced either by intimidation or a bullet. The man who knew the most about Putin, his former boss and St. Petersburg's mayor, Anatoly Sobchak, died from a sudden heart attack in February 2000. The fact that several of his aides had developed similar symptoms at the same time was a likely sign that the FSB's assassins were out of practice in deploying their deadly skills. A criminal investigation into Sobchak's death was opened and closed three months later with no result.

By December 2000, Putin's Russia had largely taken shape. It was a restoration project of both Russia's imperial glory and Soviet power led by the security services. Putin surrounded himself with former KGB officers, most of them from his St. Petersburg days, and significantly raised the salaries of the members of the security services and military. In an ominous gesture and against the objections of many, Putin revived the old Soviet anthem that was composed in 1938, at the height of Stalin's purges. Russians who dared to criticize the government were called "anti-state" and unpatriotic.

Putin's new Russia was a curios amalgam, a hybrid of the double-headed eagle of the tsars and the Soviet national anthem of the Communists. Throughout the tragic twists and turns of the twentieth century, Russia had travelled from the tsars to general secretaries and back to a tsar. Democracy remained elusive and most of the time was not needed. The prosperity of Russia's own people remained a low priority. Russia's self-esteem was measured by its geopolitical status and its ability to dominate others. Russia was entering the twenty-first century with the same basic set of principles and values it had maintained throughout the twentieth century.

Bibliography

Chapter 1

Ascher, Abraham *A Revolution of 1905: A Short History.* Palo Alto, CA: Stanford University Press, 2004.

Bartlett, Rosamund *Tolstoy: A Russian Life.* Boston, MA: Houghton Mifflin Harcourt, 2011.

Bonnell, Victoria E. ed. *Russian Worker: Life and Labor under the Tsarist Regime.* Berkeley, CA: University of California Press, 1983.

Figes, Orlando *Natasha's Dance: A Cultural History of Russia.* New York, NY: Picador, 2003.

Kizenko, Nadieszda *A Prodigal Saint: Father John of Kronsdadt and the Russian People.* University Park, PA: Penn State University Press, 2000.

Mazower, Mark *The Balkans: A Short History.* New York, NY: Modern Library, 2002.

Nathans, Benjamin *Beyond the Pale: The Jewish Encounter with Late Imperial Russia.* Berkeley, CA: University of California, 2004.

Rayfield, Donald *Anton Chekhov: A Life.* Evanston, IL: Northwestern University Press, 2000.

Sebag Montefiore, Simon *Young Stalin.* New York, NY: Vintage, 2008.

Witte, Sergei *The Memoirs of Count Witte.* New York, NY: Doubleday, 1921.

Worobec, Christine D. *Peasant Russia: Family and Community in the Post Emancipation Period.* De Kalb, IL: Northern Illinois University Press, 1995.

Zelnik, Reginal E. ed. *Workers and Intelligentsia in Imperial Russia: Realities, Representations, Reflections.* Berkeley, CA: University of California Press, 1999.

Zipperstein, Steven J. *Pogrom: Kishinev and the Tilt of History.* New York, NY: Liveright, 2018.

Chapter 2

Bowlt, John E. *Moscow and St. Petersburg, 1900–1920: Art, Life, and Culture of the Russian Silver Age.* New York, NY: Vendome Press, 2008.

Figes Orlando, *A People's Tragedy. A History of the Russian Revolution*. New York, NY: Viking, 1996.

Fitzpatrick, Sheila *The Russian Revolution*. Oxford: Oxford University Press, 1982.

Hellman, Ben *Poets of Hope and Despair: The Russian Symbolists in War and Revolution (1914–1918)*. Leiden: Brill, 2018.

Holquist, Peter *Making War, Forging Revolution: Russia's Continuum of Crisis, 1914–1921*. Cambridge, MA: Harvard University Press, 2002.

Lieven, Dominic *The End of Tsarist Russia: The March to World War I and Revolution*. New York, NY: Penguin, 2016.

Lincoln, W.. Bruce *Red Victory: A History of the Russian Civil War*. New York: NY: Simon and Shuster, 1989.

McMeekin, Sean *The Russian Origins of the First World War*. Cambridge, MA: Harvard University Press, 2011.

Melancon, Michael *The Lena Goldfields Massacre and the Crisis of the Late Tsarist State*. College Station, TX: Texas A&M University Press, 2006.

Sebag Montefiore, Simon *The Romanovs, 1613–1918*. New York, NY: Vintage, 2017.

Nickell, William *The Death of Tolstoy: Russia on the Eve, Astapovo Station, 1910*. Ithaca, NY: Cornell University Press, 2010.

Smith, Douglas *Rasputin: Faith, Power, and the Twilight of the Romanovs*. New York, NY: Picador, 2017.

Venturi, Franco *Roots of Revolution. A History of the Populist and Socialist Movements in Nineteenth Century Russia*. New York: Knopf, 1964.

Chapter 3

Ball, Alan M. *And Now My Soul is Hardened: Abandoned Children in Soviet Russia, 1918-1930*. Berkeley, CA: University of California Press, 1996.

Ball, Alan M. *Russia's Last Capitalists: The Nepmen, 1921–1929*. Berkeley, CA: University of California Press, 1991.

Bennigsen, Alexander A. and S. Enders Wimbush, *Muslim National Communism in the Soviet Union: A Revolutionary Strategy for the Colonial World*. Chicago, IL: University of Chicago, 1979.

Conquest, Robert *The Harvest of Sorrow: Soviet Collectivization and the Terror-Famine*. Oxford: Oxford University Press, 1987.

Engelstein, Laura *Russia in Flames: War, Revolution, Civil War, 1914–1921*. Oxford: Oxford University Press, 2017.

Hirsh, Francine *Empire of Nations: Ethnographic Knowledge and the Making of the Soviet Union*. Ithaca, NY: Cornell University Press, 2005.

Hoffmann, David L. *Stalinist Values: The Cultural Norms of Soviet Modernity, 1917–1941*. Ithaca, NY: Cornell University Press, 2003.

Homberger, Eric *John Reed*. Manchester, UK: University of Manchester Press, 1990.

Northrop, Douglas *Veiled Empire: Gender and Power in Stalinist Central Asia*. Ithaca, NY: Cornell University Press, 2003.

Peris, Daniel *Storming the Heavens: The Soviet League of the Militant Godless*. Ithaca, NY: Cornell University Press, 1998.

Riddell, John *To See the Dawn: Baku, 1920—First Congress of the Peoples of the East*. New York, NY: Pathfinder, 1993.

Chapter 4

Applebaum, Anne *Gulag: A History*. New York, NY: Anchor Books, 2004.

Applebaum, Anne *Red Famine: Stalin's War on Ukraine*. New York, NY: Doubleday, 2017.

Jangfeldt, Bengt *Mayakovsky: A Biography*. Chicago, IL: The University of Chicago Press, 2014.

Kelly, Catriona *The Rise and Fall of Soviet Boy Hero*. New York, NY: Granta Books, 2005.

Kotkin, Stephen *Stalin: Waiting for Hitler, 1929–1941*. New York, NY: Penguin, 2017.

Leno, Matthew E. *The Kirov Murder and Soviet History*. New Haven, CN: Yale University Press, 2010.

Patenaude, Bertrand M. *Stalin's Nemesis: The Exile and Murder of Leon Trotsky*. London: Faber and Faber, 2010.

Fitzpatrick, Sheila *Everyday Stalinism: Ordinary Life in Extraordinary Times: Soviet Russia in the 1930s*. Oxford: Oxford University Press, 1999.

Schlögel, Karl *Moscow: 1937*. New York, NY: Polity, 2013.

Slezkine, Yuri *The House of Government: A Saga of the Russian Revolution*. Princeton, NJ: Princeton University Press, 2017.

Snyder, Timothy *Bloodlands: Europe Between Hitler and Stalin*. New York, NY: Basic Books, 2010.

Chapter 5

Beevor, Antony *Stalingrad: The Fateful Siege, 1942–1943*. New York, NY: Penguin Books, 1999.

Braithwaite, Rodric *Moscow 1941: The City and Its People at War.* New York, NY: Vintage, 2007.

Holloway, David *Stalin and the Bomb: The Soviet Union and Atomic Energy, 1939–1956.* New Haven, CN: Yale University Press, 1994.

Khlevniuk, Oleg V. *Stalin: New Biography of a Dictator.* New Haven, CN: Yale University Press, 2015.

Nekrich, Alexander *The Punished Peoples: The Deportation and Fate of the Soviet Minorities at the End of the Second World War.* New York, NY: W.W. Norton, 1978.

Naimark, Norman M. *The Russians in Germany: A History of the Soviet Zone of Occupation, 1945–1949.* Cambridge, MA: Harvard University Press, 1995.

Rubinstein, Joshua *Stalin's Secret Pogrom: The Post-War Inquisition of the Jewish Anti-Fascist Committee.* New Haven, CN: Yale University Press, 2001.

Salisbury, Harrison *900 days. The Siege of Leningrad.* Da Capo Press. 2nd edition. 2003.

Vasilieva, Larissa *Kremlin Wives: The Secret Lives of the Women Behind the Kremlin Walls—From Lenin to Gorbachev.* New York, NY: Arcade Publishing, 2015.

Chapter 6

Barnes, Christopher *Boris Pasternak: A Literary Biography. Volume 2, 1928–1960.* Cambridge UK: Cambridge University Press, 1998.

Finn, Peter and Petra Couvee, *The Zhivago Affair: The Kremlin, the CIA, and the Battle Over a Forbidden Book.* New York, NY: Vintage 2014.

Jersild, Austin *The Sino-Soviet Alliance. An International History.* Chapel Hill, NC: The University of North Carolina Press, 2016.

Rubinstein, Joshua *The Last Days of Stalin.* New Haven, CN: Yale University Press, 2016.

Smith, Cathleen E. *Moscow 1956: The Silenced Spring.* Cambridge, MA: Harvard University Press, 2017.

Taubman, William *Khrushchev: The Man and His Era.* New York, NY: W.W. Norton, 2004.

Ubiria, Grigol *Soviet Nation-Building in Central Asia: The Making of the Kazakh and Uzbek Nations.* Abingdon, UK: Routledge, 2002.

Zaloga, Steven *The Kremlin's Nuclear Sword: The Rise and Fall of Russia's Strategic Nuclear Forces, 1945–2000.* Washington, DC: Smithsonian Books, 2002.

Chapter 7

Baron, Samuel H. *Bloody Saturday in the Soviet Union, Novocherkassk, 1962.*
  Palo Alto, CA: Stanford University Press, 2001.

Chukovsky, Kornei *Diary, 1901–1969.* Edited by Victor Erlich. New Haven: Yale
  University Press, 2005.

Gillespie, David C. *Russian Cinema.* Abingdon, UK: Routledge, 2002.

Kozlov, Denis *The Readers of Novyi Mir: Coming to Terms with the Stalinist
  Past.* Cambridge, MA: Harvard University Press, 2013.

Lourie, Richard *Sakharov: A Biography.* Waltham, MA: Brandeis University
  Press, 2002.

Rubinstein, Joshua *Soviet Dissidents: Their Struggle for Human Rights.* Boston:
  Beacon Press, 1980.

Solzhenitsyn, Alexander *Gulag Archipelago, 1918–1956.* The Harvill Press, 2003.

Taubman, William *Khrushchev: The Man and His Era.* New York, NY:
  W.W. Norton, 2004.

Taylor, Frederick *The Berlin Wall: A World Divided, 1961–1989.* HarperCollins,
  2007.

Chapter 8

Alexseyeva, Ludmilla and Paul Goldberg, *The Thaw Generation: Coming of Age
  in the Post-Stalinist Era.* Pittsburg: University of Pittsburg, 1993.

Azrael, Jeremy *Soviet Nationality Policies and Practices.* Santa Barbara, CA:
  Praeger, 1978.

Bialer, Seweryn *Stalin's Successors: Leadership, Stability, and Change in the
  Soviet Union.* Cambridge: Cambridge University Press, 1980.

Bloch, Sydney and Peter Reddaway, *Soviet Psychiatric Abuse: The Shadow Over
  World Psychiatry.* New York: Routledge, 1985.

Brown, Archie *The Rise and Fall of Communism.* London: Bodley Head, 2009.

Feifer, Gregory *The Great Gamble: The Soviet War in Afghanistan.* New York:
  Harper, 2010

Gilburd, Eleonory *To See Paris and Die: The Soviet Lives of Western Culture.*
  Cambridge, MA: Belknap Press, 2018.

Leffler, Melvyn M. and Odd Arne Westad eds. *The Cambridge History of the
  Cold War*, volume 2. Cambridge: Cambridge University Press, 2010.

Loth, Wilfried *Overcoming the Cold War: A History of Détente, 1950–1991.* New
  York: Palgrave McMillan, 2002.

Mirsky, George *On Ruins of Empire: Ethnicity and Nationalism in the Former
  Soviet Union.* Santa Barbara, CA: Praeger 1997.

Scammell, Michael *Solzhenitsyn: A Biography*. Boston: W.W. Norton, 1984.

Stites, Richard *Russian Popular Culture: Entertainment and Society since 1900*. Cambridge: Cambridge University Press, 1992.

Westad, Odd Arne *The Cold War: A World History*. New York: Basic Book, 2018.

Chapter 9

Garton Ash, Timothy *The Polish Revolution: Solidarity*. New York: Scribner, 1984.

Bialer, Seweryn *The Soviet Paradox: External Expansion, Internal Decline*. New York: Knopf, 1996.

Downing, Taylor *1983: Reagan, Andropov, and a World on the Brink*. Da Capo Press, 2018.

Feshbach, Murrey *Ecocide in the USSR: Health and Nature under Siege*. New York, NY: Basic Books, 1992.

Miller, Chris *The Struggle to Save the Soviet Economy: Mikhail Gorbachev and the Collapse of the USSR*. Chapel Hill, NC: University of North Carolina Press, 2016.

Parks, Jenifer *The Olympic Games, the Soviet Sports Bureaucracy, and the Cold War: Red Sport, Red Tape*. New York: Lexington Books, 2016.

Plokhy, Serhii *Chernobyl: The History of a Nuclear Catastrophe*. New York: Basic Books, 2018.

Ryback, Timothy W. *Rock Around the Block: A History of Rock Music in Eastern Europe and the Soviet Union, 1954–1988*. Oxford: Oxford University Press, 1990.

Taubman, William *Gorbachev: His Life and Times*. W.W. Norton, 2017.

Yurchak, Alexei *Everything Was Forever Until It Was No More*. Princeton, NJ: Princeton University Press, 2005.

Chapter 10

Alexievich, Svetlana *Secondhand Time. The Last of the Soviets*. New York: Random House, 2017.

Brown, Archie *The Gorbachev Factor*. Oxford: Oxford University Press, 1996.

Clover, Charles *Black Wind, White Snow; The Rise of Russia New Nationalism*, New Haven, CN: Yale University Press, 2016.

Colton, Timothy J. *Yeltsin: A Life*. New York: Basic Books, 2011.

German, Tracey C. *Russia's Chechen War*. New York: Routledge, 2003.

Gill, Graeme and Roger D. Markwick, *Russia's Stillborn Democracy? From Gorbachev to Yeltsin.* Oxford: Oxford University Press, 2000.

Myers, Steven Lee *The New Tsar: The Rise and Reign of Vladimir Putin.* New York: Alfred Knopf, 2015.

Plokhy, Serhii *The Last Empire: The Final Days of the Soviet Union.* New York: Basic Books, 2015.

Soldatov, Andrei *The New Nobility: The Restoration of Russian Security State and the Enduring Legacy of the KGB.* New York: Public Affairs, 2010.

Index

Note: Page numbers in *italics* indicate illustrations.